ABSOLUTE BEGINNER'S GUIDE

TO

the
Bible

D1403363

Tom Head

800 East 96th Street
Indianapolis, Indiana 46240

Executive Editors
Candace Hall
Rick Kughen

Development Editor
Sean Dixon

Managing Editor
Charlotte Clapp

Project Editor
Dan Knott

Production Editor
Megan Wade

Indexer
Aaron Black

Proofreaders
Mindy Gutowski
Paula Lowell

Technical Editor
Charles Henderson

Publishing Coordinator
Cindy Teeters

Interior Designer
Anne Jones

Cover Designer
Dan Armstrong

Page Layout
Toi Davis

Contents at a Glance

Table of Contents

About the Author

By day, **Tom Head** is a freelance nonfiction writer best known for his ability to turn nonexperts into experts. By night, he's a Ph.D. candidate in philosophy and religion at Edith Cowan University. A lifelong student of the Bible with years of formal training in theology, hermeneutics, and biblical languages, he is primarily interested in giving people the tools to read the Bible with confidence, regardless of their academic background or personal beliefs. "Religion can be intimidating," Tom explains, "mainly because people grow up hearing that they're not good enough to ask the kinds of questions religion asks. But the secret is that nobody's 'good enough'; whenever we start talking about God, the universe, and the meaning of life, we're all absolute beginners."

His 22 books include *Conversations with Carl Sagan* (University Press of Mississippi), *Possessions and Exorcisms: Fact or Fiction?* (Greenhaven Press), and *Freedom of Religion* (Facts on File). He also maintains www.absolutebible.com, a fun, interactive website dedicated to a host of Bible-related topics.

Dedication

To the memory of the Rev. John R. Carwile (1885–1972).

Acknowledgments

This book would not exist without my wonderful editors, Candy Hall and Sean Dixon, who have made this whole project feel like one long party. I would work with these folks for free—well, I *almost* would, anyway. If you can read this, thank our wonderful production team—including, but by no means limited to, project editor Dan Knott and production editor Megan Wade. Books are a visual medium, and I am always amazed at the beautiful works of art these folks produce. This book has also benefited from the expertise of the Rev. Charles Henderson, executive director of CrossCurrents (www.crosscurrents.org), who graciously came on board to serve as technical editor and to generally keep me honest.

I am indebted to the many professors and clergy members who have helped to guide my formal study of the Bible in recent years, including Dr. William Hagan, Dr. C. Michael Mahon, Dr. Thomas Giannotti, Dr. George Gilmore, Dr. Evelyn Thibeaux, the Very Rev. Joe Robinson, the Rev. Bill Richter, Rabbi Jim Egolf, David Kweller, and Rebecca Laskin. I would also like to thank John and Mariah Bear, for giving me my very first book deal those many long years ago, and Laurie Harper of Sebastian Literary Agency, for educating me on how the writing business works. And, as always, I'd like to extend special thanks to my family for their love and support.

We Want to Hear from You!

As the reader of this book, *you* are our most important critic and commentator. We value your opinion and want to know what we're doing right, what we could do better, what areas you would like to see us publish in, and any other words of wisdom you're willing to pass our way.

As an executive editor for Que Publishing, I welcome your comments. You can email or write me directly to let me know what you did or didn't like about this book—as well as what we can do to make our books better.

Please note that I cannot help you with technical problems related to the topic of this book. We do have a User Services group, however, where I will forward specific technical questions related to the book.

When you write, please be sure to include this book's title and author as well as your name, email address, and phone number. I will carefully review your comments and share them with the author and editors who worked on the book.

Email: feedback@quepublishing.com

Mail: Rick Kughen
              Executive Editor
              Que Publishing
              800 East 96th Street
              Indianapolis, IN 46240 USA

For more information about this book or another Que Publishing title, visit our website at www.quepublishing.com. Type the ISBN (excluding hyphens) or the title of a book in the Search field to find the page you're looking for.

INTRODUCTION

Scholars say that the biblical tradition as we know it probably started about 3,000 years ago. Life was incredibly hard in those days. Babies often died before they were old enough to even become children; children often died before they were old enough to become adults; and those who made it to adulthood were already lucky—luckier still if they made it to see their 30th birthday. And those brief, fragile, painful lives were washed away like dust in the rain whenever they encountered forces like war, famine, disease, floods, storms, and wild animals. They had no medicine, unreliable harvests, and poor shelter. And they faced the constant threat of horrible, bloody war.

The ancient Near East was ravaged by conflict as empires assembled: The Sumerians, the Babylonians, the Assyrians, the Egyptians, were all ruled by ancient generals who had no concept of ideas that we take for granted now. Cruel and unusual punishment was considered an effective deterrent; torture, a standard operating procedure; death of civilians, a natural consequence of war. Men were men, in all their violent and obscene glory. Women were often reduced to property, captured and raped and beaten and killed.

And in these angry cultures rose stories of angry gods. In the time before creation, as the ancient Sumerians wrote, the primeval cosmos was caught in a struggle against the beast Tiamat, who fought alongside an army of bloodthirsty sea creatures against the gods. But one god—Anu or Marduk, depending on which version of the story you read—defeated her in battle and tore her corpse in two. One half became the sky; the other half became the earth. By the standards of the ancient Near East, that was a pretty normal creation story.

Every empire had its gods, and when one empire defeated another, it would often assimilate the old religion into the new. Gods were as interchangeable as vacuum cleaner parts. Sometimes the followers of these religions produced works of great and lasting wisdom, but more often the connection between religion and ethics generally boiled down to a single principle: Obey. Obey Pharaoh, the god-man who wielded power over the earth. Obey Baal-Hadad, who demanded the blood of children to satisfy his wrath. And most of all, obey the man with the axe or spear who stood for Pharaoh, or who stood for Baal-Hadad, or who stood for Marduk, who could just as easily make earth and sky of your own body if you belonged to the wrong tribe.

In the midst of this were 12 tribes, 12 factions claiming common ancestry as the children of Abraham (Hebrew for "the father of many") and Sarah (Hebrew for "the princess") and of Abraham and Sarah's grandson Israel ("wrestles with God"), and they followed a deity they called Yahweh ("the one who is"). At first, it would have been possible to mistake Yahweh for any of the countless other gods of the time, but this one was different. This was a god who, stories say, was disobeyed and still forgave, who was defied but often spared those who defied him. This was a god that human beings of no particular physical power could argue with, wrestle with, and doubt. And the stories of Yahweh, the stories of Israel, were passed faithfully from mother to child and from father to child. These stories created cultures and a vibrant, powerful nation: Judah.

One day, in 586 B.C., this nation met an end. Its capital, Jerusalem, fell. The Babylonians swept in and destroyed the holy temple of Yahweh, and they did what nations of that time generally did to conquered cities. To Judah's king, Zedekiah, they issued special treatment: They killed his sons before his eyes and then, to make sure that was the last thing he would ever see, they tore his eyes out. He was exiled with thousands of others to Babylon. Yahweh, the triumphant god of Judah, had not spared them from the Babylonians. Their religion, Judah-ism—what we now call *Judaism*—seemed to be at an end.

But in Babylon, Jerusalem's former religious leaders did something remarkable. Not knowing how long they would be exiled, or the pressure their children and grand-children and great-grandchildren might face to conform to the local gods, they gathered up all that they could of what had been written of their people and of Yahweh and wrote down what they had received that had not yet been written. They told the story of Yahweh—or Adonai ("the LORD"), as he was more commonly called because his name was too holy to pronounce—putting into writing the stories they had faithfully received. Fifty years later, Cyrus the Great of Persia would let them return to Jerusalem with their battle-hardened faith, their new books, and their newfound appreciation for their old books. Even though only 1 of the 12 tribes remained, and even though that tribe would not have an independent nation again until the founding of Israel in 1948, those old books, those precious books that relate the stories of Adonai, form the core of what we now call the Bible.

Quick Start: How to Find a Specific Bible Book

Roaming for Romans? Jonesing for Jonah? Hunting for Habakkuk? Look no further:

Bible Book	Where to Find It
Acts	Page 227
Amos	Page 125
Baruch	Page 177
1 Chronicles	Page 107
2 Chronicles	Page 107

How This Book Is Organized

I've sliced up this book into eight easy pieces:

- ◼ **Part I, "An Introduction to the Bible"**—Puts you on the road to being a Bible expert. By the time you've finished reading this part of the book, you'll discover something shocking about 12% of the U.S. population, you'll be exposed to a good range of views on where the Bible came from, and you'll find out helpful strategies that can help make the Bible a snap to read.

- ◼ **Part II, "The Books of Moses"**—Guides you through the first five books of the Bible—books which, according to an old tradition, were written by Moses. In Judaism, these five books—often referred to as the *Torah*, or "the teaching"—are the core of scripture. You'll learn the full biblical account of the origins of humanity, the Jewish people, and the Ten Commandments. Along the way, you'll learn what scientists believe happened 13.7 billion years ago, who the heck Lilith was, and why people say Onan never played well with others.

- ◼ **Part III, "Prophets and Kings"**—Tells you about the biggest part of the Hebrew Bible (Old Testament)—the 29 books that relate the story of what happened to the 12 tribes of Israel after they left Pharaoh for the Promised Land. In the midst of all this bloody war, anarchy, chaos, and palace intrigue, you'll learn what it was Samson said that brought down the house, why King David spent so darned much time up on the roof, why Jonah was sent off to swim with the fishes, and how Naomi got her groove back.

- ◼ **Part IV, "Poetry and Wisdom Literature"**—Wraps up our discussion of the Hebrew Bible by talking about its philosophical and literary texts—the books that aren't really about history. From the existential angst of Ecclesiastes to the practical advice of Proverbs, from the 150 (or 151) Psalms to God to the risqué Song of Solomon, this is the stuff dreams—or, in the case of Job, nightmares—are made of. You'll also learn whether Hebrew poetry rhymes, how to find just the right Psalm for a social occasion, and what the devil used to do for a living.

■ **Part V, "Beyond the Bible"**—A short section covering the Bible books you never knew you had. From the books and passages that can be found only in Catholic and Eastern Orthodox Bibles (such as Judith and the Wisdom of Solomon) to the books that can't be found in *any* Bibles (such as the Testament of Abraham and the Book of Adam and Eve) to the ancient Dead Sea Scrolls, Part V covers the books your family Bible might not include—and gives you links to great websites where you can find them.

■ **Part VI, "The Life of Christ"**—Begins our discussion of the New Testament by covering Matthew, Mark, Luke, and John—the four Gospels, telling Jesus' entire life (and death and resurrection) story. Here you'll encounter the whole story of Jesus—his birth, his miracles, his parables, the Sermon on the Mount, and why crucifixion was a particularly rotten way to die. You'll also find out about Jesus' grooming habits, the B.C./A.D. calendar, and the secret of the Holy Grail.

■ **Part VII, "The New Covenant"**—Covers the rest of the New Testament (Acts, the Epistles, and Revelation) and goes a little further to tell us what, according to tradition, happened to the 12 apostles after the New Testament ended. Here you'll find out which apostle lived to a ripe old age, why Paul stopped hanging out with stoners, and what the number 666 is all about.

■ **Part VIII, "Appendixes"**—Made up of six extra resources that don't fit into other parts of the book: Biblical phrases we use every day, great passages from the Bible, the top 25 Bible websites, 12 good books based on the Good Book, 12 must-see Bible movies, and a special section on how to choose a new study Bible.

…and if that's *still* not enough, visit www.absolutebible.com for even more special features you can't find anywhere else.

Special Elements Used in This Book

Wonder what all those little boxes are for?

note

Notes give you extra nuggets of information you might find interesting or relevant.

Controversy

No book is more controversial than the Bible, and every now and then I point out a reason why.

Biblically Speaking

"If you see a Biblically Speaking box, that means I'm quoting the Bible. Or, occasionally, quoting another source. Or, in this case, quoting myself in the third person. (Hey, writing is a lonely business.)"

—Tom Head

PART i

AN INTRODUCTION TO THE BIBLE

1

GETTING TO KNOW THE BIBLE

The Bible is the bestselling and most influential book ever published. It is the core document of Western civilization, the pinnacle of world literature, and the backbone of three major world religions. To know the Bible is to know the world—and, many say, to know much more than the world. So if you're relatively new to all this, how do you get started?

The Greatest Story Never Told

The Bible is the most influential volume in the Western world. It has inspired the rise and fall of empires and the creation and destruction of entire religious traditions. It has shaped the traditions of the Western world and the Near East and has had a profound effect on the rest of the world as well. Its power as a written document can be traced well over two millennia into the past and shows no signs of waning. Yet the Bible comes with a paradox: It is both widely discussed and widely ignored.

According to an April 2005 Rasmussen poll, 63% of Americans believe that the Bible is an infallible document written by God. The 63% figure is interesting because, in a 1990 Barna survey, exactly the same percentage of Americans were unable to name Matthew, Mark, Luke, and John as authors of the four Gospels. It gets stranger: According to a November 2003 CNN/USA Today/Gallup poll, 77% of Americans support setting up Ten Commandments monuments in government buildings. But how many Americans can actually name five or more of these commandments? A mere 42%. The Bible is always at the center of American social policy debate. Why, then, do only 14% of Americans attend Bible study groups? Why do 38% believe that the Hebrew Bible (Old Testament) was written after Jesus' death? Why do 12% believe that Noah's wife was Joan of Arc?

> **Biblically Speaking**
>
> "The Bible is endorsed by the ages. Our civilization is built upon its words. In no other Book is there such a collection of inspired wisdom, reality, and hope."
>
> —Dwight D. Eisenhower

It isn't that odd that people attach great importance to the Bible. It forms the basis of Judaism, Christianity, and Islam; it's the greatest anthology of ancient literature ever compiled; and it has been the central document of American and European culture. What *is* odd is that despite all the interest in what the Bible says about specific social issues, there seems to be relatively little interest in learning more about what it actually says. Many people love the Bible from a comfortable distance but don't want to get too close.

Obstacles to Reading the Bible

If you feel a little nervous or bored with the whole idea of studying the Bible, I can understand why.

Problem: The Bible is *huge*; I don't have time; or it just isn't that interesting. Depending on which edition and translation you use, you're looking at an anthology made up of 66–73 separate works totaling 750,000–1,000,000 words. Reading the Bible cover to cover is akin to reading the Gettysburg Address 3,000 times—or, rather, 3,000 *different* documents of roughly the same length as the Gettysburg Address, all of them written in the style of ancient Jewish literature.

Solution 1: Don't read the Bible from cover to cover. The Bible is not a book; it's a collection of books. The books don't usually flow into each other in such a way as to indicate that they're meant to be read one after the other. So, when you sit down to read the Bible, start with what interests you. Sitting down to read the Bible from beginning to end is sort of like going to the biography shelves of your local library and reading all the books in chrono-logical order, starting with the person who died first.

Solution 2: Find a new translation. In Chapter 3, "How to Read the Bible," I describe some of the most popular English translations of the Bible. Bottom line: Unless you have religious reasons for doing so, you don't have to stick with the King James Version. It's amazing how much difference a new translation can make.

Solution 3: Find a good Bible group. It's a lot easier to work through the Bible when you're not going it alone—and hearing other points of view can only improve your under-standing of the text.

> ## Biblically Speaking
>
> "The Bible is good enough for me, just the old book under which I was brought up. I do not want notes or criticisms, or explanations about authorship or origins, or even cross-references. I do not need or understand them, and they confuse me."
>
> —Grover Cleveland

Solution 4: Use this book. Okay, that might sound just a *little* self-serving, but bear with me here: The whole point of this book is to help you understand the Bible, or at least become more comfortable with it. So, by all means, flip to a random sec-tion and start reading.

Problem: The Bible is scary. For those of us who find religious meaning in the Bible, there's always the danger of flipping to a not-yet-discovered verse and finding something that will challenge our beliefs.

Solution 1: Have a little faith. Jewish and Christian religious leaders are, as a rule, intimately familiar with the Bible. Ministers of most denominations have to attend semi-nary for three years, which usually includes at least a year of Bible study (often in the original languages). So, it's safe to say that if you *do* find something really creepy that you've never seen before, somebody will be able to explain what it means. Remember that there are multiple interpretations of practically every verse in the Bible; whatever you find, odds are good that people have argued for centuries about what it really

> ## Biblically Speaking
>
> "The Bible wasn't part of my reading. It was part of my life."
>
> —Toni Morrison

means. If you want more than one point of view on a passage of scripture, the websites listed in Appendix C, "The Top 25 Bible Websites," are a good place to start.

Solution 2: Look it in the eye. If the Bible has religious meaning for you, hiding from it means hiding from an important part of your own faith.

Whatever your religious point of view (or lack thereof), knowing the Bible a little better will come in handy. It has incredible cultural and religious significance, it includes arguably the greatest of great literature, and it can be a pretty fun read. If you want violence and intrigue, try the Book of Esther. If you want brutally honest meditations on the meaning of life, try Ecclesiastes. If you want pillow talk, try the Song of Solomon. Even 2,000 years after its debut, the Bible has something for everyone.

> **Biblically Speaking**
>
> "The Bible is no mere book, but a Living Creature that conquers all that oppose it."
>
> —Napoleon Bonaparte

THE ABSOLUTE MINIMUM

- Both Judaism and Christianity are organized around the Bible, and the story it tells also forms the basis of Islam.

- Although the Bible is very highly regarded and always at the center of Western social policy debate, relatively few people seem to know much about it.

- If you'd like to get to know the Bible better but find it difficult or unpleasant to read, there are ways around those problems.

RESOURCES

- **The American Bible Society**—www.americanbible.org
- **The Bible @ Beliefnet**—bible.beliefnet.com
- **bible.org**—www.bible.org
- **Biblenotes**—www.biblenotes.net

IN THIS CHAPTER

- A history of the development of the Hebrew Bible (Old Testament)

- A history of the development of the New Testament

- How the Bible was assembled

- How and why the Bible became more widely available during the Protestant Reformation

2

WHERE DID THE BIBLE COME FROM?

The Bible wasn't born yesterday. Drawn from millennia of oral tradition and compiled by church leaders over a period of centuries, it has taken shape slowly, gradually, and sometimes painfully. The story of how the Bible became what it is today is a testimony in and of itself.

Disputed Questions

If you ask most members of the Jewish or Christian faith where the Bible came from, you will encounter some pretty strong feelings on the matter. Some believe that God wrote the Bible and that human beings functioned as little more than stenographers, while others believe that the Bible is a human record of religious experience. On the liberal margins of the Jewish and Christian faiths, and outside of those traditions, you will find others who consider it a completely human product with little religious significance of its own.

You're reading the most controversial chapter of this book. It's controversial because the origins of the Bible are central to the question of its authority. If God wrote the Bible exactly as it stands, then it becomes much harder to say that the world was not created in six days or that Moses did not really part the Red Sea. If human beings wrote the Bible, then it becomes much harder to say that Jewish and Christian value concepts based on the Bible are infallible and timeless ways of approaching the divine. Today, most religious conflicts in the Jewish and Christian tradition can be ultimately reduced to the question of who wrote the Bible and what its intended purpose is.

For our purposes, I've divided perspectives on the Bible's origins into three basic categories (loosely based on a model provided by one of my old professors, religion scholar William Hagan). Not all views on the Bible can be classified neatly into one of these categories, but they are broad enough to encompass the majority of perspectives:

> ## Biblically Speaking
>
> "I have learned to hold those books alone of the Scriptures that are now called canonical in such reverence and honor that I do most firmly believe that none of their authors has erred in anything that he has written therein. If I find anything in those writings which seems to be contrary to truth, I presume that either the codex is inaccurate, or the translator has not followed what was said, or I have not properly understood it."
>
> —St. Augustine of Hippo

- **Fundamentalism**—Fundamentalists believe that God is the author of the Bible and human beings are merely the tools by which it was written. Fundamentalists reject secular scholarship suggesting that the Bible was written by human authors over a long period of time, believing instead that it was *revealed* to us by God. Although most fundamentalists accept that some portions of Scripture are metaphorical and were not intended to be taken literally, fundamentalists do not believe that the Bible has any flaws. They believe that it is *inerrant*—completely without error.

- **Modernism**—Modernists believe that human beings were inspired by God to write the Bible, but that God is not its author. The modernist point of view allows room for secular scholarship and even concedes that the Bible might contain errors, but it also grants the Bible special status as a holy document.

■ **Secularism**—Secularists believe that the Bible is strictly a product of the human imagination and that God did not reveal or inspire it in any way.

MORE ABOUT FUNDAMENTALISM

During the late nineteenth and early twentieth centuries, the "higher criticism" movement—based on secular and historical study of the Bible—began to gain influence in the universities of Europe and the United States. In reaction to this movement, a group of conservative Christians published a series of 12 pamphlets titled *The Fundamentals* (1909) and distributed millions of copies throughout the world. The pamphlets became so well known that the conservative Christian response to modernist challenges became known as fundamentalism. The five fundamentals, as described at the time, are

■ **The inerrancy of Scriptures**—According to fundamentalism, both the Hebrew Bible and the New Testament are the perfect and infallible revelation of God.

■ **The deity of Jesus**—The belief that Jesus Christ is the Son of God and was born to the Virgin Mary through the Holy Spirit.

■ **Substitutionary atonement**—The belief that Jesus Christ's death on the cross atones for humanity's sins and that the only way to achieve salvation is to personally accept Jesus Christ as one's savior.

■ **The bodily resurrection**—The belief that, following his crucifixion, Jesus Christ returned from the grave in the flesh and not in spirit form.

■ **The Second Coming**—The belief that the end of the world will arrive as prophesied in the Revelation of St. John and that Jesus will return to achieve final victory over evil.

Today, the word *fundamentalism* has taken on a derogatory meaning in some circles. In truth, however, a fundamentalist is merely somebody who upholds the traditional fundamental beliefs of his or her faith and rejects modern, scientific challenges to those beliefs.

The Story of the Hebrew Bible

The Hebrew Bible predates the New Testament by centuries, although scholars are not completely in agreement regarding its age. The earliest known engravings of individual verses from the Hebrew Bible date back to 600 B.C., and most scholars believe that the stories behind the Bible had been developing through oral tradition for many centuries before they were written down.

In Judaism, the Hebrew Bible is known as the *Tanakh* (essentially "T.N.K.," an acronym for *Torah*, or "teachings"; *Nevi'im*, or "prophets"; and *Kethuvim*, or "writings"). In Christianity, it is known as the Old Testament. Today, most scholars refer to it as the *Hebrew Bible*, a neutral term that affirms its continuing relevance to both faiths.

One story that supports this idea is the history of King Josiah, who ruled Judah (the Southern Kingdom of Israel) during the seventh century B.C. in a time of great religious confusion, when Jews frequently worshipped Assyrian and Babylonian fertility deities and relied on the king's support to build temples accordingly. Two biblical accounts (2 Kings 22:3–13 and 2 Chronicles 34:14–22) state that Josiah's high priest, Hilkiah, accidentally ran across a written record of Mosaic law while cleaning out the temple treasure room. When the priest brought the document—probably the Book of Deuteronomy—to Josiah's attention, he was horrified and began a process of reform to return Israel to the standards of his ancestors.

> **note**
>
> For more on the origins of the Hebrew Bible—particularly the first five books of the Hebrew Bible (called the Pentateuch of Torah)—see Chapter 5, "Who Wrote the Torah?"

Most scholars believe that the book of the law was some version of Deuteronomy. During Josiah's reign and over the centuries that followed (as shown in Figure 2.1), the Torah began to take shape. This became particularly crucial after Jerusalem fell to Babylonian invaders in 586 B.C. and exiled Jewish religious leaders began to transcribe oral traditions for the benefit of future generations.

FIGURE 2.1

Timeline of the Hebrew Bible.

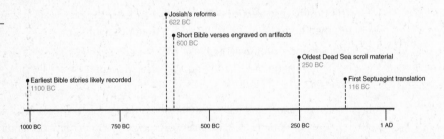

Proving any hypothesis regarding the origins of the Torah is exceptionally difficult. This is because, until very recently, the oldest substantial manuscript—not counting individual verses engraved on amulets and such—was the Nash Papyrus of approximately 150 B.C., a liturgical document (that is, a document used to direct religious services) that includes the *Shema* (Deuteronomy 6:4–9 and 11:13–21, along with Numbers 15:37–41) and the Ten Commandments. The discovery of the Dead Sea Scrolls in the years 1947–1956 helped matters tremendously because they include a complete Book of Isaiah and fragments of every book of the Hebrew Bible except for the Book of Esther. Still, the absolute earliest date that could be provided for documented texts of significant length would be 250 B.C., some 400 years after Josiah's death.

Table 2.1   Ancient Editions of the Hebrew Bible

	Language	Dates	Notes
Masoretic Text	Hebrew	The oldest complete Hebrew Bible is the Leningrad Codex (1009 A.D.), but Hebrew manuscripts of individual books as old as 100 B.C. have been discovered, as have individual Hebrew verses and fragments dating back to 600 B.C.	The most widely used edition of the Hebrew Bible, accepted as authoritative in the Jewish tradition and by most Protestant denominations. It does not include the Deuterocanonical Books/Apocrypha.
Dead Sea Scrolls	Hebrew, Aramaic, Greek	Between 150 B.C. and 70 A.D., depending on the text.	Oldest extant texts of the Hebrew Bible. Discovered in 11 caves east of Jerusalem, in the years 1947–1956. They contain fragments of every Hebrew Bible book (except Esther), but the only complete biblic Dead Sea Scroll text is the Book of Isaiah. For more information on the Dead Sea Scrolls, see Chapter 20, "The Search for the Historical Jesus."
Septuagint	Greek	The Septuagint has existed since at least 116 B.C., and may date back to 300 B.C. The oldest discovered fragments of the Septuagint date to the second century B.C., and the oldest complete Septuagint dates to the fourth century A.D.	Until the discovery of theDead Sea Scrolls, the Septuagint was the oldest extant translation of the Hebrew Bible and the edition quoted by New Testament authors. Although it has been replaced by the Masoretic Text in most traditions, it is still accepted as authoritative by Eastern Orthodox churches. It includes the Deuterocanonical Books/Apocrypha.
Targumim	Aramaic	Developed during the second century B.C., with evidence that a written edition existed before 200 A.D.; the earliest discovered version dates to the fourth century A.D.	Loose translations and paraphrases of the Bible in Aramaic for use by laypersons. Never universally accepted as canonical, but useful for purposes of interpretation, context, and so forth.

Literature of the Early Christian Church

Although the Gospels come first in the New Testament, they are not its oldest books. The author of Luke admits as much when he points out that his Gospel is a second-generation document, recorded based on s tories told by the actual witnesses to Christ's life.

The oldest Gospel is most likely the Gospel of Mark, written near 65 A.D. Matthew and Luke followed about 20 years later, around 85 A.D., and John followed about 10 years after that. This is not to say, however, that the Gospels were not based in part on earlier sources—they almost certainly were. But in their final, written form, they are among the youngest books in the New Testament.

The oldest book in the New Testament is probably 1 Thessalonians, which most scholars believe they can pinpoint to 51 A.D.—a mere 18 years after the death of Jesus—because of historical references contained in the letter. The majority of the other New Testament letters (Galatians, Philippians, 1 and 2 Corinthians, Romans, and Philemon) attributed to Paul were probably written by Paul himself between 51 A.D. and his death in 67 A.D., making them the oldest collection of documents in the New Testament.

Biblically Speaking

"While they were bringing out the money that had been brought into the house of the LORD, the priest Hilkiah found the book of the law of the LORD given through Moses.... The secretary Shaphan informed the king, 'The priest Hilkiah has given me a book.' Shaphan then read it aloud to the king.

When the king heard the words of the law he tore his clothes. Then the king commanded Hilkiah, Ahikam son of Shaphan, Abdon son of Micah, the secretary Shaphan, and the king's servant Asaiah: 'Go, inquire of the LORD for me and for those who are left in Israel and in Judah, concerning the words of the book that has been found; for the wrath of the LORD that is poured out on us is great, because our ancestors did not keep the word of the LORD, to act in accordance with all that is written in this book.'"

—2 Chronicles 34:14, 18–21

By 90 A.D., the New Testament was almost complete. It lacked only the Gospel and Revelation of John; the epistles 1, 2, and 3 of John; and the second epistle named for Peter (which could not have been written by Peter himself because it refers to documents that were not written until after his death). Every document had been written by 100 A.D., but assembling the documents into a single book was another story entirely.

FIGURE 2.2

Timeline of the New Testament.

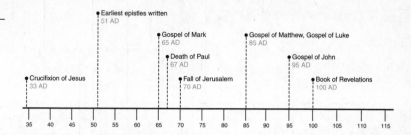

Councils and Canons

Most scholars believe that the Jewish canon developed organically after the destruction of the Temple in 70 A.D. In Jamnia, a city west of Jerusalem, Rabbi Johanan ben Zakkai established a teaching school where, between 90 and 100 A.D., the rabbis in attendance began to examine Jewish religious literature closely and to decide which books should not be accepted as holy.

It is important to note that the Jewish concept of canonicity was based on the sacredness of the book, not on questions of authorship as such. Ancient rabbis said of sacred books that they "stain the hands," that their holiness leaves an almost tangible mark on readers.

The early Christian canon developed based on the Septuagint, the Greek translation of the Hebrew Bible that began to be widely adopted in the second century B.C. The Septuagint includes seven books that are not adopted as part of the Jewish canon, and which would later be rejected by Protestants during the sixteenth century.

Today, the Roman Catholic version of the Hebrew Bible is made up of 46 books, the Protestant version has 39, and the *Tanakh* (Jewish Bible) includes 24. The Jewish Bible is shorter than the Protestant Old Testament by virtue of the fact that it has one book of Kings (merging 1 Kings and 2 Kings) and one book of Chronicles (merging 1 Chronicles and 2 Chronicles) and because it treats the 13 minor prophets in one book, but the two canons are otherwise identical.

Biblically Speaking

"Since many have undertaken to set down an orderly account of the events that have been fulfilled among us, just as they were handed on to us by those who from the beginning were eye-witnesses and servants of the word, I too decided, after investigating everything carefully from the very first, to write an orderly account for you, most excellent Theophilus ["lover of God"], so that you may know the truth concerning the things about which you have been instructed."

—Luke 1:1–4

note

For more on the history of the four Gospels, see Chapter 21, "Before He Was Christ."

FIGURE 2.3

Timeline of the
New Testament
canon.

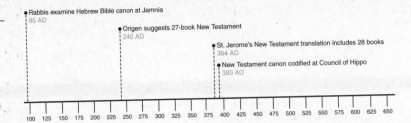

The Roman Catholic, Greek and Russian Orthodox,
and Protestant churches all generally rely on the
same 27-book canon (authorized version) of the
New Testament today, but for most of Christian
history this was not the case. Writers in the early
church frequently omitted more recent epistles
(especially 2 Peter) from their lists of canonical
texts. The first theologian to describe the 27-book
canon was the church father Origen Adamantius
(182–251 A.D.), but his list was not formally set
out. Even the standard Latin translation of the
Bible, the Vulgate of St. Jerome (384 A.D.), initially
contained a New Testament made up of 28 books:
the commonly accepted 27 plus the Epistle to the
Laodiceans (which is no longer recognized as part
of the canon).

A formal list of the 27 was approved at the
Council of Hippo (393 A.D.), but after that date
there were still many dissenting regional churches
and Bible editors who favored omitting one or
more books (usually the Book of Revelation/
Apocalypse of St. John) and adding others (usually the epistles of Clement of
Alexandria). Even in recent centuries, the Ethiopian Orthodox Church has relied on
a 35-book New Testament.

The Public Bible

Although St. Jerome's Latin Vulgate was the Bible
of choice until the Protestant Reformation, the
Bible has—contrary to conventional wisdom—
traditionally been available in other languages.
Followers of Jesus who could not understand
Hebrew very likely read or were read to from one
of the *Targums*, or Aramaic paraphrases of the

note

Today, writing a letter
and signing someone
else's name to it with-
out that person's permission is a
pretty rude thing to do—and,
depending on the context, may
even be illegal. But during the
New Testament era, it was considered a sign of humility and
respect to write philosophical
works in the name and spirit of
a deceased mentor. It was a way
of carrying the mentor's legacy
forward and demonstrating that
some people continue to influence the world long after their
deaths.

note

For more on the
Deuterocanonical
Books, see Chapter
17, "The Books of Tradition."

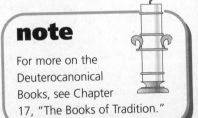

Bible. The ancient Septuagint that provided the basis for the Vulgate translation was written so that Hellenized Jews, literate in Greek but not Hebrew, would have access to scripture. And while John Wycliffe's Bible of 1384 is the first complete English translation known to us, a scholar named Altheim produced what was at least a partial Old English translation in 700 A.D., shortly after the conversion of England to Christianity. Caedmon, a contemporary of Altheim, also wrote numerous Old English songs retelling Bible stories in verse.

FIGURE 2.4

The Bible and the Protestant Reformation.

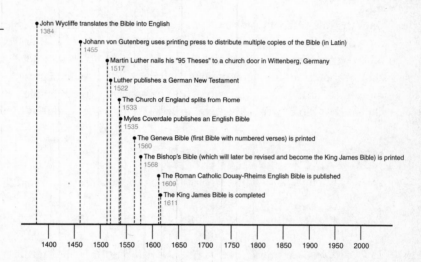

John Wycliffe translates the Bible into English
1384

Johann von Gutenberg uses printing press to distribute multiple copies of the Bible (in Latin)
1455

Martin Luther nails his "95 Theses" to a church door in Wittenberg, Germany
1517

Luther publishes a German New Testament
1522

The Church of England splits from Rome
1533

Myles Coverdale publishes an English Bible
1535

The Geneva Bible (first Bible with numbered verses) is printed
1560

The Bishop's Bible (which will later be revised and become the King James Bible) is printed
1568

The Roman Catholic Douay-Rheims English Bible is published
1609

The King James Bible is completed
1611

1400 1450 1500 1550 1600 1650 1700 1750 1800 1850 1900 1950 2000

Although many have framed the Protestant Reformation as the era during which the Bible was first made available in the language of the people, the church has a long and distinguished history of producing new translations under very difficult circumstances. The Bible became more widely available during the Protestant Reformation not because the Roman Catholic Church had somehow deprived readers of their Bibles, but instead because the literacy rate increased, more printed Bibles became available, and the Protestant Reformation placed greater emphasis on individual Bible study.

Theology

The Catechism of the Catholic Church teaches that "Both Scripture and Tradition must be accepted and honored with equal sentiments of devotion and reverence." The Catholic tradition has historically given clergy the responsibility to read and interpret scripture, to present it in a manner that is relevant to the laity, and to preserve traditional interpretations of scripture.

The Protestant Reformation placed greater emphasis on the individual's relationship with God. Using biblical proof-texting as their basis, Protestant leaders such as John Calvin and Martin Luther relied on public availability of the Bible to justify their theological positions.

Literacy

It's impossible to read the Bible if one cannot read at all. Although no statistics exist on literacy rates in sixteenth-century Europe, we know that, until the last 200 years or so, most Europeans were illiterate. For the most part, only clergy and nobility were taught to read.

Technology

Until the mid-fifteenth century, copying a book meant hundreds of hours of work for scribes who had to produce each copy by hand, letter by letter. For this reason, Bibles were scarce—there simply weren't very many to go around. This all began to change thanks to Johann Gutenberg, who in 1455 invented Europe's first printing press and distributed a print run of 180 two-volume Vulgate Bibles. But even Gutenberg's Bibles were expensive; only the wealthy could afford them.

THE ABSOLUTE MINIMUM

- Although parts of the Hebrew Bible probably date back to at least 1100 B.C., scholars believe that it was compiled over a period of centuries. The earliest manuscripts of complete Bible books currently intact trace back to 100–150 B.C.

- The New Testament was written between 50 A.D. and 100 A.D., although the church did not formally decide which books would form the New Testament until the Council of Hippo in 393 A.D.

- The Bible became widely available for individual reading during the Protestant Reformation, thanks to advances in printing technology, an incrementally increasing literacy rate, and a greater emphasis on personal study of Scripture as promoted by the fathers of the Reformation.

RESOURCES

- **The Development of the Canon of the New Testament**—www.ntcanon.org

- **The Fundamentals**—www.geocities.com/Athens/Parthenon/6528/fundcont.htm

- **The Skeptic's Annotated Bible**—www.skepticsannotatedbible.com

- **The Skeptic's Annotated Bible Refuted**—www.tektonics.org/sab/sab.html

- **Who Wrote the Bible? @ The Straight Dope**—www.straightdope.com/mailbag/mbible1.html

3

HOW TO READ THE BIBLE

There are as many different ways to read the Bible as there are people to read it. Whether you and the Bible have barely met or are trying to rebuild an old relationship, a fresh perspective can work wonders. Without pretending to exhaust all the possibilities involved in Bible reading, this chapter skims some of the options every reader has when approaching or reapproaching this massive, diverse, and frequently misunderstood book.

Three Ways of Looking at the Bible

Most people read the Bible in at least one of three ways:

- As holy scripture
- As history
- As literature

As Holy Scripture

In the previous chapter, we discussed various beliefs regarding where Scripture comes from and classified them into three basic categories:

- **Fundamentalism**—Holds that God is the author of the Bible. Biblical fundamentalists believe that the Bible is a holy and divine product and means what it says at face value (except in cases where the metaphorical intent is clear, such as when Jesus tells his parables).

- **Modernism**—Holds that the Bible was written by human beings inspired by their relationships with God. Biblical modernists also tend to see the Bible as holy, but believe that context, metaphor, and the limitations of its human authors should be taken into account.

- **Secularism**—Holds that the Bible is purely a product of human creativity. Biblical secularists believe that the Bible represents a literary tradition that has a great deal to say about human nature and the history and culture of the ancient Middle East, but they do not believe that God was involved in its origins.

Whether you believe that the Bible is the work of God, the work of human beings, or a combination of the two, it can still be a useful devotional aid. And if you believe that the Bible is a holy book, it has an additional virtue: It brings you closer to God.

There are many ways to read Holy Scripture, but everyone who draws religious meaning from the Bible does so as part of a group, individually, or through some mix of the two approaches.

There are several important advantages to group Bible reading: It exposes you to the viewpoints of others and gives you a way of expressing and clarifying your own understanding of the Bible. Group Bible reading is practiced in almost every church, but it receives particular attention in the Roman Catholic Church and in most mainline Protestant churches. These churches use *lectionaries*—books that reorganize the Bible into short readings that function well for church use, either during formal services or during small group prayer. The Jewish tradition also uses a lectionary approach; every week, one is given a *parsha* ("portion") of the Torah to read and study, preferably in a group setting.

The most common place to read the Bible as Holy Scripture in a group setting is in a house of worship, although it is not always necessary to join a religious community to participate in its Bible study programs. When in doubt, it is always a good idea to call and ask.

In Judaism, individual Torah study has always been encouraged. Within Christianity, however, individual study of the Bible is a relatively new phenomenon that came about during the fifteenth century and the height of the Protestant Reformation. Until that time, most people did not own a Bible or read it as they would a book—primarily because most people were illiterate. (Then again, at that point in history very few people had books, either.)

> **note**
>
> For most of its history, the Bible has been read aloud—heard rather than examined. Reading the Bible aloud or hearing it read (as it often is in religious services) is a wonderful way to connect to this ancient approach to Scripture.

Individual Bible study can be challenging for those of us who cannot read Hebrew or Greek and do not fully grasp the context of each Bible verse. Fortunately, a good study Bible can solve this problem. In Appendix F, "Choosing a Study Bible," I've listed a few of my personal favorites. Online Bibles (such as those described in Appendix C, "The Top 25 Bible Websites") can also be useful, because they allow you to search the entire Bible for a word or phrase with only a few keystrokes.

LECTIO DIVINA

The ancient Christian meditation practice of *lectio divina*, or "sacred reading," has recently gained newfound popularity (particularly among Roman Catholics). Although lectio divina is best learned with a community of other practitioners, the four basic steps involved are easy to learn:

1. *Lectio* **(reading)**—Slow, contemplative reading of a text. (If you're having trouble choosing one, try one of the passages in Appendix B, "Great Quotations from the Bible.") Do not spend much time rationally analyzing the text, and do not try to work through it quickly; instead, let your mind linger on the individual words as if you're listening to someone speak slowly and calmly. For this example, let's use Ecclesiastes 1—one of the most depressing chapters in the entire Bible.

2. *Meditatio* **(meditation)**—At some point during the process of *lectio*, one passage should speak to you more than others. Spend time repeating the passage, silently or aloud, letting it sink in. My mind settles on the second half of verse 8: "The eye is not satisfied with seeing, or the ear filled with hearing."

3. ***Oratio* (prayer)**—With your mind still focused on *meditatio*, recite the passage over and over. The words become random syllables, voice music, nothing more. But on some level, the idea behind the words is still rattling around in my mind. If the words begin to mean something again, if they register as if another person is speaking them, I recite them more quickly until they become syllables again; if I completely lose focus, I recite the passage more slowly so that the idea can sink in again.

4. ***Contemplatio* (contemplation)**—If you feel yourself drifting into a meditative state, let go of all words and silently settle into the experience.

As History

Although the Bible was not written to function as a history book in any contemporary sense of the term, it is the only book of its time to study the Christian movement in depth and the only book to chronicle the history of ancient Israel in any meaningful way. Reading the Bible as history can be a compelling experience, placing you in the mind of the ancient writers in a way that few ancient texts can.

Judges, 1 and 2 Kings, 1 and 2 Chronicles, the Gospel of Luke, and the Book of Acts are especially useful for those seeking to study the Bible as history because these books are, in effect, histories. Judges, Kings, and Chronicles essentially tell the story of ancient Israel after the time of Joshua; the Gospel of Luke is the most objective and historical of the four Gospels; and the Book of Acts (written by the same author as Luke) tells the story of the early church in a fairly direct way. Few books of the Bible are *completely* devoid of history, but some are more oriented toward history than others. Proverbs and Ecclesiastes, for example, cannot be read as historical narratives, and neither can most of the New Testament epistles.

Controversy

Even among people who find religious meaning in the Bible, there is a great deal of disagreement over whether it is meant to provide an accurate history. Fundamentalists tend to argue that every event mentioned in the texts happened exactly as described; modernists tend to argue that the Bible was not meant to function as a history book; and secularists tend to see biblical histories as flawed but interesting products of their time.

As Literature

Whatever anyone might believe about the Bible's religious value or historicity, few can deny that the Bible is one of the greatest literary anthologies ever produced. The Hebrew Bible is certainly the pride of the ancient Near East; nowhere else can the same level of complex characterization, the same detailed plots, and the same varying literary forms be found.

Even the Bible's harshest critics acknowledge its literary merits. Books particularly well-loved by literary scholars include Exodus, Ruth, Job, Ecclesiastes, the Song of Solomon, Isaiah, the Gospel of Luke, the Gospel of John, and the Revelation (Apocalypse) of St. John.

Lost in Translations

I still remember that day in Sunday school class. I was about six years old, listening to a middle-aged woman tell Bible stories to us. I don't remember what it was that week—Adam and Eve, Noah and the Flood, Abraham and Sarah, Moses, Samson and Delilah, Mary and Joseph, or perhaps some of the other long-dead people in brightly colored bathrobes who talked to God—but I distinctly remember what my teacher asked me: "Do you understand the Bible, Tommy?" I paused for a minute. "I think so," I said a little cautiously, watching her face carefully to see whether I got the answer right. "Except for the *thee's* and *thy's* and *thou's*," I said.

> **note**
>
> A great resource for comparing Bible translations side-by-side is the Unbound Bible at Biola University (unbound.biola.edu).

I'm still working on that. The King James Version (KJV) is beautiful and poetic, much like Shakespeare (for good reason—it was written in Shakespeare's English), and every now and then I want my KJV. But most of the time I would rather read a more contemporary translation, where *thou art you* and *yours* is *thine*. Choosing an English translation of the Bible is always an interesting experience because an astonishing number of translations are available. The vast majority of them are not listed here, but it's likely that one of the Bibles on this list will speak to you—or to *thee*.

The King James Version (1611)

The good news: It's full of beautiful, flowing seventeenth-century English prose.

The bad news: It's full of beautiful, flowing seventeenth-century English prose.

The King James Bible is generally regarded as the strongest English literary translation of the Bible, and it still defines the biblical tone of voice for most readers.

The Douay-Rheims Bible (1609)

The Douay-Rheims is a Roman Catholic contemporary to the King James Version, translated from the Latin Vulgate translation of St. Jerome rather than directly from the Hebrew and Greek. Because of the consistently Latinate sentence structure, this version has a liturgical sound—almost a chant—to it.

Sometimes the Latin gets a little tricky, though. Perhaps the most famous of Jerome's errors was his mistranslation of Exodus 34:35, which is preserved in the Douay-Rheims: "the face of Moses when he came out was horned" (the Hebrew states that Moses' face shone, not that it had horns).

The New International Version (1984)

The best-selling contemporary English Bible, this is widely used in Protestant churches. The language is very warm and approachable.

The Jewish Publication Society Tanakh (1985)

This is the most widely used English Jewish Bible translation. It contains no New Testament (it would be a little strange if it did), but the writing style is straightforward and very true to the original Hebrew. The word *Tanakh* refers to the entire Hebrew Bible and is an acronym for the *Torah* (Pentateuch), *Nevi'im* (Prophets), and *Kethuvim* (Writings).

The New Revised Standard Version (1989)

This smooth, scholarly, gender-neutral translation is owned by the National Council of Churches and is the Bible of choice for mainline Protestant denominations.

The New American Bible (1990)

This new Catholic Bible translation is remarkably readable and has been used by Catholics and non-Catholics alike.

The New Living Translation (1996)

Patterned on the 1971 Living Bible (a paraphrase of the Bible written for contemporary readers), this translation is extremely readable—even for children—and is widely used as a private devotional translation.

THE ABSOLUTE MINIMUM

■ No two people read the Bible in exactly the same way. If you would like to gain a better understanding of the Bible but don't enjoy reading it, a different approach (or a different translation) might be beneficial.

■ The Bible is most often read through the lens of Scripture, history, and literature.

RESOURCES

■ **BiblePlan: Helping You Read the Bible**—www.bibleplan.org

■ **Bible Translations**—www.geocities.com/bible_translation

■ **The Unbound Bible**—unbound.biola.edu

■ **Lectio Divina (From the Order of St. Benedict)**—www.osb.org/lectio

■ **Read the Bible in a Year by Email**—www.bibleinayear.org

PART

THE BOOK OF MOSES

- How the Torah is understood and interpreted in the Jewish tradition
- An overview of Jewish law (*halakha*)
- The major Jewish festivals
- Two classic Jewish prayers that come from the Torah

4

THE MEANING OF TORAH IN JUDAISM

In Judaism, Torah ("the teaching" or "the law") is not just the name given to the first five books of the Bible, but is also the name given to the code of conduct it inspires. It towers over other portions of the Hebrew Bible, which are not generally given equal weight, and forms the basis of the traditional Jewish worldview, culture, and system of ethics.

Torah Study in Judaism

In Judaism, biblical commentary is a supreme art form. The commentaries of Judaism's philosophical giants—such as Rashi (Solomon ben Isaac) and Rambam (Moses Maimonides)—are literary masterpieces in their own right, studied in depth by all rabbinical students.

In Judaism, commentary on a text is called *midrash*. Approaches to midrash are described as *pardes*, an abbreviation for *peshat* (the plain meaning), *remez* (the implied meaning), *derash* (the deeper meaning), and *sod* (the secret meaning). To explain how they work, let's begin by looking at Deuteronomy 34:5: "Then Moses, the servant of the LORD, died there in the land of Moab, at the LORD's command."

note

Jewish congregations study Torah on a weekly basis, moving through all five books in a year. Each week's designated portion of the Torah is called a *parsha*. Usually, the *parsha* is accompanied by a selected reading from one of the prophets, referred to as that week's *haftorah* ("dismissal").

THE TANAKH

Just as Christian canons divide the Bible into the Old and New Testaments, Jewish Bibles are organized into three parts:

- **Torah ("instruction" or "the Law")**—Genesis, Exodus, Leviticus, Numbers, and Deuteronomy
- **Nevi'im ("the Prophets")**—Joshua, Judges, Samuel, Kings, Isaiah, Jeremiah, Ezekiel, Hosea, Joel, Amos, Obadiah, Jonah, Micah, Nahum, Habakkuk, Zephaniah, Haggai, Zechariah, Malachi
- **Kethuvim ("the writings")**—Psalms, Proverbs, Job, the Song of Songs, Ruth, Lamentations, Ecclesiastes, Esther, Daniel, Ezra, Nehemiah, and Chronicles

The three sections are abbreviated TNK in Hebrew—which form the word *Tanakh*, used to refer to the Hebrew Bible as a whole.

The Plain Meaning (*Peshat*)

The literal meaning of the text, called *peshat*, is generally studied before more advanced interpretation is employed. In this case, the verse states rather clearly that Moses died, that Moses died in the land of Moab rather than in the Promised Land, that Moses died at God's command rather than by an accident of nature, and that Moses was still God's servant when he died.

The Hinted Meaning (*Remez*)

The hinted meaning (*remez*) of a text is its potential meaning—the meaning not formally stated in the text, explicitly or implicitly, but seen with a sideways glance. For example, the rabbinic text *Beresheis Rabba* asks, "How did Moses know where to die, when it is written [in verse 34:6] that no one knows where he was buried?" The answer: Moses ascended the mountain, just as he had been told to before (most notably at Mt. Sinai, where he had received God's commandments).

> **note**
>
> Because the meanings of *midrash*, *derash*, and *remez* overlap, scholars sometimes disagree on the type of interpretation that falls into each category.

The Deeper Meaning (*Derash*)

Next, it's useful to examine the implied meaning of the passage. In this case, we can look at the commentary of the thirteenth-century Spanish scholar Rabbi Bachya ben Asher, who points out the fact that the text identifies Moses as *ebed* ("servant")—the first time this designation is ever used to describe him in the Torah. In Deuteronomy 33:1, for example, he is called *iysh-elohim* ("man of God")—not quite the same thing. It is only at Moses' death, it appears, that he is completely disconnected from the world and can grant God his undivided attention, becoming his servant.

The Secret Meaning (*Sod*)

The *sod* (rhymes with *toad*) of a text is its secret meaning, discovered only through mystical contemplation. The sod of a text typically involves complex terminology drawn from Jewish mysticism. One frequently cited example deals with Genesis 1. The *Mishnah* (an authoritative Jewish text cited in the following) states that the world was created with 10 statements—but Genesis 1 lists only 9. The authors of the *Mishnah* knew perfectly well how to count, so from where did they draw the other statement? According to some rabbis, the secret lies in the *sod* of the phrase "In the beginning…" (1:1)—that what this phrase represents, among other things, is God's creation of existence itself.

> **Biblically Speaking**
>
> "If your law had not been my delight,
>
> I would have perished in my misery.
>
> I will never forget your precepts, for by them you have given me life."
>
> —Psalm 119:92–93

The Other Torah

In Orthodox Judaism, it is believed that an oral tradition centering on practical application of the law was given to Moses at the same time as the written Torah. The Oral Torah was memorized by religious leaders and transcribed as the *Mishnah* ("repetition") sometime around 200 A.D., when the Palestinian Jewish community was threatened and it was feared that the tradition could be lost. Over the next 400 years, rabbinic scholars wrote commentaries on the *Mishnah*, called *gemara* ("completion"). Two editions of the *Mishnah* with *gemara* were compiled: the Jerusalem Talmud (compiled around 350 A.D.) and the Babylonian Talmud (compiled around 550 A.D.). Each Talmud is organized into six *seders* ("orders"):

- **Zeraim ("seeds")**—Concerns agriculture
- **Moed ("festivals")**—Concerns the Sabbath and festivals
- **Nashim ("women")**—Concerns marriage
- **Nezikin ("damages")**—Concerns civil and criminal law
- **Kodshim ("holy matters")**—Concerns the Temple, sacrifices, and *kosher* law (addressing which foods are acceptable to eat)
- **Tohorot ("purities")**—Concerns ritual purity

note

One of the most remarkable features of Jewish law is that no one is above it; even the most esteemed figures in the Jewish tradition, Moses and David, were punished severely for breaking the law. This brings Mosaic law into sharp contrast with other legal codes of the ancient world, which did not restrict the most powerful in society. The ancient *Epic of Gilgamesh*, for instance, begins by mentioning (without a trace of moral outrage) that one of King Gilgamesh's hobbies was serial rape—a crime that he could commit with impunity because he was the king. Not so in Israel.

The Talmud includes two types of writing: *halakha*, which directly involves Jewish law and ethics, and *haggadah*, writing on other matters. *Haggadah* frequently includes rich stories, parables, and aphorisms that make for fascinating reading, even for people who have no serious interest in matters of Jewish law. Rabbinic Judaism is commentary oriented and has produced one of the most impressive collections of commentary one can imagine—with everything from matters of criminal law to outrageous humor, from deep philosophy to recipes. It is possible for a scholar to spend a happy lifetime studying rabbinic texts, and many scholars have. Comparisons between rabbinic literature and the Internet have been made: Both are driven by cross-references, both contain vast amounts of material on a wide range of topics, and both are far too large for any one human mind to exhaust.

But in the end, all the Jewish commentaries orbit the written Torah in much the same way that the planets orbit the Sun. *Halakha* is built around the 613 commandments given in Leviticus, Numbers, and Deuteronomy; most *haggadah* stories deal with biblical personalities; and, as shown in Table 4.1, every major Jewish holiday (with the exception of Hanukkah) is directly based on a biblical mandate. Judaism is the religion of Abraham and Sarah, Isaac and Rebecca, Jacob and Rachel, and Moses, Aaron, and Miriam. Judaism is the faith received from the ancestors of the Jewish people, and the written Torah is the story of their lives.

Table 4.1 Major Jewish Festivals

Festival	Description	Relevant Bible Verses
Hanukkah	The Festival of Lights. According to the Talmud, a group of oppressed Jews desperately needed light but had enough oil to burn their lamps for only one day. Miraculously, the oil lasted eight. An eight-day festival was celebrated not long afterward and soon became part of the Jewish tradition. Today, the holiday is observed with candles—one candle is lit on the first night of Hanukkah, two on the second, and so forth until eight candles are lit. Hanukkah was traditionally regarded as a minor holiday but has taken on a new meaning in recent centuries. Because it usually occurs in December or early January, contemporary Jews tend to observe Hanukkah in much the same way that Christians observe Christmas—by feasting, spending time with relatives, and exchanging gifts.	2 Maccabees 1:18–36 advocates the celebration of Hanukkah but tells a completely different story of its origin from the one given here (which comes from the Talmud and is more widely accepted). It is worth mentioning that 2 Maccabees is not considered holy scripture in the Jewish tradition.
Pesach (Passover)	Passover celebrates the Hebrews' escape from slavery at the hands of the Egyptians.	Exodus 12:1–20
Purim	In the Book of Esther (discussed in Chapter 16, "Mortal Questions"), the wicked Haman plots the mass execution of the Jewish people but is thwarted by Esther and pays for his scheming with his life. Purim is the wildest holiday in the Jewish year, a joyous festival that involves song, dance, feasting, drinking, and large doses of humor and irreverence.	The entire Book of Esther.

Table 4.1 (continued)

Festival	Description	Relevant Bible Verses
Rosh Hashanah	The Jewish calendar's New Year, celebrated in a somber and low-key way. Jewish law encourages those who observe the holiday to do so by practicing introspection and repenting of their sins.	Leviticus 23:24–25.
Shavu'ot	This holiday celebrates the first revelation of Jewish law on Mt. Sinai.	Exodus 19:16–25, 20:1.
Simchat Torah	On Simchat Torah, the *parsha* (Torah reading) schedule for the year starts over again. This holiday also celebrates the revelation of the Torah itself.	n/a
Sukkot	The feast of the tents. This seven-day holiday recalls the 40 years that the ancient Hebrews spent wandering in the desert. Those who observe the holiday often build temporary outdoor shelters themselves and (weather permitting) eat and sleep in them.	Leviticus 23:33–36.
Tisha B'Av	The bleak holiday of Tisha B'Av acknowledges the oppression the Jewish people have experienced, most notably on the ninth day of the month of Av. According to tradition, it was on this day that both the first (586 B.C.) and second (70 A.D.) temples were destroyed.	2 Chronicles 36:17–19.
Tu B'Shevat	No longer widely observed, Tu B'Shevat celebrates the harvest of fruit previously forbidden under the tithing schedule outlined in Leviticus.	Leviticus 19:23–25.
Yom Kippur	The day of atonement. On this somber day, worshippers confess their sins against God and plead for forgiveness.	Leviticus 23:26–32.

Two Essential Prayers from the Torah

If you open a *siddur* (Jewish prayer book), you will find plenty of prayers inspired by biblical passages. But two particularly well-known prayers *are* biblical passages, drawn from the Torah no less.

The Shema

The Shema ("hear") is the central prayer of the Jewish faith, as well as its central creed. It is recited at every traditional religious service, testifying to the reality of one God and the importance of his law. It begins with the unforgettable words: *Sh'ma, Yisrael: Adonai elohaynu, adonai echad.* The word *elohaynu* means "**our** God"; the prayer asserts a direct, concrete relationship with God. The word *echad* means "one"; it embraces the First Commandment to have no other gods, standing in loyalty to one and only one.

> ## Biblically Speaking
>
> "Hear, O Israel: The LORD is our God, the LORD alone. You shall love the LORD your God with all your heart, and with all your soul, and with all your might. Keep these words that I am commanding you today in your heart. Recite them to your children and talk about them when you are at home and when you are away, when you lie down and when you rise. Bind them as a sign on your hand, fix them as an emblem on your forehead, and write them on the doorposts of your house and on your gates."
>
> —Deuteronomy 6:4–9

The portion I've quoted here is only the beginning of the Shema; the prayer continues with Deuteronomy 11:13–21 and Numbers 15:37–41, which deal with the importance of keeping the law. The Shema highlights the central message of Judaism: One God, and the law as the means of relating to God. The two ideas are inseparable; the Jewish philosophy of religious law is centered not on fear or power, but on living life as a response to God.

The Song of Miriam

Many scholars believe the Song of Miriam—expanded in Exodus 15:1–18 as the Song of Moses—is one of the oldest verses in the Bible. It also has powerful things to say about the role of women in the ancient Jewish world. Miriam is described as a prophet and leads a crowd of people in song and dance. Like many women of the Bible, Miriam is assertive and—when the situation calls for it—capable of leading.

The verse contains two important parallels, also pointed out by scholars. The first is the religious imagery of the sea. In the ancient Near East, the sea represented the chaos conquered by the gods. In Genesis 1:1–2, God is credited for conquering the waters of chaos. So, what does He do to protect His people? He throws their enemies into the sea—into the chaos, into the destructive forces they represent.

The second parallel is the role of women. In Exodus 1:15–22, it is women who are oppressed by Pharaoh in a particularly horrific way: Egypt's midwives, who must answer to the Pharaoh's laws, are instructed to kill all male infants by throwing them into the river almost as soon as they are out of the womb. In the story of Exodus, how many of the women dancing behind Miriam lost their sons in this ghoulish way? And how many appreciate the irony of watching Pharaoh's terrifying, invincible soldiers as they are thrown out into the water to drown, just as their newborn sons had been?

Biblically Speaking

"Then the prophet Miriam, Aaron's sister, took a tambourine in her hand; and all the women went out after her with tambourines and with dancing. And Miriam sang to them:

'Sing to the LORD, for he has triumphed gloriously;
horse and rider he has thrown into the sea.'"

—Exodus 15:20–21

THE ABSOLUTE MINIMUM

- Jewish commentaries approach verses from the Torah on four levels: *peshat* ("literal meaning"), *daresh* ("deeper meaning"), *remez* ("hinted meaning"), and *sod* ("secret meaning").

- Jewish tradition teaches that God revealed two sets of laws at Mount Sinai: The Written Law, or 613 commandments, and the Oral Law, or *Mishnah*. The Mishnah was first transcribed sometime around 200 A.D.; two commentaries on the Mishnah, referred to as the *Gemara*, were written by rabbinic scholars over a period of centuries and were compiled with the Mishnah to form the Jerusalem Talmud and Babylonian Talmud, respectively.

- Jewish law is referred to as *halakha* ("the way"); material in the Talmud and other rabbinic writings not focused on issues of law is referred to as *haggadah* ("lore").

continues

- The *Shema* ("hear") is the central prayer of the Jewish tradition, used at all traditional services. It affirms worship of one God and remembers the obligation Jews have to keep their ancestral covenant with Him.

- The Song of Miriam is one of the oldest verses in the Hebrew Bible, possibly dating as far back as 3000 B.C.

RESOURCES

- **Jewish Law Research Guide**—library.law.miami.edu/jewishguide.html
- **Judaism 101**—www.jewfaq.org
- **Parshas Hashavua**—www.shemayisrael.co.il/parsha
- **Project Genesis**—www.torah.org

IN THIS CHAPTER

● The traditional view that
  Moses wrote the Torah

● The contemporary, scholarly
  view that a multitude of
  authors wrote the Torah

● A description of the four
  traditions that scholars
  believe produced the Torah

5

WHO WROTE THE TORAH?

Over the past century, scholars have reexamined the authorship of the
Bible in general and the Torah (the first five books of the Bible) in particular. The emergence of the *four sources hypothesis* has provided an
alternative explanation to the theory that Moses wrote or transcribed
the Torah. The disagreement over the authorship of the Torah is a
central issue in the larger controversy over the Bible's origins.

The Books of Moses

According to Jewish and Christian tradition, the first five books of the Bible were transcribed by Moses. The Torah itself credits him with at least transcribing the law given to him on Mount Sinai (in Exodus 17:14, 24:4, and 34:27; Leviticus 1:1 and 6:8; and Deuteronomy 31:9 and 31:24–26), twice in other parts of the Hebrew Bible (Joshua 22:5 and 2 Chronicles 34:14), eight times by Jesus (Matthew 19:7–8 and 22:24; Mark 7:10 and 12:24; Luke 24:44; and John 1:17, 5:46, and 7:23), and twice in other New Testament writings (Acts 26:22 and Romans 10:5). As the phrase *the Law* can be used to refer to the actual laws of Sinai or to the books of the Torah as a whole, the meaning of these verses is not entirely clear.

Historically, both Jewish and Christian scholars have believed that Moses did not write the *entire* Torah—Deuteronomy 34, recounting Moses' death, is attributed to other authors. But most have argued that he wrote the bulk of it, including the laws, the history, and the story of creation. It is the Torah that grants Moses his status as the Hebrew Bible's greatest prophet because the Torah is central to the Jewish faith and plays a crucial (if less central) role in the Christian faith as well.

Although the Bible never explicitly states that Moses wrote any portion of the Torah other than the legal code, the Torah as a whole is so strongly identified with the law of Moses that history has generally credited him as its author.

> ## Biblically Speaking
>
> "The Lord said to Moses: Write these words; in accordance with these words I have made a covenant with you and with Israel. He was there with the Lord forty days and forty nights; he neither ate bread nor drank water. And he wrote on the tablets the words of the covenant, the ten commandments."
>
> —Exodus 34:27–28

More recent biblical scholars disagree, however. They point to evidence of diverse grammatical styles and other identifying characteristics that suggest the central stories of the Torah were passed down by oral tradition for centuries, written down, and then later assembled into a single document by scribes and rabbis of ancient Israel. They also identify some unusual references in the text that would seem inconsistent with the Mosaic authorship theory:

- As supporters of the theory have generally acknowledged, Deuteronomy 34:6 refers to Moses' death in the past tense.

- Two references in Genesis—verses 13:7 and 50:10—suggest that the author has already arrived in the Promised Land; according to the Bible, Moses died en route.

- There are references to the Philistines in Genesis chapter 26, but Moses would not have had any reason to know who the Philistines, the future enemies of Israel, were.

Four Groups of Authors

Although there had been some doubt for centuries regarding the authorship of the Torah, it was not until Julius Wellhausen published his *Prolegomena to the History of Israel* (1883) that a single, cohesive, alternative theory of biblical authorship was presented. Arguing that the Bible was compiled based on at least four sources—the Yahwist (J), Elohist (E), Deuteronomistic (D), and Priestly (P) traditions—Wellhausen provided a new, convincing model of Torah authorship based on an extensive study of the Hebrew text. In addition to the differences noted in Table 5.1, the verses identified with the J, E, D, and P sources use different Hebrew vocabularies and syntax. Scholars also believe that there are contradictions and redundancies in the text that can be explained only by multiple sources.

Controversy

Most fundamentalists still believe that Moses was the author of the Torah and wrote the five books under God's guidance. They argue that the special knowledge Moses received from God would more than adequately explain idiosyncrasies in the text, and they tend to reject recent theories of biblical authorship as misguided attempts to reduce the experience of God to human social forces.

Table 5.1 The Four Traditions That Created the Torah

Source	Authorship	Nature of God	Recurring Themes
Yahwist (J)	Southern Kingdom (Judah), about the ninth century B.C.	Called "Yahweh" (the name of God, never spoken aloud); walks with and talks to human beings; has a physical form; manipulates the world by hand (forming human beings from clay, for example)	God's personal relationship and dialogue with human beings; greater attention to stories that tell of the ascendancy or moral superiority of the younger son (representing the younger, Southern Kingdom); dialogue that tends to be earthy and unpretentious (imagine an ancient Jewish version of Ernest Hemingway)
Elohist (E)	Northern Kingdom (Israel), about the eighth century B.C.	Called "Elohim" ("Lord"); supreme being; has no body; cannot deal directly with humanity, relating to them instead through angels and other intermediaries	Worship, fear, and recognition of God as supreme being

Table 5.1 (continued)

Source	Authorship	Nature of God	Recurring Themes
Deuterono-mistic (D)	Seventh century B.C.	All-powerful; fearsome; concerned primarily with obedience; levels harsh punishment for disobedience; grants great rewards for obedience	Obedience to religious law; preservation of Israel; loyalty to, and fear of, God
Priestly (P)	Sixth century B.C. or earlier	God is called "Elohim" or "El Shaddai" (usually translated as "Almighty God," but the literal meaning is "God of the Cosmic Mountain"); all-powerful; distant; very appreciative of proper worship, including animal sacrifice; concerned with legal codes	Atonement of sin; sacrifices; keeping the law, including the Sabbath and circumcision; genealogies; consistency and order

One of the best examples is the dual creation account in Genesis 1 and Genesis 2. In the Genesis 2 version, God (identified here as "Yahweh") physically molds Adam from dust and then creates Eve by plucking out flesh from his side and forming her from it. In the Genesis 1 version, God (identified as "Elohim") creates humanity by proclaiming its existence, creating man and woman at the same time. In the Genesis 2 account, dry land exists and God nurtures it with water; in the Genesis 1 account, the earth is entirely water and God raises up land. In the Genesis 1 account, animals are created before humanity is created; in the Genesis 2 account, animals are created later, to keep humanity company.

Although the four sources hypothesis is not universally accepted, it provides—at the very least—a good model that can be used to understand the recurring literary themes of the Bible. Until a more widely accepted theory emerges, it will continue to define secular biblical scholarship in much the same way that the Mosaic authorship theory has defined traditional Jewish and Christian religious attitudes concerning the Torah.

USING THE FOUR SOURCES HYPOTHESIS FOR FUN AND PROFIT

Applying the four sources hypothesis in a scholarly context usually involves study of the original Hebrew text, supported by an understanding of the literary forms of ancient Israel. But why let that spoil the fun? The four sources hypothesis is wonderfully adaptive; nothing breaks up the monotony of a dull conversation like saying, "I hear Yahwist strains in what you're saying, but the Deuteronomistic undercurrent is too strong to ignore."

Let's say you're reading along and you come across this difficult passage:

> Little Miss Muffett sat on a tuffet
>
> eating her curds and whey.
>
> Along came a spider, who sat down beside her,
>
> and frightened Miss Muffett away.

Some people might dismiss this as a children's nursery rhyme, but we know better, don't we?

"Little Miss Muffett sat on a tuffet" is clearly drawn from Elohist sources because it represents the ascendancy of the Northern Kingdom. The word *tuffet*, which refers to a low bench but can also be used to refer to a clump of grass, obviously signifies the throne—but it is also a veiled reference to the Southern Kingdom of Judah and King David's background as a shepherd.

The phrase "eating her curds and whey" is clearly liturgical and drawn from Priestly sources. The curds represent the firmament; the whey, the seas. By having Little Miss Muffett consume both the firmament and the seas, the poem reminds us that humanity holds dominion over earthly creation.

The line "Along came a spider, who sat down beside her" is clearly Yahwist because the image represents the ascendancy of the younger son; the spider, who is much younger and smaller than Miss Muffett, sits beside her as an equal. Scholars believe that this line was probably composed earlier than the first line; in the original version, Miss Muffett and the spider were most likely sitting on the ground, not on a tuffet.

The tragic conclusion, "and frightened Miss Muffett away," is obviously a Priestly reference to defeat and oppression at the hands of the Babylonians. The spider, once representative of the younger son, becomes a symbol of the Mesopotamian spider-goddess Uttu. The invasion of the menacing outsider forces Little Miss Muffett from the tuffet, driving her away to a foreign land. The author yearns for the day when Little Miss Muffett finally returns to claim her rightful tuffet, and to eat her curds and whey in peace.

Controversy

Fundamentalists, and some modernists, argue that the two creation accounts complement each other. From a fundamentalist point of view, the hand of God is in the passages—and criticizing them would be the height of human arrogance.

But even from a modernist perspective, the two descriptions of the creation account may say very positive things about the Bible. The ancient scribes and rabbis who compiled the Bible were very aware of what they were doing—they knew that they were providing two different accounts of the creation narrative, and they chose to include both accounts anyway. Perhaps this is because both traditions were already important to the Jewish faith, and they respected both traditions too much to change them. It is clear from the structure of the Bible as a whole that the original authors were comfortable with ambiguity and diversity; they did not want, or need, a single, unified narrative. Instead of treating the Bible as a solo performance, they treated it as a choir—giving many voices, many points of view, on God's relationship with humanity.

THE ABSOLUTE MINIMUM

- The legendary author of the Torah was Moses. The theory of Mosaic authorship is still accepted as valid by many religious Jews and Christians.

- Most contemporary scholars favor what is called the *four sources hypothesis*, arguing that the Torah was produced from four documentary traditions: the Yahwist tradition (favoring a close, personal God), the Elohist tradition (favoring a more distant God), the Deuteronomistic tradition (favoring obedience and threatening punishment), and the Priestly tradition (placing emphasis on liturgy and genealogies).

RESOURCES

- **The Documentary Hypothesis**—ccat.sas.upenn.edu/rs/2/Judaism/jepd.html

- **Torah (from the Catholic Encyclopedia)**—www.newadvent.org/cathen/14779c.htm

- **Who Wrote the Pentateuch?**—www.religioustolerance.org/chr_tora.htm

6

THE CREATION AND THE FLOOD

The first nine chapters of the Book of Genesis tell the story of humanity's origins, from the creation of the world in a seven-day week to its watery doomsday. Although these chapters are among the most controversial in the Bible, clashing with most widely accepted scientific theories regarding the origins and development of life, they present a vision of creation that has survived for thousands of years and shows no signs of fading.

And the Earth Was Without Form

Astronomers believe that, in the beginning, all matter and energy that exists now was compressed into an unimaginably small object of unimaginably high density. And then there was light: 13.7 billion years ago, the unstable object exploded into existence, pushing outward into the surrounding void in all directions in an event scientists call the Big Bang. The explosion was so powerful that matter is still being pushed away from the center of the universe to this day. Driven by gravity and other natural forces, the matter gathered into itself to form stars, planets, and other celestial objects. On one planet, orbiting a star, microbial life slowly developed over a period of several billion years. Single-celled organisms became multicelled organisms, and one species of multicelled organisms, *homo sapiens*, advanced neurologically to the point where it was both aware of its own existence and able to reason out how that existence came to be.

The story told in the first two chapters of Genesis, as shown in Table 6.1, is strikingly different in many ways. Although there are some parallels (including the eerie similarity between the Big Bang of science and the biblical description of primordial chaos illuminated by sudden light), both the timeframe and the sequence of events seem to be drastically different. Further, the overall biblical cosmology—as shown in Figure 6.1—seems to clash with contemporary science. For those who believe that the Bible was written by human beings, this is not surprising; it would seem unfair and unrealistic to expect a culture almost three millennia old—a culture so ancient that it could not even rely on telescopes—to come to the same conclusions regarding cosmology as twenty-first-century astrophysicists. But for those who believe that God revealed the Bible to humanity, the disparity poses a problem.

Table 6.1 Biblical Creation and Contemporary Science

	The Bible	Contemporary Science
The primordial state of the universe	A formless void covered by darkness.	Before the Big Bang, nothingness; after the Big Bang, primarily a formless void covered by darkness.
First known event	God breathed over the waters and said "let there be light," and there was light. Genesis 1:2–3	The Big Bang: Matter and energy, compressed into an object of unimaginably small size and unimaginably great density, exploded into an expanding universe. Light from the explosion is still visible today, 13.7 billion years later.
The nature of the earth	Matter surrounded by a dome, which floats in the midst of the primordial waters (see Figure 6.1). Genesis 1:6–7, 9–10	A spherical cluster of matter surrounded by an atmosphere, surrounded by a vacuum.

	The Bible	Contemporary Science
The age of the earth	About 6,000 years, based on biblical genealogies tracing back to Adam. Some Bible scholars argue that gaps in genealogical record might allow the for a much older world.	About 4.55 billion years, based on chemical and geological evidence.
Day and night	Created by God immediately after light, but before the Sun, Moon, or stars. Genesis 1:4–5, 14–18	An effect created by the Earth's rotation. The part of the Earth facing the Sun experiences day, and the part of the Earth not facing the Sun experiences night. The Earth takes about 24 hours to complete a full rotation.
The sky	The name of the dome separating the Earth from the surrounding waters, created on the second day. Genesis 1:6–8	The name of the Earth's atmosphere.
Stars	Small lights in the dome of the sky, created on the fourth day to provide some natural light at night. Genesis 1:14–15	Massive bodies of incandescent light around which planets, such as ours, sometimes orbit. The earliest stars formed shortly after the universe came into being.
Sun	A greater light placed in the dome of the sky to "rule the day," although it is not responsible for daylight. Genesis 1:3–5, 16–18	A nearby star that formed about 5 billion years ago and creates daylight.
Moon	A lesser light placed in the dome of the sky to "rule the night." Genesis 1:16–18	A mass of rock and minerals orbiting the Earth, which shines only because it reflects light from the Sun.
Bacteria and other microorganisms	Never directly mentioned in the creation account (although it's worth mentioning that in Genesis 2, humanity *is* described as being created out of dust).	The earliest forms of life, which ruled the Earth for more than 2 billion years.
Vegetation	According to the Genesis 1 account, all forms of vegetation were created together on the second day (although the Sun was not created until the fourth day). According to the Genesis 2 account, the Earth was	

Table 6.1 (continued)

	The Bible	Contemporary Science
	barren until after Adam was created, at which point God created plants and placed them in the Garden of Eden Genesis 1:11–12, 2:4–5, 8–9	The first plants, single-celled blue-green algae, evolved from other single-celled microbes about 3 billion years ago. The first multicellular plants began to evolve about 1–1.5 billion years ago. Plants live by transforming sunlight into energy, a process known as *photosynthesis*.
Animals	According to the Genesis 1 account, sea creatures and birds were created on the fifth day and all other animals (including humans) were created on the sixth day. According to the Genesis 2 account, land animals and birds were created after Adam in order to keep him company.	The first animals evolved between 650 and 550 million years ago; the first reptiles evolved about 300 million years ago; the first mammals evolved about 200 million years ago; and the first human beings evolved about 250,000 years ago.

Particularly problematic is the theory of evolution proposed by Charles Darwin in *The Origin of Species* (1859), which relies on fossil evidence in making its case that complex life on Earth evolved from simpler forms of life over a vast period of time. This theory, which seems to directly contradict the creation account described in Genesis 1–2, has provoked widespread controversy over the past century and a half. Those who reject Darwin's theory of evolution in favor of the biblical creation account are generally called *creationists*, while those who accept Darwin's theory are generally called *evolutionists*.

In the Jewish tradition, the seventh day of creation—the Sabbath, or *Shabbat*—was originally a more serious issue than the first six. Under the captivity of foreign nations, Jews continued to observe circumcision and the Sabbath, distinguishing themselves from the dominant gentile culture and helping to preserve their culture against the pressure to assimilate. Depending on one's point of view, the Genesis 1 creation story either indicates that the Sabbath has cosmic significance or suggests that the creation story was originally told partly to emphasize the importance of the Sabbath.

note

Although a recent Case Western Reserve University poll found that 93% of scientists believe that there is no scientifically valid alternative to the theory of evolution, the American public is more divided. According to a November 2004 CBS News poll, 55% of Americans believe that the theory of evolution is false and that God created human beings in their present form.

FIGURE 6.1

The biblical
model of the
universe.

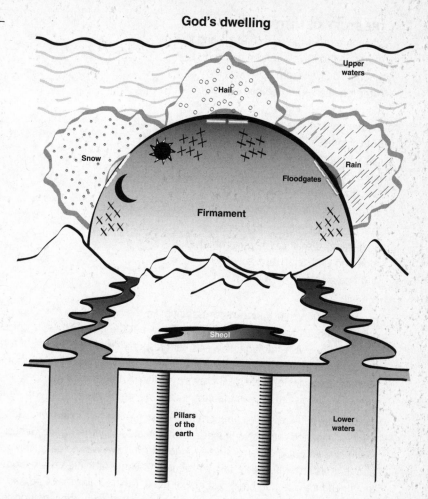

God's dwelling

Upper
waters

Hail

Snow

Rain

Floodgates

Firmament

Sheol

Pillars
of the
earth

Lower
waters

In the Garden of Eden

The creation of the universe, animals, and so forth is an interesting topic, but the
Book of Genesis is ultimately about humanity and the origins of the Jewish people.
And everyone knows the biblical origins of humanity: God shapes clay into the
form of Adam and then takes a piece of flesh from his side—designated by a
Hebrew word that is usually translated as *rib*—and makes Eve from it to keep Adam
company. Man is created in God's image, God being male for purposes of the story,
and…

No, wait, that isn't quite the way it happened. In Genesis 1:27, God explicitly creates humanity—male *and* female—"in his image." The first version of the creation
account puts forth a fairly radical proposition: Women are created in the image
of God, in the likeness of God, and therefore God (for whatever purposes we might
recognize) is both female and male.

THE STORY OF LILITH

"Inanna tended the tree carefully and lovingly
she hoped to have a throne and a bed
made for herself from its wood.
After ten years, the tree had matured.
But in the meantime...
the demon Lilith had built her house in the middle.
But Gilgamesh, who had heard of Inanna's plight,
came to her rescue...
[and] Lilith, petrified with fear,
tore down her house and fled into the wilderness."
—From *The Epic of Gilgamesh* (written ca. 2000 B.C.)

"Wildcats shall meet with hyenas,
goat-demons shall call to each other;
there too Lilith shall repose,
and find a place to rest."
—Isaiah 34:14

For over 4,000 years, various faith traditions in the Middle East have believed in the demon Lilith. Early myths regarding Lilith vary, but the oldest stories associate her with owls. In the Jewish tradition, she was held responsible for the deaths of infants who had not yet been circumcised. Special amulets were carved and sold to new or expectant mothers as means of driving Lilith away. As Jewish tradition progressed, she was seen not only as a demon but also as the mother and queen of the *lilin*, an entire race of demons.

Meanwhile, early rabbinic commentators—attempting to explain why Genesis 1 describes the first man and the first woman as being created together, while Genesis 2 describes Eve being created out of Adam's side—suggested that Eve was actually Adam's second wife and that his first wife was a failed experiment. Some rabbinic stories suggest that Adam's unnamed first wife had been cast out of Eden; others claim that God had simply failed in his first attempt to create a woman and that she was so horribly malformed and in such agony that she could not be Adam's wife.

But as far as we know, no attempt was made to connect Lilith with the stories of Adam's first wife until the satirical *Alphabet of Ben-Sira* was first distributed between 700 and 900 A.D. According to the *Alphabet*, Lilith was created soon after Adam from the dust of the Earth, just as he had been created. When they started having sex, Adam found to his annoyance that Lilith insisted on being on top. "I am to be the superior one," the Adam of *Ben Sira* bluntly stated. Less than thrilled with her sexual prospects, Lilith, according to tradition, flew away from Eden. She was pursued by the three angels Snvi, Snsvi, and Smnglof, who told her that if she fled, 100 of her children—the *lilin*—would die each day. (The *Alphabet* does not make it clear where her children came from or how they became so numerous.) She responded by saying that she would seek revenge by taking the lives of *human* infants—males up to 8 days old, females up to 20 days old—and that she would promise to leave them alone only if they were protected by an amulet bearing the names or likenesses of the three angels in pursuit.

Today, Lilith bears the odd distinction of being both a terrifying proto-Babylonian demon and a feminist icon. Contemporary retellings of the Lilith story omit the business about infanticide and the mass death of the *lilin* but mostly preserve the rest of the story. Lilith, today's retellings have it, was the original first woman and she left or was thrown out of Eden because she stood up for herself against Adam. In Eden she was replaced by the submissive Eve, drawn from Adam's side rather than from the earth, beginning a legacy of sexist oppression that continues to this day.

In 1997, singer-songwriter Sarah McLachlan created the Lilith Fair, a national tour made up entirely of female musicians. It ran successfully for three years and included such luminaries as the Indigo Girls, Sheryl Crow, the Dixie Chicks, Queen Latifah, and Christina Aguilera. The popularity of the tour—which came about in reaction to the sexist practices of concert promoters—inspired new interest in the Lilith story.

And indeed, if the story of creation had ended there, the history of women in the Judeo-Christian tradition would have probably been drastically different. But there is a second version of the creation account in Genesis 2, one that clearly establishes the primacy of man and states that the first woman was created to keep the first man company.

Reconciling these two creation accounts is made difficult for a variety of reasons (not least of which being that animals and vegetation are created before humanity in the Genesis 1 account and after humanity in the Genesis 2 account), but it is not impossible. The fundamentalist position on Genesis 1–2 has historically been that Genesis 1 is cosmic, told from the perspective of God, while Genesis 2 is more specific, told more from the perspective of the human being. Thus, the creation of humanity in Genesis 1:27 is a summary of the creation of humanity described in Genesis 2, and the animals and vegetation created in Genesis 2 are not the *first* animals and vegetation ever created. In contrast, other scholars argue that the two stories are competing accounts of the creation that were anthologized together. The Genesis 1 account, which describes God using the word *Elohim*, comes from the

> ## Biblically Speaking
>
> "Then God said, 'Let us make humankind in our image, according to our likeness; and let them have dominion over the fish of the sea, and over the birds of the air, and over the cattle, and over all the wild animals of the earth, and over every creeping thing that creeps upon the earth.'
>
> So God created humankind in his image,
>
> in the image of God he created them;
>
> Male and female he created them.
>
> God blessed them, and God said to them, 'Be fruitful and multiply, and fill the earth and subdue it; and have dominion over the birds of the air and over every living thing that moves upon the earth.'"
>
> —Genesis 1:26–28

deeply philosophical and fairly recent Priestly (P) source; the Genesis 2 account, which describes God using the sacred name (*Yahweh*), comes from the much older and earthier Yahwist (J) tradition. Where the two texts do agree is on the origin of the universe—both credit God as the supreme creator.

The story of the Tree of Knowledge, the Serpent, and the expulsion from Eden—collectively referred to as the *story of the Fall*—is interpreted in different ways by the Jewish and Christian traditions. In the Jewish tradition, it has traditionally been seen as a way of explaining why things are the way they are—why human beings must die, why serpents crawl on their bellies, why men must till the earth, and why women must experience labor pains. In the Christian tradition, they have been interpreted as supporting the doctrine of *original sin*—the idea that eating the fruit of the Tree of Knowledge condemned humanity on a collective level, so that every human being who is born bears responsibility for the first sin of Adam and Eve. Today, most theologians of both faiths see human flaws as the result of the Fall but do not believe that the human race bears collective responsibility for the sin of Adam and Eve.

> ## Biblically Speaking
>
> "[T]hen the LORD God formed man from the dust of the ground, and breathed into his nostrils the breath of life; and the man became a living being...
>
> Then the LORD God said, 'It is not good that the man should be alone; I will make him a helper as his partner'...So the LORD God caused a deep sleep to fall upon the man, and he slept; then he took one of the ribs and closed up its place with flesh. And the rib that the LORD God had taken from the man he made into a woman and brought her to the man. Then the man said,
>
> 'This at last is bone of my bones and flesh of my flesh;
> this one shall be called Woman, for out of Man this one was taken.'"
>
> —Genesis 2:7, 18, 21–23

It could be said that just as eating the fruit of the Tree of Knowledge constitutes humanity's first sin against God, Cain's murder of Abel described in Genesis 4:1–16 constitutes humanity's first sin against humanity. The importance of the story in the biblical narrative can be summed up by a tradition described in a Jewish commentary on Genesis: In the days before the murder of Abel, blood spilled on the earth—such as during an animal sacrifice or to prepare a meal—soaked into the ground instead of pooling on top. It was only after the first murder that the earth's innocence was violated, and from that day forward it refused to accept spilled blood.

> ## note
>
> For more on the authorship of Genesis 1–2, refer to Chapter 5, "Who Wrote the Torah?"

40 Days and 40 Nights

In Genesis 6–8, God becomes angry with the world—both with what it has become for its own sake and how it has affected his angels—and decrees that Earth will be flooded with water. The story, a longtime staple of Bible story books and children's Sunday school classes, is pretty easy to follow: God tells His one faithful servant, Noah, to build an ark, gather up his family and two of every creature, and load up. For 40 days and 40 nights it rains; then the rains end and God promises never to flood the earth again. As a token of his new covenant, He offers a rainbow.

note

In the ancient world, serpents were seen as symbols of earthly wisdom. They took on their reputation for deceit and cunning partly as a result of the Genesis account.

For many, the story of the Flood is more difficult to believe than the creation account. If Noah did gather 2 of every species on the ark, how did he manage to make 20 billion creatures fit and then distribute them throughout the world? The response to this is typical of the response to similarly difficult ideas: Modernists accept it as a metaphor, and fundamentalists stand by their conviction that with God, all things are possible.

THE COVENANT OF NOAH

Most moral precepts described in the first five books of the Bible are binding only on Jews; they are part of God's covenant (agreement) with Israel. What makes God's covenant with Noah—referred to as the *Noachide covenant*—stand out is that it represents God's covenant with the whole of humanity.

In Genesis 9, the covenant is rather short: It states that one should not eat the flesh of animals that are still living (once a common—and exceptionally cruel—practice) and that one should not murder another human being (because his or her blood will also be shed). The Talmud suggests that, taking into account also the moral precepts that Noah would have accepted as a given, there are actually seven Noachide laws:

- Do not murder.
- Do not steal.
- Do not worship other gods.
- Do not commit acts of sexual immorality (although the definition of sexual immorality varies).
- Do not eat the flesh of a living animal.
- Do not commit blasphemy.
- Set up honest courts, and judge offenders fairly.

But the Flood is actually one of the most well-supported miracles in the Bible because the story occurs in every tradition of the region. Babylonians, Assyrians, Egyptians—all cultures of the region—relate the story of an ancient flood that a few people survived as a result of divine intervention. This recurring theme could be attributed to catastrophic flooding of the nearby Euphrates river, which occurred quite frequently—sometimes with disastrous results. However, that would not explain why the same story recurs in indigenous European, Asian, African, and American Indian folklore, as shown in Table 6.2. Does the prevalence of these myths reflect the universal danger that flooding poses, or does it reflect shared memories of widespread, catastrophic flooding—such as the flooding that unquestionably occurred at the end of the Ice Age some 10,000 years ago?

note

The cherubim described in Genesis 3:24 are not the cute cherubs of popular tradition; they are understood, in Jewish tradition, to be fearsome angels that bear the features of both beasts and men. As one prophet describes them:

"Each [cherub] had four faces, and each of them had four wings. Their legs were straight, and the soles of their feet were like the sole of a calf's foot; and they sparkled like burnished bronze. Under their wings on their four sides they had human hands. And the four had their faces and their wings thus: their wings touched one another; each of them moved straight ahead without turning as they moved. As for the appearance of their faces: the four had the face of a human being, the face of a lion on the right side, the face of an ox on the left side, and the face of an eagle; such were their faces. Their wings were spread out above; each creature had two wings, each of which touched the wing of another, while two covered their bodies.... The living creatures darted to and fro, like a flash of lightning."

—Ezekiel 1:6–11, 14

TABLE 6.2   Other Flood Accounts

Tradition	Description
Assyrian, Babylonian, and Sumerian mythology	The gods decide to destroy humanity, but the noble Utnapishtim (sometimes called Ziusudra) is warned about their plans and escapes with his family, craftsmen, and animals in an ark.
Cherokee folklore	A man is warned by his dog that a flood is coming to cover the earth and that he must build a boat. The man takes his dog's advice, thereby saving himself, his family, and subsequently the human race.
Greek mythology	Zeus sends a flood to destroy the world. Deucalion, son of Prometheus, escapes by building an ark.
Hindu folklore	A fish seeks protection from Manu, the ancestor of the human race. Manu patiently cares for the fish, keeping it at his home in a bowl and then moving it

Tradition	Description
	to gradually larger bodies of water as it grows. When it becomes large enough and leaves for the ocean, it rewards Manu by warning him of an impending flood intended to destroy the human race, which had become wicked under the influence of the demon Hayagriva. Manu and a small group of others build an ark and use it to escape. The fish is later revealed to be an incarnation of Vishnu.
Kwaya folklore (Tanzania)	A woman owns a small pot that contains the oceans. When her daughter-in-law accidentally breaks it, the entire world is flooded.
Ottawa folklore	The world is flooded, but one man named Nanaboujou survives by floating on a piece of wood.
Zoroastrianism	The evil god Ahriman fills the world with demons, so the angel Tistar floods the earth for 30 days to destroy them. Later, the benevolent god Ahura Mazda floods the earth to reduce overpopulation; the primordial king Yima, along with his family, friends, and various animals, wait out the flood in a watertight building.

> **note**
>
> The *nephilim* ("the Fallen") described in Genesis 6:1 have historically been regarded as the offspring of human women and fallen angels ("the sons of God")—particularly in the Jewish tradition, which holds that such unions are possible. But some theologians in the Christian tradition, which has often held that angels cannot have sexual relationships (based on Jesus' statement in Matthew 22:30 that angels do not marry), instead interpret "the sons of God" as a way of describing faithful followers of God and "the daughters of men" as a way of describing nonbelievers.

THE ABSOLUTE MINIMUM

- ■ The Bible teaches that the world was created by God in six days.
- ■ The Bible includes two separate creation accounts (Genesis 1 and 2), which are regarded as complementary by some and contradictory by others.
- ■ The story of Noah and the Great Flood is remarkably similar to other flood stories that can be found in faith traditions all over the world—even in cultures that had no early contact with the Jewish people.

RESOURCES

- **Answers in Genesis**—www.answersingenesis.org
- **The Lilith Page**—ccat.sas.upenn.edu/~humm/Topics/Lilith/lilith.html
- **The Talk.Origins Archive**—www.talkorigins.org

7

RISE OF THE NATIONS

The biblical story of the Flood leaves us with Noah and his family as the last human beings on Earth. But by the time the Book of Genesis comes to a close, the world is full of nations speaking many languages and the Jewish people have established a unique relationship with God. The transition from the children of Noah to the 12 tribes of Israel is told in the later chapters of Genesis, setting the scene for the story of Moses.

Races and Nations in the Bible

For centuries, many whites used the Bible as a means of arguing for their superiority over others—particularly those with dark skin. This seems inconceivable to most people today, given that Moses married a woman of African descent (Exodus 2:16–21) and that Paul wrote that for Christians "there is no longer Jew nor Greek" (Galatians 3:28), but the size and complexity of the Bible allows for a great many arguments to be made. It is a safe bet that no matter what an individual's prejudice may be, verses can be found that support that prejudice, provided the verses are removed from their broader context and interpreted in a certain way.

The main verse cited by racists was the origin of nations described in chapter nine of Genesis—referred to as the *table of nations*.

The story: Noah, survivor of the Great Flood and subsequent ancestor of the entire human race as it exists today, had three sons named Ham, Shem, and Japheth. One day Noah got drunk and passed out naked in his tent. Ham walked in on his unconscious and less-than-dignified father and, presumably amused, brought Shem and Japheth over to share a laugh. According to the story, the two older brothers covered Noah up.

When Noah came to, he knew what his youngest son, Ham, had done—how he knew is never made entirely clear—and doles out their inheritances right then and there. Ham's son, Canaan, is to be punished—"lowest of the slaves shall [Canaan] be to his brothers" (Genesis 9:25). Shem is to be the most powerful of the three sons, but is to help and support Japheth. Nothing is actually said about Ham.

As shown in Figure 7.1, Ham's uncursed children all seem to represent nations in northern Africa. Although the descendants of Ham are clearly identified with nations and not races, white supremacists harp on the idea that Africans are in some sense "children of Ham," cursed with slavery. But they have never looked carefully enough at the text to see that Ham is never cursed with slavery or anything else and none of Ham's African sons are

note

The biblical argument for white supremacy has an obvious flaw: *The Bible contains almost no Caucasian characters.* The Hebrew Bible has no white heroes at all, and the New Testament has only a few (most of them likely to be well-tanned, dark-skinned Europeans of Greek ancestry). Abraham, Jacob, Isaac, Moses, every last one of the Prophets, Jesus, Peter, and Paul were all *Jewish*. None of them were, or plausibly could have been imagined to be, caucasian. Moses did not resemble Charlton Heston; Jesus did not resemble Jim Caviezel. The Bible was not written specifically for or about white people; most of it wasn't even written using languages and terminology an average white person of the time would have understood.

note

The word "Semitic" is derived from the name Shem.

never cursed. *Only Canaan is cursed.* This becomes particularly important later in the story because it is the Canaanites whom Joshua conquers when he enters the Promised Land. No similarly dire predictions are made about Canaan's brothers Cush ("dark") in Ethiopia, Put in Libya, or Egypt in Egypt. In fact, Cush is the only gentile nation that receives special mention in the text—as it produced the legendary Nimrod, "a mighty hunter before the LORD" (Genesis 10:9).

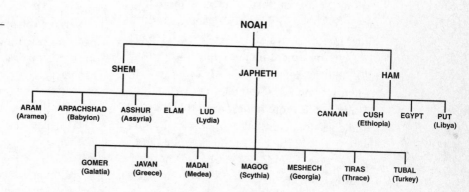

FIGURE 7.1

The table of nations.

Genesis 11 tells the story of the Tower of Babel, which explains how different languages emerged. The people of the earth, working together, are able to create a great tower that reaches the heavens. Upset at this development, God confuses their languages and then scatters them throughout the earth. The story can be read either as a competitor or a counterpart to the table of nations because it describes the origin of languages in much the same way as the table describes the origin of nations. Although a literal reading of the story suggests that God actually felt threatened by the tower and feared that the people of the world might actually march right into heaven, it has historically been read as a metaphor for human pride. Just as Icarus, the young Greek man who flew to the sky on mechanical wings, fell to his doom when he came close to the sun and the wax holding the wings together melted, those who attempted to build a tower to heaven were punished for their impudence.

Faith of the Fathers

It is in Genesis 12, however, that the primary theme of the Hebrew Bible—God's relationship with the people of Israel—begins to emerge. Abram and Sarai, an elderly and wealthy couple living in Ur, a major Mesopotamian city, are told by God to leave everything they know and create a new nation under a special covenant.

The two stop in Egypt to survive a famine, and Sarai—whom Abram describes as his sister, so the Egyptian rulers won't kill him for her—is taken by Pharaoh to be one of his wives or concubines. When God afflicts Egypt with plagues because of the Pharaoh's adultery, he responds, "Why did you not tell me that she was your wife?" (Genesis 12:18) and sends Abram and Sarai on their way. The story stands out from the rest of the text but bears an eerie resemblance to the oppression the Jewish people would later face as slaves and their deliverance out of Egypt by way of plagues. Later, in Genesis 20, Abram refers to Sarai as his sister again when visiting King Abimelech of Gerar, but Abimelech is more honest than the Pharaoh and does not actually have sexual relations with Sarai. At the end of the story, in verse 20:12, Abram explains that he was not technically lying because Sarai was his half-sister, his father's daughter by another wife. (Abram's future son Isaac probably *is* lying when he uses the exact same trick on Abimelech in Genesis 26.)

> ## Controversy
>
> Most scholars find the table of nations in Genesis 9–10 to be problematic, to say the least. The table is not comprehensive (residents of eastern Asia, Europe, Australasia, the Americas, and central and southern Africa are not listed), describing only nations with which Israel had made contact. The table also suggests that each major nation described originated as a cohesive tribe under a single common ancestor, which is not consistent with archaeological evidence.

In Genesis 16, Sarai, realizing that she is old and hasn't been able to give Abram any children, recommends that he use her slave-girl Hagar as a surrogate. He sleeps with Hagar, and she gives birth to Ishmael, Abram's oldest son and the future ancestor of "a great nation" (21:18)—the Arab people. In the Islamic tradition, Ishmael is regarded as a prophet and prominently featured in the Qur'an.

THE SINS OF SODOM

In Genesis 13:10–12, Abram and his nephew Lot decide to part ways and each heads to a separate unsettled region of what would later become Israel. Abram goes to Canaan, the land that would later be promised to Abram's descendants and delivered through Moses. Lot goes to the Jordan plains, home of the mighty cities of Sodom and Gomorrah, and stays in the ill-fated Sodom. Abraham, it is said, negotiates with God to spare the city if 10 righteous people live in it (Genesis 18:20–33)—and because 10 righteous people cannot be found, the city is destroyed.

But what were the sins of Sodom, exactly? In Latin, the slang term *peccatum Sodomiticum* ("sin of Sodom") became used to describe any unconventional sexual practice, regardless of the genders

> ## Controversy
>
> Most scholars believe that Genesis 11 was written independently from Genesis 9–10 and was meant to explain the origin of nations as well as the origin of languages.

involved. From this, the English term *sodomy* came about, which was adapted over time as a euphemism for gay sex in general and anal sex in particular. But there is no indication that the residents of Sodom ever practiced anal sex, nor is their sexual orientation particularly clear, nor are the natures of their consensual sexual relationships ever even hinted at.

In the Genesis 19 text itself, the residents of Sodom are clearly guilty of two sins: cruelty toward foreigners and attempted gang rape (once again, against foreigners). For centuries, rabbinic authors took this to mean that inhospitality is the sin of Sodom, which makes sense from a textual point of view—Lot's insistence on welcoming God's messengers into his home (19:2–3) is contrasted sharply with the attempt made by the men of Sodom to rape these visitors (19:4–11). Likewise, when Isaiah 3:8–15 refers to Sodom, it is as part of a passage condemning the rich of Israel for "grinding the face of the poor." Ezekiel 16:49 is even more explicit, stating that "this was the guilt of your sister Sodom: she and her daughters had pride, excess of food, and prosperous ease, but did not aid the poor and needy." Even if we were to reject Isaiah and Ezekiel's interpretation and assume that the sin of Sodom was gang rape, however, that still has little bearing on consensual gay sex. Gang rape by men was a common military practice at the time, conducted by ostensibly heterosexual men; it was a means of humiliating defeated opponents and demonstrating total dominance over them. Like all rape, it was motivated by a lust for power rather than a lust for sexual gratification.

> ## Biblically Speaking
>
> "Then Abram fell on his face; and God said to him...'You shall be the ancestor of a multitude of nations. No longer shall your name be Abram ['honored ancestor'], but your name shall be Abraham ['ancestor of many']; for I have made you the ancestor of a multitude of nations.... I will establish my covenant between me and you, and your offspring after you throughout their generations, for an everlasting covenant, to be God to you and to your offspring after you."
>
> —Genesis 17:3–5, 7

In more recent centuries, the text has been used to justify persecution of gay men and lesbians. There is no biblical basis for this. The text makes no reference to consensual sex of any kind, gay or straight, and it can be presumed that whatever the people of Sodom chose to do privately in their bedrooms was not considered pertinent to the story. The sins of Sodom were very public, very infamous, and very cruel: "How great is the outcry against Sodom and Gomorrah!" exclaims God in Genesis 18:20. Interpreting the story of Sodom as a commentary against consensual gay sex requires the reader to imagine an entirely new version of the story and to ignore what the Hebrew Bible itself has to say about the reasons for Sodom's destruction.

But it is in Genesis 17–18 that Abram and Sarai take on their roles as the parents of the Jewish people. God renames them—Abram ("father") becomes Abraham, "father of multitudes," and Sarai becomes Sarah, "the princess." And when God gives someone a new name, it indicates a new role. Just as Jacob ("the heel-grabber") became Israel ("he who struggles with God") in Genesis 32:28, the new "father of multitudes" and "the princess" were given their new names to signify a new chapter in their lives, and a new mission: to give birth to the Jewish people.

He promises them the land of Canaan and institutes the central *b'rith* (covenant) that Jewish males have historically observed: circumcision. It is in this exact moment, tradition teaches, that Judaism was founded. When God first tells the elderly Sarah that she will bear children, she laughs (18:9–15). This laughter gives their son his name: Isaac ("laughter").

So gentle old Abraham and Sarah finally have a child of their own, as God has promised. They have a few years together—the Bible does not say how many. And then, in one of the most disturbing passages in the entire Bible, God makes a demand of Abraham: Take your young son to a mountaintop, kill him, and offer up his burning carcass as a sacrifice. Abraham gets as far as drawing the knife before God orders him to stop and gives him a ram to sacrifice instead. Isaac is spared, Abraham's chillingly perfect faith in God is proven, and—most crucially to those most familiar with the story, who were surrounded by cultures that sacrificed human beings to pacify angry gods—the God of Abraham does not want blood sacrifice, as his specific last-minute rejection of Abraham's sacrifice is meant to demonstrate. (When God rejects a sacrifice that has already been offered, as in the case of Cain's sacrifice in Genesis 4:5, it is always a significant event.)

> ## note
>
> Converts to Judaism generally take on the Hebrew name "bat Avraham Avinu" or "ben Avraham Avinu," meaning "daughter of Abraham" or "son of Abraham," respectively. This symbolizes that by converting to Judaism, the new members of the Jewish faith have become Abraham's descendants by adoption.

> ## Biblically Speaking
>
> "Once when Jacob was cooking a stew, Esau came in from the field, and he was famished. Esau said, 'Let me eat some of that red stuff, for I am famished!'...Jacob said, 'First sell me your birthright.' Esau said, 'I am about to die; of what use is a birthright to me?' Jacob said, 'Swear to me first.' So he swore to him, and sold his birthright to Jacob. Then Jacob gave Esau bread and lentil stew, and he ate and drank, and rose and went his way. Thus Esau despised his birthright."
>
> —Genesis 25:29–34

Sarah dies of old age—at the age of 127, the according to text—and a grieving Abraham buries her in a cave. Life goes on for Isaac, who (as far as the text is concerned) never finds out how close he came to dying at his father's hand. Abraham sends a servant to find Isaac a wife from their country of birth (Genesis 24), and he returns with Rebekah. Abraham is also married, to a woman named Keturah, and they have six more children before Abraham dies. At his death, he is buried in the same cave where he buried his first wife, Sarah.

A Man Called Israel

For her part, Rebekah gives birth to fraternal twins: first Esau ("hairy," so named because he was born covered with red hair) and then Jacob ("the supplanter" or "the heel-grabber," so named because he held onto Esau's foot as he was born). Jacob, the ultimate trickster of the Jewish tradition, is the one to watch. As the (very slightly) older of the twins, Esau is entitled under Jewish law to his birthright (inheritance) and to a deathbed blessing from his father. Jacob steals both—tricking a starving Esau into trading his inheritance for a bowl of lentil soup and impersonating Esau to steal the greater blessing from their blind, dying father.

So the story of Jacob begins inauspiciously: He is a con man, deceptive and willing to lie even in the name of God (27:20). He is responsible for fathering the Jewish people, and yet at this point in the story it is difficult to see him as any kind of hero. Esau certainly doesn't: He swears to kill Jacob as soon as his father passes away. Their mother Rebekah warns Jacob and orders him to flee and take refuge with her brother, Laban, under the auspices of seeking a wife from the family homeland—just as Isaac had done. When Esau hears of his father's concern that they marry from their own tribe, he is distressed because he has already married several local Canaanite women. So, to please his parents, he marries one of his own cousins.

> ## Biblically Speaking
>
> "And [Jacob] dreamed that there was a ladder set up on the earth, the top of it reaching to heaven; and the angels of God were ascending and descending on it. And the LORD stood beside him and said, 'I am the LORD, the God of Abraham your father and the God of Isaac; the land on which you lie I will give you to you and to your offspring; and your offspring shall be like dust of the earth, and you shall spread abroad to the west and to the east and to the north and to the south; and all the families of the earth shall be blessed in you and in your offspring."
>
> —Genesis 28:12–14

Jacob's courtship isn't quite so easy. Unlike the more prolific Esau, Jacob has no wives by this point in the story—maybe because he is the kind of guy who would sell his starving brother a bowl of lentil soup—and he is about to get a taste of his own medicine. Sweet old uncle Laban has two daughters, Leah and Rachel, and Jacob is so impressed with the younger Rachel that he offers to work for Laban for seven years if he can have her hand in marriage. Laban happily agrees ("It is better that I give her to you than that I should give her to any other man," he says in 29:19). When the seven years are finally up, Jacob has a wedding feast and, tiptoeing through the dark night, goes off and steams up a nearby tent with his new bride.

In the morning, he is in for a surprise: It is the wrong bride. He has just married Laban's older daughter, Leah. "This is not done in our country," Laban helpfully explains in 29:26, "giving the younger before the older." So Jacob, the younger brother who had stolen his older brother's birthright, has just given a night of passion and a lifetime of vows to the older sister he barely knows rather than the younger sister he loves. For another seven years he works for Laban and finally earns Rachel's hand in marriage. For all this time, Jacob had been living on land owned by his uncle. But Laban had grown annoyed with Jacob, who—through a mix of divine intervention and good business practices—had claimed much of his business. After some initial disagreement, Jacob and Laban come to an understanding and part ways. Humbled and 20 years older, Jacob returns to share land with his twin brother Esau, whose birthright and blessing he had stolen. He did not know how Esau would react because he had taken so much from his older brother during their youth. The last time Esau saw Jacob, he threatened his life. How would he react after having had all those years to ruminate on what he had lost?

As he waits to meet Esau, not knowing what to expect, Jacob is visited in the night by a mysterious stranger who wrestles with him until dawn. The stranger (later identified as God) gives Jacob a new name: Israel ("he that strives with God"), for struggling with God and humanity but coming to peace with them both. Jacob the trickster has been redeemed by God—and, when his forgiving

Biblically Speaking

"Jacob was left alone; and a man wrestled with him until daybreak. When the man saw that he did not prevail against Jacob, he struck him on the hip socket; and Jacob's hip was put out of joint as he wrestled with him. Then he said, 'Let me go, for the day is breaking.' But Jacob said, 'I will not let you go, unless you bless me.' So he said to him, 'What is your name?' And he said, 'Jacob.' Then the man said, 'You shall no longer be called Jacob, but Israel, for you have striven with God and with humans, and have prevailed.' Then Jacob asked him, 'Please tell me your name.' But he said, 'Why is it that you ask my name?' And there he blessed him. So Jacob called the place Peniel ['the face of God'], saying, 'For I have seen God face to face, and yet my life is preserved.'"

—Genesis 32:24–30

brother Esau is happy to see him, he has been forgiven by humanity as well. More than that, Jacob has literally become Israel. The story of Israel had been told, and it would be the *children* of Israel who would create the new nation.

From Canaan to Egypt

According to the Book of Genesis, God is exceptionally kind to Jacob when he returns home. His father Isaac, who had been on his deathbed 20 years earlier, is still alive. Jacob also has a large family to settle down with: four wives (Rachel, Leah, and their maidservants Bilhah and Zilpah) and 13 children (6 sons and 1 daughter by Leah, who was given more children than Rachel to make up for the fact that Jacob loved her less, and 2 sons each by Rachel, Bilhah, and Zilpah). The 12 sons would form the 12 tribes of Israel (see Table 7.1).

Table 7.1   The 12 Tribes of Israel

Tribe of Reuben	Named after Leah's son Reuben, who slept with his father's concubine (Genesis 35:22). As punishment, the tribe of Reuben never achieves much prominence. It is assimilated into an Arabian tribe and vanishes during the time of Assyrian captivity in the eighth century B.C.
Tribe of Simeon	Named after Leah's son Simeon, who (along with Levi) avenged the rape of his sister Dinah by slaughtering her rapist, her rapist's father, and every male under their rule (Genesis 34:1–31). Simeon's tribe is quickly absorbed into the tribe of Judah.
Tribe of Judah	One of only two tribes to remain intact following the Assyrian captivity of the eighth century B.C. Named after Leah's son Judah, this tribe—along with the Tribe of Benjamin—comprised the Southern Kingdom of Israel. After assimilating the tribe of Benjamin, it became the only land-owning tribe of Israel. It is from *Judah* that the words *Jew* and *Judaism* are derived.
Tribe of Zebulun	This tribe (named after Leah's son Zebulun) settled in coastal regions and achieved some measure of financial success. Like most of the other tribes, however, it vanished following the Assyrian captivity.
Tribe of Issachar	The tribe named after Issachar, son of Leah, received money from the tribe of Zebulun, and its scholars were well known. Jacob's blessing in Genesis 49:14–15 also suggests that its members were subjected to slavery at one point. Like most other tribes, Issachar vanished after the Northern Kingdom fell to the Assyrians.
Tribe of Dan	The tribe of Dan ("judge"), son of Bilhah, which produced Samson and other figures described in the Book of Judges, settled near what is now the Israeli capital of Tel Aviv. Although it initially vanished during the Assyrian captivity, a group of Ethiopian Jews claims ancestry from the tribe of Dan.

Table 7.1   (continued)

Tribe of Gad	Little is known about the tribe of Gad, son of Zilpah, although Jacob's blessing has it that the tribe "shall be raided by raiders, but he shall raid at their heels" (Genesis 49:19). It vanished from history during the period of Assyrian captivity.
Tribe of Asher	Genesis 49:20 says that the tribe of Asher, son of Zilpah, produced good harvests and "royal delicacies." It, too, disappeared during the period of Assyrian captivity.
Tribe of Naphtali	The tribe of Naphtali, son of Bilhah, was the most economically powerful of the 10 tribes making up the Northern Kingdom, but it fell to the Assyrians and ostensibly dissolved.
Tribe of Ephraim	One half of the House of Joseph (son of Rachel), this tribe (along with the tribe of Manassah) received Jacob's strongest blessing. Ephraim—named after Joseph's youngest son—ruled the Northern Kingdom until power shifted to Judah in the south. When the Northern Kingdom fell to Assyria, the tribe of Ephraim vanished. Christians of the Church of Jesus Christ of Latter-day Saints (Mormon) denomination claim that many of their leaders are descendants of the tribe of Ephraim.
Tribe of Manasseh	Named after Joseph's older son, the tribe of Manasseh was largely overshadowed by Ephraim but still wielded considerable influence in the Northern Kingdom in the years leading up to the Assyrian captivity.
Tribe of Benjamin	The tribe of Benjamin, son of Rachel, achieved some early prominence but was ultimately assimilated into the tribe of Judah.
Tribe of Levi (Levites)	Originally the 12th tribe of Israel (named after Levi, son of Leah), the Levites lost their status as a land-owning tribe and became a special caste of Israelites responsible for religious duties. (To make it an even 12, the House of Joseph had been divided between his sons Ephraim and Manasseh.) Levites were not permitted to own land but were paid a tithe by members of other tribes. *Levi* is a common Jewish surname indicating some Levite ancestry, as are the derivations *Levine* and *Lewinsky*.

After they arrive in Canaan, Rachel gives birth to her last child: Benjamin. Jacob's beloved Rachel dies in childbirth, and Isaac dies soon afterward. At this point in the story, Jacob becomes an old man and the story focuses on his son Joseph.

THE RAPE OF DINAH

In Genesis 34, after Jacob and his family return to the land of his birth, Dinah—Jacob's only daughter by Leah—is raped by Shechem, a regional prince. When Shechem's father arrives asking that Dinah marry his son, her brothers Simeon and Levi—who had obviously inherited their father's deviousness—devise a plan to get revenge. They say they will give her in marriage only if every man in Shechem's tribe is circumcised. The king complies, and then as the men are healing, Simeon and Levi launch a full assault on Shechem's tribe, slaughtering all the men and conquering the town. Jacob is not pleased at the barbaric form their vengeance has taken, but the damage has already been done.

Joseph's brothers didn't like him very much. At 17, he was obviously the favorite son, wearing a coat of many colors that his father had made for him (37:3); he tattled on his brothers (37:1–2); and, because he still wasn't obnoxious enough, he began to have dreams in which inanimate objects, sometimes representing his brothers, bowed down to him in reverence (37:5–11). Naturally, his brothers' first inclination was to kill him and throw him in a pit, but the level-headed Reuben talked them out of it. Then Judah had an idea: They could sell Joseph into slavery. The original idea was to sell him to the tribe of Ishmael (founded by Isaac's cousin), but he ended up in the hands of the Egyptians.

ONAN THE BARBARIAN

Genesis chapter 38 features the story of Onan, son of Judah. When we meet Onan as an adult, his brother Er has died, leaving a widow named Tamar. According to the custom of the time, men were expected to impregnate their brothers' widows to produce children on their behalf. Onan willingly has sexual relations with Tamar, but he chooses to practice *coitus interruptus*, interrupting the sexual act before pregnancy can take place and denying his brother an heir. For refusing to fulfill his duty, Onan is struck dead by God. Since that time, masturbation has been referred to as *Onanism*, even though Onan's sin was a little more complicated than that. Under the pretense of performing a solemn duty, Onan used natural birth control to get the fringe benefits of sleeping with his brother's wife without actually producing any offspring on his brother's behalf, showing a profound lack of respect for both his grieving sister-in-law (who presumably would not have otherwise consented) and his deceased brother.

Joseph is initially successful as an Egyptian slave. However, after being falsely accused of attempted rape because he spurned an advance from his master's wife, he soon finds himself in prison. There he becomes a model prisoner, just as he had been a model slave. Wherever Joseph is—as a child of Jacob, as a slave, or as a prisoner—he has a knack for blooming where he was planted. He quickly becomes well known as an interpreter of dreams; when he interprets a dream of the Pharaoh's as a sign of seven years of harvests followed by seven years of famine, he is given a high rank in Egypt. From there, he is able to supply his family—including his father Jacob—with goods during the years of famine, and they move from Canaan to the plain of Goshen in Egypt, where they settle down. Joseph is credited with saving the Jewish people from famine by bringing them into Egypt. From here, the story winds down: Jacob dies of old age, as eventually does Joseph.

When the Book of Genesis ends, the stage is set for Moses: The children of Israel are living in Egypt, and—to avoid famine—have fled from Canaan, the land promised to Abraham, Isaac, and Jacob. It is the escape from Egypt, the return to Canaan, and the reestablishment of a new nation of Israel in Canaan that form the basis of the next four books of the Torah.

THE ABSOLUTE MINIMUM

- According to the Bible, Noah, the sole survivor of the Great Flood, had three sons—Ham, Shem, and Japheth—from whom every nation on Earth can claim ancestry.

- God promises the land of Canaan and the nation of Israel to Abram (later known as Abraham) in Genesis 12.

- Jacob, the greatest trickster in the Bible, is redeemed through a series of character-building experiences.

- Jacob's son Joseph rescues the Jewish people from starvation by bringing them from Canaan into Egypt, but over time they are enslaved—setting the stage for the Book of Exodus and the return to the Promised Land of Canaan.

RESOURCES

- **Racism, Racial Issues, and Christianity** www.christiananswers.net/race.html

- **What Was the Sin of Sodom?**—www.iwgonline.org/docs/sodom.html

- **Lost Tribes of Israel**—www.pbs.org/wgbh/nova/israel/

8

FROM SLAVERY TO THE PROMISED LAND

Moses towers above all other human figures in Judaism. It was Moses who was chosen to lead the Jewish people back to their ancestral homeland of Canaan, Moses who confronted Pharaoh, Moses who was given the unimaginable privilege and responsibility of transcribing the law, Moses who enjoyed a relationship with God that appears to have been more informal and personal than any prophet before him or since—it was, after all, Moses who was the first biblical figure to know God's name. In the latter four books of the Torah (the first five books of the Bible), the supreme holy scripture in Judaism, Moses represents the human side of the relationship between God and humanity. This is his story.

Under Pharaoh's Rule

At the end of the Book of Genesis, famine had forced the 12 tribes of Israel from their ancestral homeland of Canaan into a friendly, thriving Egypt. Joseph, great-grandson of the patriarch Abraham, was favored by the Pharaoh of the time and given a prominent place in the Egyptian administration; from there, he was able to watch out for his kin and encourage other Egyptians to do the same.

But things had changed drastically by the time of the first chapter of Exodus. According to the Bible, the 12 tribes of Israel had gone from being a small group of rural shepherds who refused to worship Egyptian gods to a large, cohesive bloc of cultural outsiders who refused to worship Egyptian gods. Baby panthers are cute, but they grow mighty big teeth as they get older. Pharaoh, it is said, was frightened. To break down and assimilate the 12 tribes of Israel into the larger order of society, he enslaved them and put them to work on construction projects. When they rebelled, he took more drastic measures, including ordering the death of all Hebrew male infants.

In the midst of this, a young Levite woman named Jochebed gave birth to a little boy. Fearing for his life, she and her husband Amram hid him for three months. As time went on, it became clear that she would not be able to protect him forever, so she made a watertight basket and left her son there by the river that Pharaoh's daughter, among others, bathed in. Her oldest daughter, Miriam, watched out for the infant. Pharaoh's daughter, it is said, found the baby and adopted him as her own. He was given the Egyptian name *Moses* ("son"), which renders in Hebrew as *Moshe*, or "he who draws out."

> ## Biblically Speaking
>
> "Then Joseph died, and all of his brothers, and that whole generation. But the Israelites were fruitful and prolific; they multiplied and grew exceedingly strong, so that the land was filled with them. Now a knew [new] king arose over Egypt, who did not know Joseph...."
>
> —Exodus 1:6–8

> ## note
>
> It is not clear that the word translated as *Hebrew* is meant to refer only to the Israelites; the Hebrew term is *ibri*, or "those who came from across the river," and the similar Egyptian term *Apiru* was probably used to describe both Israelites and others who had emigrated from the Mesopotamian region.

THE PHARAOH AND I

Scholars disagree about the identity of the pharaohs to which the Book of Exodus refers. The traditional view has been that the pharaoh confronted by Moses was Rameses II (who ruled from ca. B.C. 1279 to 1213), but a good case can be made that it was his son, Merneptah I (who ruled from ca. B.C. 1213 to 1203), or virtually any pharaoh of the period.

Rameses II (a.k.a. Rameses the Great) tends to get a great deal of attention for three reasons: because he reigned for 66 years (longer than any other pharaoh of the period), because Exodus 1:11 describes the construction of a city named after him, and because he built an astonishing number of monuments (making slave labor useful).

In the case of Merneptah, the primary evidence is a 7-foot monument called the Merneptah Stela, which was carved during his reign. Boasting of his achievements, it includes the first documented use of the word Israel:

The princes are prostrate, saying: "Mercy!"

Not one raises his head among the Nine Bows...

Plundered is the Canaan with every evil;

carried off is Ashkelon;

seized upon is Gezer;

Yeno'am is made as that which does not exist;

Israel is laid waste, his seed is not;

Hurru is become a widow for Egypt!

All lands together, they are pacified;

everyone who was restless has been bound...

When Moses was a young man, he became disheartened by the treatment Hebrew slaves received at the hands of the Egyptians. When he witnessed an Egyptian beating a slave, he took matters into his own hands by killing the Egyptian and hiding the body. Word traveled quickly, and Moses fled to the land of Midian, where he settled down with a woman named Zipporah and raised a family. For many years (40, according to tradition), he remained there. But as he grew older, his life took an unexpected turn—one that would send him back to Egypt, under amazing circumstances.

Let My People Go

While Moses is tending to his father-in-law's sheep, he finds himself on a mountain called Horeb (3:1), better known as Mount Sinai. There, he encounters a bush that is on fire but will not burn. It glows with flames but seems to be completely impervious to the heat. From this bush, God speaks to Moses and declares that He has come down to Earth to fulfill His covenant to Abraham,

Biblically Speaking

"After a long time the king of Egypt died. The Israelites groaned under their slavery, and cried out. Out of the slavery their cry for help rose up to God. God heard their groaning, and God remembered his covenant with Abraham, Isaac, and Jacob. God looked upon the Israelites, and God took notice of them."

—Exodus 2:23–25

Isaac, and Jacob and to rescue the Israelites from Egyptian slavery. Moses is to go to Pharaoh and demand that he free God's people.

Moses, who had fled Egypt years ago after killing a guard, is understandably a little apprehensive about this whole idea. According to Exodus, he has four objections:

1. "Who am I that I should go to Pharaoh, and bring the Israelites out of Egypt?" (3:11) God responds that Moses will not go alone—he and God will go together.

2. "If I come to the Israelites and say to them, 'The God of your ancestors has sent me to you,' and they ask me, 'What is his name?' what shall I say to them?" (3:13) This was an important question. In the ancient Near East, gods—from benign household idols to the Canaanite fertility god Baal to the Egyptian goddess Isis— were plentiful. To say "I come in the name of God" would be much like saying "I come in the name of my home country"; to mean something to the audience, it needs to be more specific. Here God introduces Himself for the first time in the Bible, giving the name YHWH (usually transliterated "Yahweh" or "Jehovah"), which will become known as the sacred *Tetragrammaton* ("four letters")—the holy name of God, never to be taken in vain.

> **Biblically Speaking**
>
> "God said to Moses, 'I AM WHO I AM.' He said further, 'Thus you shall say to the Israelites, "I AM has sent me to you."' God also said to Moses, 'Thus you shall say to the Israelites, "The LORD [YHWH], the God of your ancestors, the God of Abraham, the God of Isaac, and the God of Jacob, has sent me to you":
>
> This is my name forever, and this is my title for all generations.'"
>
> —Exodus 3:15

3. "But suppose they do not believe me...?" (4:1) God offers Moses three demonstrations of divine power: A staff that turns into a snake, Moses' ability to turn his hand leprous and then cure the leprosy instantly, and his ability to turn water into blood. These seem like three fairly definitive demonstrations, but Moses has one more worry....

4. "O my Lord, I have never been eloquent... [but] I am slow of speech and slow of

> **note**
>
> When the name of God (YHWH) appears in the Hebrew Bible, it is translated as "LORD" (all caps). Even when read from the original Hebrew, it is not pronounced—readers say "Adonai" ("Lord") instead.

tongue…. O my Lord, please send someone else." (4:10, 13) At this point, "the anger of the LORD was kindled against Moses" (4:14)—all these concerns started to sound suspiciously similar to excuses. But to alleviate Moses' worries, God offers him a priest to speak for him: Moses' brother Aaron, who is very eloquent. Moses will be the intermediary between God and Aaron, and Aaron will be the intermediary between Moses and other human beings.

> **note**
>
> Some believe that Moses' reference to being "slow of speech and slow of tongue" is actually meant to suggest that he suffered from stuttering or another speech impediment, about which he was extremely self-conscious.

These concerns addressed, Moses makes the arduous journey to Egypt and prepares to confront the most feared and powerful political leader of the ancient Near East. Pharaoh is not amused.

10 Plagues and a Holiday

When Moses and Aaron travel to Egypt, they spread word of their ancestral faith among the Israelite slaves. Having had great success, they face Pharaoh. They arrive representing the Israelites and demanding that Pharaoh allow them to leave to celebrate a festival in God's honor. They announce that they ask this in the name of YHWH, to which Pharaoh essentially says, "Never heard of him." Deciding that the slaves must have entirely too much time on their hands if they're getting religion, Pharaoh demands that they gather their own straw to make bricks (4:7–8), without reducing their brick production. Israelites who cannot meet the quota are beaten (4:14).

SONGS OF FREEDOM

The problems the ancient Israelites faced were in many ways universal problems, and since that time many have used the terms of the Hebrew Bible as code when criticizing an oppressive regime. In the New Testament, for example, Rome is frequently referred to as Babylon (1 Peter 5:13), the oppressor of the Jewish people of days past. And in nineteenth-century America, the language of Exodus—ethnic slavery under foreign kings and the quest to escape it—framed slaves' yearning for freedom.

But it wouldn't have worked for slaves to sing songs about escaping from their masters because that sort of talk could get people killed. Under such laws as Virginia's 1669 Act on the Casual Killing of Slaves, masters could kill their slaves with impunity provided that they did so "accidentally" while administering punishment—and with the slave rebellions that began to dominate the news media during the early nineteenth century, one sure way to be punished was to stir up antislavery sentiment.

On the other hand, many slave masters saw religious belief as an effective way to make slaves more docile and were delighted to hear them singing hymns while working in the fields. A mix of African musical tradition and local flavors of Christianity, a new genre known as the *spiritual* began to emerge. Early spirituals often included subtle antislavery messages, usually relying heavily on the story of Exodus. In "Go Down, Moses," for example, slaves sang:

When Israel was in Egypt land,

let my people go.

Oppressed so hard they could not stand,

let my people go.

Go down, Moses,

way down in Egypt land;

tell old Pharaoh,

let my people go.

The story of Exodus became in many ways the framework that abolitionists kept in mind as they did their work. In keeping with the similarities between the Exodus and the northward escape of countless slaves on the informal network of safe houses called the Underground Railroad, Harriet Tubman—the Railroad's best-known operative—was nicknamed "Moses."

By this point, Pharaoh has already turned away two appeals to his conscience: Moses and Aaron's initial demand that the slaves be allowed to worship God in a festival (5:1) and the pleas of Israelites who protest his unjust labor standards (5:15–16). Pharaoh's stubbornness is the central feature of this portion of the story. Exodus reports that God hardens Pharaoh's heart to necessitate increasingly more dramatic plagues against his people (7:3 and onward), a troubling concept given the human cost of the Pharaoh's refusal to comply. However, when read from a broader perspective, it seems clear that the story is meant to suggest that it is the Pharaoh's own arrogance and stubbornness that are his undoing.

Controversy

Most scholars are skeptical that the 10 plagues could have happened because their combined effects would have devastated Egypt and no archaeological evidence of this devastation has been found.

Because asking nicely doesn't work, Moses and Aaron initially try the snake staff trick. Pharaoh's magicians are able to reproduce the effect, but their snakes are eaten by Aaron's snake—an indication that their sorcery is no match for the power of God. Still, Pharaoh doesn't budge. So God sends 10 plagues on the Egyptians, each time giving Pharaoh the opportunity to let the Israelites go:

1. **The plague of blood (7:17–24)**—Moses strikes the water of the Nile with his staff, and the entire river turns to blood. Pharaoh is not particularly impressed.

2. **The plague of frogs (8:1–7)**—Egypt, both indoors and outdoors, is infested with countless frogs. Pharaoh offers to let the Israelites go to get rid of the frogs but turns back on his word after the frogs are gone.

3. **The plague of gnats (8:15–20)**—The dust of Egypt turns into gnats, which seem to infest every living creature. Pharaoh stands his ground.

4. **The plague of flies (8:20–32)**—Flies infest every region of Egypt except Goshen, where the Israelites live. As he did with the frogs, Pharaoh promises to let the Israelites go but ignores his promise once the flies are gone.

5. **Mass death of livestock (9:1–7)**—Egyptian livestock mysteriously drops dead, but Israelite livestock is spared. Pharaoh still doesn't budge.

6. **Festering boils (9:8–12)**—Egyptians and animals in the region are covered with painful, oozing skin infections. Pharaoh stands firm.

7. **Storms and hail (9:13–27)**—Moses warns Egypt of a large, deadly hailstorm. The entire country is covered in deadly hail except for the Goshen region populated by Israelites, which is spared. Pharaoh initially offers to let the Israelites go but once again goes back on his word as soon as the hailstorm ends.

8. **The plague of locusts (10:3–20)**—Locusts invade Egypt and eat all the remaining fruits, vegetables, and grains. Pharaoh begs Moses to drive the locusts away in exchange for Israel's freedom but then fails to fulfill his end of the bargain one last time.

9. **The plague of darkness (10:21–29)**—Egypt falls under cover of darkness for three days. This time, Pharaoh is so angered he threatens Moses' life.

10. **The death of the firstborn sons (11:1–12:50)**—All of Egypt's firstborn sons suddenly die during the night—even the Pharaoh's—while those of the Israelites are spared.

Controversy

Exodus reports that 600,000 Israelite men (12:37) fled Egypt; counting women and children, this would suggest an Israelite population of approximately 1.5 million. Historians are skeptical of this figure, which would have made the Israelite population higher than that of most large nations of the period. Many theologians suggest that it was a symbolic number intended to demonstrate that all the tribes of Israel were represented, which would also explain why only men (who functioned as tribal leaders) were included in the tally.

As soon as he discovers his son's body, the grieving Pharaoh angrily sends the Israelites on their way. The 12 tribes of Israel leave quickly, stunned and disheveled, in the middle of the night, carrying with them gold and silver from their Egyptian neighbors and bowls of bread dough that has not yet had time to leaven. The Jewish holiday of *Pesach*, or Passover, is still celebrated today just as the Hebrew Bible commands (12:1–11), and those celebrating it still eat *matzoh*, or unleavened bread, reenacting their ancestors' flight from Egypt.

Parting the Waters

Pharaoh changes his mind and sends his feared chariots to chase down the fleeing Israelites as they near the impassible Sea of Reeds, prompting one of the greatest moments of dark humor in the entire Bible: "Was it because there were no graves in Egypt," a refugee complains to Moses, "that you have taken us away to die in the wilderness?" (14:11) But God orders Moses to keep the Israelites moving toward the sea, where it appears they will be cornered by Pharaoh's chariots.

God appears as a whirlwind to stand between the Egyptians and the Israelites. Then, in the single most iconic moment of the entire Exodus story, Moses raises his staff and the Sea of Reeds parts to let the Israelites through. They march through and reach the other side; then Moses lowers his staff, and the water rushes in to drown the pursuing charioteers and their horses. Moses' older sister, the same one who watched out for him as he floated in a wicker basket as an infant, leads the women of Israel in singing and dancing, rejoicing in their escape. The Song of Miriam (Exodus 15:21), one of the most ancient passages of the entire Bible, sums up the Exodus story:

> Sing to the LORD, for he has triumphed gloriously;
>
> horse and rider he has thrown into the sea.

From here the Israelites marched to Mount Sinai to receive the new laws given through Moses.

note

It has generally been said that God parted the *Red* Sea. The Hebrew term, however, is *yam suph*—the "sea of reeds." It is not entirely clear to which body of water *yam suph* refers; the text could still refer to the Red Sea (and most translations of the Bible render *yam suph* as "Red Sea" as a nod to tradition), but it seems more likely, given the location, that the sea of reeds was a river branching off from the Nile.

note

For more on the Song of Miriam, refer to Chapter 4, "The Meaning of Torah in Judaism."

The 613 Commandments

From this point on, the Torah is primarily concerned with one question: How can the Israelites, and their spiritual descendents, live into their covenant with God? In Exodus 20, as the children of Israel arrive at Mount Sinai (the place where Moses first encountered the burning bush), God speaks directly to the Israelites, giving them the Ten Commandments. The Israelites do not actually see God because they remain at the base of the mountain (only Moses and Aaron ascend). However, the Israelites find the indirect signs of God's appearance (thunder and lightning, a trumpet, and large quantities of smoke and heat) so terrifying that they plead for Moses to serve as their intermediary from this point forward (20:18–19), which he does.

THE TEN COMMANDMENTS

Then God spoke all these words:

1. I am the LORD your God, who brought you out of the land of Egypt, out of the house of slavery; you shall have no other gods before me.

2. You shall not make for yourself an idol, whether in the form of anything that is in heaven above, or that is on the earth beneath, or that is in the water under the earth. You shall not bow down to them or worship them; for I the LORD your God am a jealous God, punishing children for the iniquity of parents, to the third and the fourth generation of those who reject me, but showing steadfast love to the thousandth generation of those who love me and keep my commandments.

3. You shall not make wrongful use of the LORD your God, for the LORD will not acquit anyone who misuses his name.

4. Remember the Sabbath day, and keep it holy. Six days you shall labor and do all your work. But the seventh day is a Sabbath to the LORD your God; you shall not do any work—you, your son or your daughter, your male or female slave, your livestock, or the alien resident in your towns. For in six days the LORD made heaven and earth, the sea, and all that is in them, but rested the seventh day; therefore the LORD blessed the Sabbath day and consecrated it.

5. Honor your father and your mother, so that your days may be long in the land that the LORD is giving you.

6. You shall not murder.

7. You shall not commit adultery.

8. You shall not steal.

9. You shall not bear false witness against your neighbor.

10. You shall not covet your neighbor's house; you shall not covet your neighbor's wife, or male or female slave, or ox, or donkey, or anything that belongs to your neighbor.

—Exodus 20:1–17 (retold, using slightly different wording, in Deuteronomy 5:6–21; compare also to the Ritual Decalogue, discussed in a later section)

The two tablets containing the Ten Commandments are stored in the Ark of the Covenant (Exodus 25:10–22), an ornate box carried by the Israelites as they moved to the Promised Land. Although it is referred to in the historical books, it vanishes from history at that point; its exact whereabouts are unknown. The Ark and the possibility that it might contain supernatural properties formed the basis of the first Indiana Jones movie, *Raiders of the Lost Ark* (1981).

The Israelites find the experience so terrifying (20:18–19) that they ask Moses to act as intermediary between the people and God. The remainder of the Torah describes the 613 laws of Moses, which scholars divide into five categories: the Covenant Code, the Ritual Decalogue, the Priestly Collection, the Holiness Code, and the Book of the Law.

The Covenant Code (Exodus 20:22–23:33)

This is the most basic covenant between God and the Israelites and is probably the oldest collection of laws in the Torah. It includes commandments pertaining to

- Murder, assault, and other causes of death or injury (21:12–36)—The Covenant Code clearly distinguishes between murder and manslaughter and gives special protection to the weak and marginalized, such as non-Israelites resident in the land (22:21 and 23:9) and widows and orphans (22:22–24). Slaves who lose an eye or a tooth due to abuse at the hands of their masters are immediately granted freedom (21:26–27).

- Property, theft, and arson (22:1–15).

- Preparation of an altar (20:22–26).

- The basics of kosher (food) law (22:31, 23:19).

> **Biblically Speaking**
>
> "You shall not oppress a resident alien; you know the heart of an alien, for you were aliens in the land of Egypt."
>
> —Exodus 23:9

The Ritual Decalogue (Exodus 34:1–26)

This is a separate version of the Ten Commandments, given to Moses after the incident with the Golden Calf (see the following). They are slightly different from the Ten Commandments we're familiar with, and scholars tend to believe that they come from a separate tradition. They are as follows:

1. You shall not make treaties with hostile tribes of the land of Canaan because they will corrupt and assimilate your religious tradition.

2. You shall not make idols.

3. You shall keep the festival of *Pesach* (Passover).

4. You shall offer all firstborn livestock as a sacrifice to God.

5. You shall not ever appear before God's altar without a sacrifice.

6. You shall observe the Sabbath.

7. You shall not eat leavened bread on Passover.

8. You shall burn any leftovers from the Passover lamb.

9. You shall offer the first fruits of the harvest to God.

10. You shall not cook meat and milk together.

> ## note
>
> Due to a mistranslation of Exodus 34:29 ("As [Moses] came down from the mountain with the two tablets of the covenant in his hand"), St. Jerome's Latin translation of the Bible described Moses as coming down from the mountaintop with horns on his head. The error was repeated in some subsequent translations, and as a result many Renaissance paintings of Moses portray him with horns.

The Priestly Collection (Leviticus 1:1–16:34, 27:1–34)

The Priestly Collection makes up the bulk of the Book of Leviticus, focusing primarily on religious rituals and the proper forms of sacrifice. It discusses the following topics, among others:

- Sacrifices to God (1:1–5:26). According to Leviticus, there are five kinds of ritual sacrifice:

  - **Holocausts**—Burnt offerings of livestock given to God in the spirit of worship, which must be completely consumed by fire, with none of the flesh eaten.

  - **Cereal offerings**—Offerings of fruits, vegetables, or grains in the spirit of worship.

  - **Peace offerings**—Livestock that can be partially burned and partially eaten.

  - **Sin offerings and guilt offerings**—Both refer to livestock slaughtered as an act of repentance; the distinction between the two was clear to the author of Leviticus but has been lost over time.

- Kosher law as it pertains to clean and unclean animals (11:1–47). The only animals that can be eaten are

- Land animals that chew their cud and that have cleft feet or hooves
- Aquatic animals with fins and scales
- Nonpredatory birds

- Laws concerning the important holiday of Yom Kippur (16:1–34).

Scholars regard chapter 27 as a series of clarifications regarding earlier legal codes, inserted by editors as an appendix of sorts.

The Holiness Code (Leviticus 17:1–26:46)

The Holiness Code is a self-contained portion of Leviticus that deals primarily with preserving the Jewish tradition against foreign influences. It deals with means by which Israel may remain *holy*, or distinct from other nations, and includes discussions of

- **Animal sacrifices (17:1–16)**—Particularly the means by which animal sacrifices can be offered that clearly distinguish such sacrifices from those given to local deities, such as "goat-demons" (17:7).
- **Sexual purity (18:1–20 and 22–23, 20:10–21)**—This section includes the only biblical prohibition against homosexuality (specifically, sexual relations between two men); it also outlaws sexual contact during menstruation and marriage between half-brothers and half-sisters.
- **Rules governing priests (21:1–24)**—They are forbidden from touching the dead. Priests, if they marry, must marry virgins; they are prohibited from marrying widows.

The Book of the Law (Deuteronomy 12:1–26:15)

The Book of Deuteronomy as a whole often stood alone in the Jewish canon, and it reads marvelously well as a self-contained narrative. It restates many of the laws given in the previous sections along with new laws, formulating the collection into a coherent whole. It discusses a wide range of topics, including

- Rules concerning judges (16:18–18:22).
- More rules concerning violent crimes (19:1–21:23), with additional emphasis on cities of refuge (special cities where those guilty of manslaughter could flee to avoid blood revenge).
- The laws of war (20:1–21:14). Most of the passages are extremely challenging for contemporary readers (the call for the annihilation of six tribes in 20:17 is particularly chilling), but it also includes humanitarian ideas, such as the preservation of fruit trees for the benefit of civilians (20:19–20).

40 Years in the Wilderness

The first concerns the Israelites faced in the wilderness were biological: They needed food and water. The food was provided by God in the form of *manna* (a kind of cereal) falling from the sky (16:4–36), and the water was provided when Moses struck rocks with his staff (17:1–7). Later, as we will discuss in a moment, he would go about this in the wrong way—at great personal cost.

The primary theme of the wilderness journey is conflict and rebellion. God and Moses suppress nine major crises within the Israelite community:

- **The Golden Calf incident (Exodus 32:1–34:35)**—After God delivers the Ten Commandments to the Israelites, Moses ascends the mountain to talk to God, and the refugees immediately melt down their gold to build a giant calf representing their deliverer, which they proceed to worship. God is infuriated and determined to destroy the Israelites, building a new nation from Moses alone, but Moses successfully barters for their safety by reminding God of his covenant with Abraham and by asking what the Egyptians would think if God's people died in the wilderness as soon as they fled slavery (32:11–14). The Israelites still pay dearly, however: Moses orders the Levites to kill their brethren in repentance (32:25–29), and 3,000 fall by the sword. At this point, God forgives the survivors of their sins and sends them toward Canaan.

- **Aaron's oldest sons, Nadab and Abihu, are both ordained as priests**—They then burn strange fire in a censer before God, in a way that ostensibly violates earlier commandments (Leviticus 10:1–10). God burns them to death with holy fire.

- **Many of the Israelites grow tired of *manna***—They then harass Moses, demanding meat (Numbers 11:1–15, 18–25, 31–34). God delivers quail and with the quail a great plague, which suppresses the rebellion.

- **Aaron and Miriam ridicule Moses for marrying a Cushite ("dark") woman of another tribe (Numbers 12:1–15)**—When they do this, God afflicts Miriam with leprosy for a week as punishment but then heals her.

- **Four Israelites (Korach, Dathan, Abiram, and On) challenge Moses' authority and threaten a rebellion (Numbers 16:1–50)**—God swallows the insurrectionists up in the earth. When a larger number of Israelites blame Moses for the rebels' deaths and attempt to overthrow him, God sends another plague to suppress them.

- **Moses' sister Miriam dies in Numbers 20:1**—There is no real detail on the circumstances surrounding her death, but rabbinic tradition has it that she died because of "a kiss from God"—that God brought about her death gently and at the appointed time, as He would later do in the cases of Aaron and Moses. Tradition has it that God had given Miriam the power to give the

Israelites fresh drinking water by striking a rock, a resource they lost when she died.

- **The grieving Moses finally gets an earful from his followers and does something he'll live to regret (Numbers 20:2–13)**—When God orders him to strike a rock and bring water for the Israelites, he snaps at them and strikes the rock twice to produce more than the usual amount of water. For disobeying God and violating their status as the representatives of the Israelites before God, Moses and Aaron are told that they will not live to enter the Promised Land. Aaron dies soon afterward.

- **On the way to the plains of Moab bordering the Promised Land, the Israelites once again complain about the lack of food (21:4–9)**—God responds by sending poisonous serpents to bite them. They plead to Moses for assistance, and under God's command he fashions a bronze serpent; by looking at the serpent, victims of snakebites can be healed. Scholars believe that this story was written as an explanation for the presence of a snake image in the Temple of Jerusalem (2 Kings 18:4).

- **The apostasy in Shittim (Numbers 25:1–18)**—This takes place when Israelite men and Moabite women of other faiths have sexual relationships, and the Israelite men begin worshipping other gods. God afflicts the Israelites with a plague; a zealous priest named Phinehas runs a couple through with a spear for their apostasy, in hopes that this will constitute a suitable sin offering and lift the plague. God obliges.

There are also five military conflicts to deal with:

- **Attacks orchestrated by the Amalekites (Exodus 17:8–16), a group of bandits who attack the Israelites as they march to Sinai**—According to Jewish tradition, the Amalekites are so despised by God because they had attacked the Israelites' flank, killing the old and infirm.

- **When Israel reaches the territory of the Amorites, King Sihon refuses to let them pass (Numbers 21:21–32)**—They pass by force, though, conquering much of his territory as they go.

- **Immediately after defeating Sihon, the Israelites are confronted by King Og of Bashan and his army (Numbers 21:33–35)**—According to a literal reading of the text, all of the people of Bashan—men, women, and children—are slaughtered.

- **It is implied that Israel goes to war with the Moabites, whose territory the Israelites must pass near to enter the Promised Land**—Most notable is the story of Balaam (Numbers 22:2–24:25), a Mesopotamian seer with no significant ties to the Israelites. Balak, king of Moab, calls on Balaam to issue a prophecy against the Israelites. With the aid of his donkey (who speaks and alerts him to the presence of an angel), Balaam temporarily becomes a prophet of sorts and foretells the victory of Israel. Balaam is later presented as a villainous figure who is killed by the Israelites during their siege of Midian (31:8).

■ **Israel also goes to war with the Midianites (Numbers 25:16–18; 31:1–54)**—After conquering the Midianite territory, they slay the men but keep the women and children as prisoners. In one of the most disturbing passages of the Bible, the army of the Israelites decides that all nonvirgin women and male children should be slaughtered; only girls and virgin women are spared. Scholars suspect that this text was inserted from a more obscure tradition than most others (because it refers to Balaam as a villain and also to a plague at Peor, which is never directly described earlier in the text).

At the end of the story, Moses ascends a mountain one last time—Mount Nebo, in the plains of Moab—and God shows him the Promised Land. He anoints the military hero Joshua, Son of Nun, as his successor and then lies down to die. The Israelites enter the Promised Land, presumably carrying the bones of Joseph with them so they can be buried there (Exodus 18:19). After more than 400 years in Egypt, the 12 tribes of Israel have returned to the land promised to Abraham, Isaac, and Jacob—the Promised Land of Canaan.

Biblically Speaking

"Never since has there arisen a prophet in Israel like Moses, whom the LORD knew face to face. He was unequaled for all the signs and wonders that the LORD sent him to perform in the land of Egypt, against Pharaoh and all his servants and his entire land, and for all the mighty deeds and all the terrifying displays of power that Moses performed in the sight of all Israel."

—Deuteronomy 34:10–12

THE ABSOLUTE MINIMUM

■ After the death of Joseph, the leaders of Egypt enslaved and mistreated the Israelites. The Israelites escaped after God inflicted 10 plagues on the Egyptians.

■ Jewish law is rooted in the 613 commandments described in Exodus, Leviticus, Numbers, and Deuteronomy.

■ The Israelites faced grave challenges, both internal and external, on their way to the Promised Land.

RESOURCES

- **Moses (Wikipedia)**—en.wikipedia.org/wiki/Moses
- **A List of the 613 *Mitzvot* (Jewfaq)**—www.jewfaq.org/613.htm

PART III

PROPHETS AND KINGS

- The concept of Chosenness in the Jewish tradition

- The covenant, or contract, between God and humanity as expressed in the Hebrew Bible

- The Deuteronomistic cycle of grace, betrayal, punishment, and repentance

9

COVENANTS BROKEN AND COVENANTS RENEWED

The historical and prophetic books, generally referred to in the Jewish tradition as the Prophets (*Nevi'im*), tell the story of the people of Israel and their relationship with God. In the prophetic books this relationship is understood as a *covenant*, or contract, between God and Israel: He will be their God, and they will be His people.

A Chosen People

Judaism has historically been a religion of covenants based on friendships between God and ancient biblical figures who served as representatives of the human race. Orthodox Judaism teaches that there are two covenants:

- **The covenant of Noah (Genesis 9:1–17)**—Applicable to the entire human race, wherein God offers animals as food and promises never again to destroy the world with a flood but declares that blood is sacred and that anyone who takes the life of another human being should die.

- **The covenant of Abraham (Genesis 12:1–3 and 22:15–19)**—Applicable only to the Jewish people, which establishes Judaism as a holy nation (*goy kadosh*) blessed and set apart by God.

This blessing comes with a price, however: The Jewish people obey a stricter set of laws than members of other nations—613 commandments in all. The special relationship between God and the Jewish people comes with both advantages and disadvantages: a unique blessing, but also greater responsibility. Because Judaism teaches that Jews and non-Jews both have a share in the world to come, the *Chosenness* of the Jewish people is a challenge, not a privileged status. To be God's people is to be subject to more of his attention, both positive and negative. Many who obey the law see it as a joyous opportunity to live in a stronger relationship with God, but in the books of the Prophets, straying from the law brings harsh consequences.

Controversy

Over the centuries, anti-semites have misunderstood the concept of chosenness. Chosenness does *not* imply that Jews are superior to non-Jews in any way. Instead it refers to special responsibilities, and special transformative experiences, that come with living in the unique covenant that God has made with the Jewish people. Judaism teaches that Jews and non-Jews are loved equally by God, and have an equal share in the world to come.

Biblically Speaking

"It was not because you were more numerous than any other people that the Lord set his heart on you and chose you—for you were the fewest of all peoples. It was because the Lord loved you and kept the oath that he swore to your ancestors ..."

—Deuteronomy 7:7–8

The Deuteronomistic Cycle

Although the Chosenness of the Jewish people is unconditional, God's blessing of Israel and the Jewish people in the Hebrew Bible is contingent on faithfulness.

In the Books of the Prophets, the relationship between God and the Jewish people operates according to what is generally described as the *Deuteronomistic Cycle*:

1. **Blessing**—The Jewish nation is subject to special favor, freely conquering other nations and defending its own sovereignty. They gratefully obey God's laws.

2. **Betrayal**—Inevitably, those blessed by God become complacent and take his blessings for granted. They begin to ignore the law by worshipping idols, neglecting the poor, or violating the law in other ways on a widespread basis. Prophets urge lax Jews not to neglect God's laws; otherwise, the entire nation may be punished.

3. **Punishment**—The Jewish nation is collectively punished, usually by conquest at the hands of an invading force (such as the Assyrians or Babylonians), and forced into horrific oppression. Prophets urge repentance.

4. **Repentance**—The people of the Jewish nation repent of their past sins and begin following God's laws again, and God resumes his blessings.

The theme of the Deuteronomistic Cycle is the basic idea behind the teachings of nearly all Prophets of the Hebrew Bible and plays a role in other books as well. It recurs almost constantly, and its importance to the Bible as a whole is difficult to overstate.

A good example of the Deuteronomistic Cycle can be found in the Book of Amos, which is well worth reading as an introduction to the Prophets because it's fairly short and addresses concerns that people living today will find easy to understand.

> **note**
>
> Not all traditions of Judaism still include the concept of Chosenness as a core doctrine. Reconstructionist Judaism, for instance, teaches that God does not have a special relationship with any nation, a view held by many Reform Jews as well.

> **Biblically Speaking**
>
> "Therefore because you trample on the poor and take from them levies of grain, you have built houses of hewn stone, but you shall not live in them; you have planted pleasant vineyards, but you shall not drink their wine.
>
> "For I know how many are your transgressions, and how great are your sins—you who afflict the righteous, who take a bribe, and push aside the needy in the gate...
>
> "I hate, I despise your festivals, and I take no delight in your solemn assemblies.
>
> "Take away from me the noise of your songs; I will not listen to the melody of your harps.
>
> "But let justice roll down like waters, and righteousness like an ever flowing stream."
>
> —Amos 5:11–12

According to tradition, Amos was a farmer in Judah—Israel's Southern Kingdom—during the eighth century B.C. Israel thrived and expanded under the rule of King Jeroboam II, a far cry from the horrors Israel had experienced in the past and would soon experience again. The wealth and stability of Israel was seen as a *blessing* from God.

The rich ruling class of the Northern Kingdom betrayed God, however, through bribery and profound, heartless oppression of the poor. Comfortable and happy in their own wealth and security, the aristocrats of the Northern Kingdom ignored the suffering within their midst. Amos railed against this *betrayal*.

He also prophesied *punishment*. Channeling the anger of God, Amos cried out that "the high places of Isaac shall be made desolate, and the sanctuaries of Israel shall be laid waste, and I will rise against the house of Jeroboam with the sword" (7:9). Israel would be completely destroyed, Amos prophesied, and its aristocracy exiled to a foreign land. He cited a recent earthquake (9:1) as evidence of God's anger with the Northern Kingdom aristocracy.

But when Israel *repented* of its sins, it would once again experience *blessing*. The old cities would be rebuilt, its prosperity would return, and the people of Israel would never again experience exile.

> ## Biblically Speaking
>
> "The time is surely coming, says the Lord, when the one who plows shall overtake the one who reaps, and the treader of grapes the one who sows the seed; the mountains shall drip sweet wine, and all the hills shall flow with it.
>
> "I will restore the fortunes of my people Israel, and they shall rebuild the ruined cities and inhabit them...
>
> "I will plant them upon their land, and they shall never again be plucked up out of the land that I have given them, says the LORD your God."
>
> —Amos 9:13–15

The Absolute Minimum

- The traditional Jewish concept of Chosenness holds that the physical and spiritual descendants of Abraham hold a special relationship with God, binding them to a stricter set of principles than those governing non-Jews.

- The books of the Prophets teach that the nation of Israel had a special contract with God, based on the Chosenness of the Jewish people: If Israel collectively obeyed God's commandments, He would fulfill His part of the agreement and the nation would thrive; but if Israel collectively disobeyed God's commandments, the nation would collectively suffer.

- Prophets interpreted the fate of Israel based on the Deuteronomistic Cycle of blessing, betrayal, punishment, and repentance. If graced by God, the Israel of the Prophets would collectively forget His commandments and betray Him, suffer punishment, return to God's laws in desperation, and then be subject to grace once again.

- For this reason, the books of the Prophets generally describe one of two pleas: either to avoid complacency in the face of success or to return to God's laws in the face of despair.

Resources

- **History of Ancient Israel and Judah (Wikipedia)—** en.wikipedia.org/wiki/History_of_ancient_Israel_and_Judah
- **The Nevi'im (Wikipedia)—**en.wikipedia.org/wiki/Nevi'im

IN THIS CHAPTER

- Joshua leads the Israelites in their reconquest of Canaan, the Promised Land

- After the death of Joshua, Israel is itself conquered by local Canaanite tribes and repeatedly falls under foreign occupation for a period lasting more than 400 years

- During this time, God sends 15 judges (*shoftim*) to relieve the oppression of the Israelites, although none make Israel into an independent nation

10

CONQUESTS AND CHAOS

The death of Moses left the Israelites on the cusp of Canaan, the Promised Land. Actual conquest of the land fell on a military man named Joshua, who was anointed Moses' successor. Joshua would be successful, but after his death he left no clear successor and Israel, lacking leadership, fell into anarchy. During more than 400 years of captivity, 15 judges (*shoftim*) would rise from the ranks of the struggling new nation to offer their leadership.

This Land Is My Land

According to Deuteronomy 34, Joshua is the anointed (divinely authorized) successor to Moses. Unlike Moses, who came from a non–military shepherd's background, Joshua is described mainly as a warrior—in the Torah, he is most prominently featured for leading an army to battle the Amalekites (Exodus 17:9–14). He is a natural choice to lead the conquest of an occupied region and emerges from the Book of Joshua as arguably the most potent military commander in the entire Hebrew Bible. Joshua 12:9–24 credits him with defeating no fewer than 31 enemy kings during his military career.

THE GODS OF CANAAN

Even though the ancient original inhabitants of Canaan did not preserve an oral tradition comparable to that of the Israelites, much can be learned about them by way of archaeology and translation of ancient texts. The Egyptians, who referred to the Canaanites as "Kanana," depicted them as well-armed and formidable soldiers.

In the Bible, the Canaanites are the descendants of Canaan, the cursed grandson of Moses (Genesis 9:25). They are described as worshipping a god called Baal, but this is somewhat vague because the term, loosely translated as "lord," can be used to refer to any number of figures. The Bible most likely refers to worship of Baal-Hadad ("Lord Hadad"), god of thunderstorms and patron of fertility, who was represented by a bull. Ashtart (Hebrew "Ashtoreth"), his female counterpart, was more completely oriented toward fertility and represented by snakes. Canaanite religion was very much oriented toward revered statues of *Baal-Hadad* and Ashtart, placing it squarely in the category of idolatry by Israelite standards.

Conventional wisdom has it that the Canaanites also practiced child sacrifice as a means of appeasing angry gods, and this is almost certainly true; child sacrifice was a fairly common practice in the region at the time. It was most likely not a universal practice even among the Canaanites, but the Israelites' wholesale rejection of child sacrifice was remarkable.

From a contemporary perspective, the Book of Joshua can be difficult to absorb. It is often violent, describing the slaughter of men, women, and even children as if they were acts of obedience toward God (6:21, 8:22–26, 10:28–32), and it describes political conflicts and realities set thousands of years in the past, in a world that most of us cannot imagine.

RAHAB, YOU DON'T HAVE TO PUT ON THE RED LIGHT

Plenty of movies rely on the cliche of the prostitute with a heart of gold, but one clear biblical example is Rahab (Joshua 2:1–21). When Joshua sends spies to scout out the Jericho region, they hide out in the home of Rahab, a Canaanite prostitute—a questionable character on at least two counts. But she saves their lives by hiding them under the flax on her roof, and in repayment they agree to allow her and her descendants to coexist peacefully among the Israelites, even though they are Canaanites. In Jewish tradition, she is regarded as an ideal convert and a possible ancestor of Ezekiel; in the Christian tradition (drawing on the Aramaic biblical commentaries that had come into wide use by that time), she is considered the wife of Salmon (Matthew 1:5), the great-great grandmother of David, and subsequently an ancestor of Jesus Christ himself.

For the new residents of Canaan, however, a more immediate challenge poses itself: maintaining order. The death of Joshua creates a power vacuum, leaving Israel surrounded by hostile tribes and overflowing with dissent from within as more Israelites begin to adopt Canaanite religious practices and abandon the god of their ancestors.

Here Come the Judges

As the new nation of Israel lapses into idolatry and oppression at the hands of foreign nations, Judges records that God felt merciful and began to inspire new heroes, or judges (*shotfim*), to alleviate the suffering of the Israelites. (These are not necessarily judges in the legal sense of the term; it would probably be more accurate to understand them as leaders of society.) Many of these 15 figures, whose stories are told in the Book of Judges and summarized in Table 10.1, are among the most captivating and complex in the entire Bible. I have chosen to focus on 5: Ehud, Deborah and Barak, Jephthah, and Samson.

Table 10.1 The Judges

Judge	Verses	Description
Othniel	Judges 3:9–11	After Israel's 8-year captivity under the Babylonian king Cushanrishathaim ("double-wicked"; probably not the name he called himself), the military leader Othniel leads an army to fight off the invaders, granting Israel 40 years of independence.
Ehud	Judges 3:15–4:1	The left-handed Benjaminite warrior fights off the Moabites, granting Israel 80 years of independence. (More on Ehud in this chapter.)
Shamgar	Judges 3:31	Shamgar killed 600 Philistine invaders with an oxgoad, or primitive cattle prod.
Deborah	Judges 4:4–5:31	A prophetess who judges cases while Israel is under Canaanite oppression, she orders Barak to rout the armies of the Canaanite military commander Sisera. Their attack gives Israel 40 years of independence. (More on Deborah in this chapter.)

Table 10.1 (continued)

Judge	Verses	Description
Barak	Judges 4:6–5:31	A powerful military leader who serves the prophetess Deborah and defeats the armies of the Canaanites. (More on Barak in this chapter.)
Gideon	Judges 6:11–8:35	Anxious, physically weak, and full of doubts, Gideon nevertheless leads a campaign that successfully throws off Israel's Midianite oppressors and grants his people 40 years of independence.
Abimelech	Judges 8:31–9:57	Abimelech, son of Gideon, is a particularly wicked judge—he attempts to claim the kingship of Israel by claiming divine lineage from Gideon. To make the decision easier, he murders his 70 brothers and slaughters civilians who question his authority (9:46–49). After only a 3-year reign, he is killed when an Israelite woman standing high above him on a tower throws a stone on his head, crushing his skull. (Not to be confused with the Abimelech mentioned in the Book of Genesis, who was a different figure entirely.)
Tola	Judges 10:1–10:2	Judges Israel for 23 years.
Jair	Judges 10:3–10:5	Judges Israel for 22 years.
Jephthah	Judges 11:1–12:7	The son of a prostitute, the mercenary leader Jephthah takes command of his family's army to defeat the invading Ammonites. (More on Jephthah in this chapter.)
Ibzan	Judges 12:8–12:10	Judges Israel for 7 years.
Elon	Judges 12:11–12:12	Judges Israel for 10 years.
Abdon	Judges 12:13–12:15	Judges Israel for 80 years.
Samson	Judges 13–16	The legendary biblical strongman, who kills thousands of Philistine soldiers but falls prey to the seductive Delilah. (More on Samson in this chapter.)
Samuel	1 Samuel	The final prophet, a man of deep integrity who wields immense religious and political power and anoints Israel's first king, Saul. (Discussed in the next chapter.)

Ehud the Benjaminite (3:15–4:1)

When Ehud comes on the scene, Israel faces oppression at the hands of the Moabites. The corpulent King Eglon rules over the Moabite invaders, demanding tribute from his Israelite subjects. Ehud, a left-handed Benjaminite warrior, has an idea of how he might put an end to the Moabite oppression: He hides a double-edged blade on his right leg, under his clothes, and goes to meet Eglon to deliver tribute. There he catches Eglon off guard, assassinates him, and flees before the body is discovered—then he launches a full-scale attack against the vulnerable Moabite forces. They are routed, and Israel is saved—for the time being.

> **Biblically Speaking**
>
> "When Ehud had finished presenting the tribute [to King Eglon]…[he] said, 'I have a secret message for you, O king.' So the king said, 'Silence!' and all his attendants went out from his presence. Ehud came to him, while he was sitting alone in his cool roof chamber, and said, 'I have a message from God for you.' So he rose from his seat. Then Ehud reached with his left hand, took the sword from his right thigh, and thrust it into Eglon's belly…."
>
> —Judges 3:18–22

Deborah and Barak (4:4–5:31)

Deborah, a prophetess who judges cases in Canaanite-occupied Israel, receives word from God that it is the right time to attack the opposing forces. She calls on Barak, a military commander, to engage the armies of Sisera, the Canaanite military leader. She warns Barak that his forces will not be able to kill Sisera themselves, however, because she has been told by God that he will die at the hands of a woman. Indeed he does; Jael, a woman of the non-Israelite Kenite ethnicity, finally tires of his behavior and kills him with a tent stake.

Jephthah the Outlaw (11:1–12:7)

When we first meet Jephthah, son of a prostitute, he has been cast out of his family and become known as a feared mercenary commander. But when Israel is invaded by the Ammonites, his family pleads with him to come back and lead their military forces. Jephthah makes a promise to God: If He grants victory over the Ammonites, then Jephthah will offer the first creature that leaves his property when he returns home as a burnt offering. Jephthah defeats the Ammonites but faces tragedy when he returns home and his daughter rushes out to greet him.

Samson the Nazirite (13–16)

No story in the Book of Judges is better known than that of Samson, the deadly strongman with a weakness for inquisitive women. His story begins with his parents, who are infertile but are visited by an angel with an offer they can't refuse: They will be given a child, but he will be dedicated to God as a *nazirite* (Numbers 6:1–21), which means he must be kept away from unclean animals, corpses, and fermented food and drink and that his hair must never be cut. He violates most of his vows—most remarkably in 14:8–9, where he eats fermented honey from the corpse of an unclean animal—but still receives superhuman strength from God, which allows him to slaughter thousands of enemy Philistines.

After he falls madly in love with an unscrupulous Philistine named Delilah (16:4–17), she convinces him to tell her the secret of his strength—his uncut hair. His hair is trimmed, his eyes are gouged out, and he is held captive in Jericho—but, in a final moment of strength, he brings down the pillars of the temple, taking his own life and the lives of thousands of Philistines with him.

note

The Philistines were a coalition of tribes in southern Palestine who frequently clashed with Israel during the first centuries of its existence. However, they largely vanished from history from that point on. Today the term *Philistine* is often used to refer to people who have no appreciation for the arts—a usage that dates back to seventeenth-century Germany, where those who studied at universities referred to hostile townspeople as *Philistines*.

Horrors of Anarchy

The Book of Judges ends with three horror stories meant to demonstrate the lawlessness and barbarity of the era of the judges, which is not authorized by God:

■ **The Levite's concubine (19:1–30)**—In a story reminiscent of Lot's experience in Sodom (Genesis 19), a Levite staying in the Benjaminite town of Gibeah receives out-of-town guests who are promptly threatened with gang rape. Just as Lot offered his virgin daughters, the Levite offers his concubine—but this time, the townspeople accept his offer. His concubine is raped until she collapses, unconscious, on his doorstep. Outraged at the way she has been treated, he cuts her into 12 pieces—the text leaves the impression that she was still alive,

Biblically Speaking

"In those days there was no king in Israel; all the people did what was right in their own eyes."

—Judges 21:25

albeit unconscious, until this point—and sends each piece to representatives of each of the 12 tribes of Israel.

■ **The Benjaminite slaughter (20:1–48)**—The 12 tribes of Israel assemble; goaded on by the Levite, all but the Benjaminites agree to attack the men of Gibeah and slaughter them for what they have done. But the Benjaminites take up arms in defense of Gibeah, resulting in a bloody conflict. The majority 11 tribes defeat the Benjaminite armies and then slaughter their people. There are no Benjaminite women left to bear children, so the tribe is in danger of extinction.

■ **The atrocities of Jabesh-gilead and the rape of Shiloh (21:1–24)**—It is noted that the city of Jabesh-gilead sent no representatives to the assembly of the 12 tribes, so it is decided that Jabesh-gilead would be the ideal location to find women for the Benjaminites. A massive army is assembled and slaughters every male and every nonvirgin woman in the city. The 400 virgin girls who survive are kidnapped and forced into "marriages" with their Benjaminite captors. When it becomes clear that this number is too low to replenish the Benjaminite stock, young Benjaminite men are given the go-ahead to forcibly abduct young women attending the annual religious festival at Shiloh and take them away as wives.

At this point in the story, one fact becomes clear: Israel needs new leadership. Fortunately, the final judge—Samuel—is about to provide it.

THE ABSOLUTE MINIMUM

■ It is written that Joshua, the successor of Moses, conquered most of the Promised Land by force and established the nation of Israel.

■ Shortly after Joshua's death, Israel descended into anarchy and began to adopt Canaanite practices. It soon became easy prey for invaders.

■ Fifeen leaders (*shoftim*, or "judges") emerged to fight for Israeli independence, with mixed results.

RESOURCES

- **The Canaanites (*Catholic Encyclopedia*)** www.newadvent.org/cathen/03569b.htm

- **Rahab (*Jewish Encyclopedia*)**—www.jewishencyclopedia.com/view.jsp?artid=71&letter=R

- **The Gideons International**—www.gideons.org

- ***Samson Agonistes* by John Milton**—darkwing.uoregon.edu/~rbear/samson.html

IN THIS CHAPTER

- The judge-prophet Samuel and the first four kings of Israel: Saul, Ishbaal, David, and Solomon

- The division of Israel into two kingdoms, north (Israel) and south (Judah), and their respective histories

- The destruction of the two kingdoms at the hands of foreign invaders and the aftermath

11

THE ERA OF KINGS

After the conquests of Joshua and the chaos of the Judges period, the people of Israel pursued stability by organizing the 12 tribes of Israel into a single kingdom ruled by a single king. According to Judges and 1 Samuel, this arrangement was generally regarded as a vast improvement over the violence and anarchy of earlier periods, but it would be short-lived. Within a century, Israel would experience civil war and split into two kingdoms.

The United Kingdom (1020–920 B.C.)

The Books of 1 and 2 Samuel deal primarily with the first kings of Israel rather than with Samuel himself, but he is certainly a pivotal figure in the Bible. In the years preceding his public ministry, Israel was overseen on a regional basis by a series of religious leaders called *shoftim*, or judges. The last of the major judges described in the Bible is Samuel, who is also a prophet. He notes the threat that the people of Israel face at the hands of the better-organized Philistines and attempts to give more structure to the nation of Israel by establishing a dynasty of sorts, setting his sons up as judges over the people (1 Samuel 8:1–3). This idea is rejected, and the people demand a king.

At this point, Israel is just a loose confederation of 12 tribes united by a common culture and religious ancestry. They have no significant shared government, and there is no single ruler who holds dominion over all 12 tribes. There is only their shared belief in God as king, which inspires them to take the Ark of the Covenant—containing the Ten Commandments given to Moses—to the battlefield, where it has invariably granted victory to the Israelites in the past (4:1–22). The Israelites lose the battle and the Ark, no doubt prompting many to wonder whether God had abandoned His people.

But as it turns out, the Ark is not a blessing to the Philistines. It spreads death and disease in every city it is sent to; in desperation, the Philistines return it to the Israelites. Unfortunately, the Ark has the same effect even in Israel. The effects stop only when the Ark is placed in Jerusalem.

By describing these two scenarios, the First Book of Samuel provides justification for two ideas: the appointment of a king and the establishment of an Israeli capital in Jerusalem.

Saul and the Rise of David

The Bible reports that Saul was a Benjaminite, considered at the time to be the weakest and least reputable of the 12 tribes of Israel (1 Samuel 9:21), and a shepherd of a lower-class family at that. But he was championed and anointed by the judge and prophet Samuel to serve as Israel's first king, falling out of favor when he disobeyed a series of divine orders, relying instead on his own judgment.

The prophet Samuel tires of King Saul's routine displays of disobedience and is ordered by God to find a new king. He is sent out into the wilderness, where he declares that the torch will be passed to the shepherd boy David (1 Samuel 16:1–13), who is also handy with the lyre (a musical instrument resembling a small harp). King Saul, who knows nothing of Samuel's excursion, hires David (who has already been secretly anointed as Judah's next king) as a court musician. He is so impressed with David's skill that he eventually appoints him royal armor-bearer, an esteemed position that ensures that David would always be in Saul's company.

The story of David and Goliath comes in 1 Samuel 17. The chapter seems to be independent of the rest of 1 Samuel because no mention is made of David's position in chapter 16 as Saul's armor-bearer, a military position that sometimes involved combat, and David is introduced to Saul after he arrives to witness the fight between the Philistine giant Goliath and the not-yet-chosen champion of Israel. David ends up petitioning King Saul to let him challenge the giant, and when Saul reluctantly agrees, David kills the mighty Philistine warrior with a rock fired from a sling.

At this point, David begins to be accepted as a full member of Saul's military and builds a close friendship with Saul's son Jonathan. Soon the stories of David's military successes begin to outshine those of Saul himself (1 Samuel 18:7), and the jealous king plots David's demise. After making several direct attempts on his life, a disgusted Saul decides to send David away for extended campaigns leading the Israeli army, where David's fame only increases (18:13–16). An increasingly desperate Saul then offers David his own daughter, Michal, in marriage in exchange for 100 Philistine foreskins—no simple request. Because circumcision was (and for the most part still is) an important symbol of Jewish identity, and because having one's foreskin cut off without any anaesthesia isn't a pleasant experience, a Philistine warrior hostile to the tribes of Israel would give up his foreskin only when David pried it from his cold, dead...fingers.

So, this would appear to be a suicide mission—David is being asked to kill or subdue 100 Philistine warriors, a task Saul believes will make short work of the young prodigy. This, of course, does not happen, and David cheerfully greets his soon-to-be father-in-law with a disturbingly large pile of dismembered skin.

When it becomes clear that this sort of indirect approach won't work, Saul begins to take matters into his own hands, forcing the young king-to-be into hiding. After David takes shelter with the priests of Nob (21:1–22:23), who are not aware of his refugee status, Saul has them slaughtered; the only survivor, Abiathar, hides with David and his men as they settle in among the Philistines. Saul, meanwhile, has

note

Goliath is fairly huge according to the Hebrew text—six cubits and a span, or about 9'9". The earliest Greek manuscripts have Goliath at a mere four cubits and a span, or 6'9", which would have still been astonishingly tall by ancient Near Eastern standards. His armor would have weighed in at "five thousand shekels of bronze" (16:5), or about 125 pounds, and the tip of his spear, at "six hundred shekels of iron" (16:7), would have weighed about 15 pounds.

note

It would be a mistake to look at the sling as a mere toy—slings were the firearms of the ancient world and deadly in the hands of well-trained soldiers.

troubles of his own: Philistines are gathering and Samuel, on whom he has relied to discern the outcome of battles, is dead. So Saul decides to contact Samuel the only way he knows how: by finding a psychic who can contact the dead.

Because he has banned such psychics within the kingdom of Israel, they're a bit scarce—but he hears of one in the city of Endor and goes in disguise to visit her (1 Samuel 28:3–25). She puts him in touch with Samuel, who offers him unwelcome news: Saul and most of his sons will be joining Samuel the next day.

Having run out of options, the terrified Saul awaits his destiny.

> **note**
>
> The medium, or witch, of Endor is portrayed in a very positive light, lovingly feeding and comforting Saul (28:20–25), who is paralyzed by fear after hearing Samuel's message. This is rather unusual because the Bible is generally fairly hostile toward witches, sorcerors, and other practitioners of magic.

Samuel's prophecy comes true: Saul meets his fate the next day. Two accounts of Saul's death are given. One suggests that he fell on his own sword rather than risk falling into the hands of the Philistines (1 Samuel 31:5), and the other suggests that a sympathetic Amalekite put the mortally wounded Saul out of his misery (2 Samuel 1:7–9). Some scholars have harmonized these passages by suggesting that Saul's attempt at suicide was unsuccessful. In either case, Saul's death releases David from his loyalty oath and allows him to ascend to the throne. At first, he is portrayed as an exemplary king, avenging Saul's death (2 Samuel 1:1–16) despite their less-than-friendly history and avenging the death of Saul's son Ishbaal (4:9–12), who had attempted to wrest the kingdom from David.

His conquests become the stuff of legend, and he establishes Israel's capital in Jerusalem, which from this point on would be the world capital of Judaism. But then King David suffers the fate of so many of the world's most powerful men: He can control massive armies and cities hundreds of miles away, but he cannot control his own hormones.

> **Controversy**
>
> The Bible provides two different accounts of Saul's death. In 1 Samuel 31:1–4, a wounded Saul falls on his own sword to prevent the encroaching Philistines from having the privilege of killing him. In 2 Samuel 1:4–10, an Amalekite armor scavenger tells David that he had encountered a mortally wounded Saul on the battlefield and killed him out of mercy.

The Legacy of David

The view from the top of David's house, towering as it does over the rest of the city, is magnificent. But one afternoon, it is more magnificent than usual—a beautiful woman, Bathsheba, is bathing not far away. She is married, but that's no obstacle to a king, especially when the husband is out in battle. David sends messengers to invite her to the palace, where the pair finish the day on a memorable note. Then David sends her home and goes about his own business. A few days later, he is in for a shock: Bathsheba is pregnant, and it is only a matter of time before her pregnancy will be impossible to hide—and her husband Uriah the Hittite, absent at war, will know that he could not be the father.

Panicked, King David calls Bathsheba's husband in from the battlefield and orders him to go home and sleep with his wife. Uriah has probably received tougher assignments in his time, but in obedience to the military policies of the Israelites (which require all soldiers to observe celibacy near combat dates), Uriah refuses and sleeps outside the front door of the castle instead. King David's next attempt to resolve the situation is comical: He, the king of Israel, gets Uriah drunk in hopes of sending the soldier home to be seduced by his own wife. That doesn't work, either, so David takes drastic—and, let's face it, downright evil—measures: He pulls a Saul and tries to get the guy killed by sending him on an impossible assignment (2 Samuel 11:14–16) so he can then marry his widow. In this case, he sends sealed orders (carried by Uriah himself) that Uriah's fellow troops back away, leaving him alone on the battle to face the Philistines. Loyal Uriah never opens the envelope to read his own death warrant and meets a bloody death on the battlefield. King David—now an adulterer *and* a murderer—thus wins the hand of fair Bathsheba. According to the Bible, Bathsheba does not know of David's treachery; she mourns for her husband (2 Samuel 11:26–27), one of many casualties of war, before she is carried off to become David's wife.

But God reveals the whole story to the prophet Nathan, who challenges David for his sin (2 Samuel 12). The punishment will be harsh: Bathsheba's newborn son, the result of her afternoon with David, dies (12:15–23)—and he will not be the last of David's children to suffer. David's daughter Tamar is raped (2 Samuel 13) by his oldest

> ## note
>
> David ordered Uriah: "Go down to your house, and wash your feet" (2 Samuel 11:8). In the ancient Jewish world, "feet" was a common euphemism for genitals, so "wash your feet" comes with an implicit wink and nudge.

> ## Biblically Speaking
>
> "The king said to the Cushite, 'Is it well with the young man Absalom?' The Cushite answered, 'May the enemies of my lord the king, and all who rise up to do you harm, be like that young man.' The king was deeply moved, and went up to the chamber over the gate, and wept; and as he went, he said, 'O my son Absalom, my son, my son Absalom! Would I had died instead of you, O Absalom, my son, my son!'"
>
> —2 Samuel 18:32–33

son, Amnon, who is in turn killed by David's younger son, Absalom, in revenge (2 Samuel 13:23–29). The ambitious Absalom flees, assembles an army, and attempts to take over the entire nation of Israel from his father—dying at the hands of David's soldiers, despite explicit orders from David to spare his son (2 Samuel 18:9–15).

David is still remembered today as the ideal king of Israel, despite his faults, and he would establish the longest-serving dynasty in the history of Israel—a dynasty that would continue despite the loss of Amnon and Absalom. But he is perhaps best remembered as the legendary author of the Psalms, a collection of hymns to God (see Chapter 15, "Psalms and Proverbs").

When David reaches old age, one of his sons inherits the kingdom: Solomon, the second son he had with Bathsheba. Solomon arguably does as much as David to create the legacy of Israel as a united kingdom, building the great Temple in Jerusalem (1 Kings 6:1–38), which more permanently establishes the city as the capital of Judaism. He also becomes renowned for his wisdom and is credited as the author of Proverbs (see Chapter 15), along with Ecclesiastes and the Song of Songs (see Chapter 16, "Mortal Questions"). But after Solomon's death, the story of Israel as a united kingdom comes to an end.

Civil war divides the kingdom in two, both of which eventually fall to foreign invaders.

Two Kingdoms

According to 2 Samuel, every insurgency David faced—from the challenge of Ishbaal (2:12–32) to the rebellion of Absalom (15–18) to the short-lived revolt of Sheba (20)—split the kingdom between north and south. This is not particularly surprising when one considers the geography of Israel; the southern half, Judah, was isolated from foreign empires by the Salt Sea to the east and northern Israel to the north. Northern Israel, on the other hand, lined up along the Assyrian border; it was therefore more vulnerable to attack and more susceptible to foreign influence, a distinction that would become even more important when the

> **note**
>
> The stories of the Northern and Southern Kingdoms are told in Kings and in Chronicles (each broken into two parts). The books are not arranged in chronological order; instead, they represent two points of view about the history of the two kingdoms. Both were written in Southern Israel, or Judah, but at different times: Kings was probably written between the reign of Hezekiah in 715–680 B.C. and the Babylonian exile of 586 B.C. (a turbulent period in which Judah's rulers faced constant threats from foreign empires), whereas Chronicles was probably written between 540 and 332 B.C., when Judah was occupied by Persia (a relatively calm period in Israel's history). Kings was probably produced by the same tradition that compiled Deuteronomy and 1 and 2 Samuel; and Chronicles, by the tradition that compiled the books of Ezra and Nehemiah.

Temple in Jerusalem, in Southern Israel, became the center of the Jewish faith. The ethnic differences were also substantial; 10 of the 12 tribes of Israel were located in the northern half of the country, while the southern half was controlled by the tribe of Judah, with a Benjaminite minority (which was steadily shrinking due to assimilation and would eventually disappear entirely).

David and Solomon were able to keep Israel united, but under Solomon's son, Rehoboam, the differences between Northern and Southern Israel become irreconcilable. They become two separate nations: Israel, representing Northern Israel and 10 of the twelve tribes, and Judah, representing Southern Israel and the tribes of Judah and Benjamin. The more vulnerable Israel struggles along for a violent and difficult 200 years under 19 different kings (as shown in Table 11.1) before finally falling to its neighbors the Assyrians in 721 B.C. Ten of the twelve tribes of Israel are assimilated into Assyrian society, and their fate remains a mystery to this day.

Table 11.1 The Kings of Israel (the Northern Kingdom)

King	Verses	Description
Jeroboam I	1 Kings 11:26–14:30 and 2 Chronicles 10:1–16	Ruled ca. 920–900 B.C. Jeroboam had attempted to become king when the kingdom was still united but was able to achieve power only after Solomon's death when the 10 revolting tribes of northern Israel sought new leadership. His first leadership crisis: With Solomon's temple in Jerusalem in the Southern Kingdom, how could he lay claim to the religious authority so important to his people? His solution, according to the Hebrew Bible, was to build golden calf icons in the cities of Dan and Bethel and encourage worship of God at the foot of the golden calves. This forbidden practice would be continued by all the rulers of the Northern Kingdom as a means of compensating for the loss of Solomon's temple.
Nadab	1 Kings 14:20, 15:25–32	Jeroboam's son, who reigned for about 2 years at some point near 900 B.C. Nadab's time on the throne was exceptionally brief thanks to the mutinous Baasha, who made short work of Nadab and everyone else in his line of succession, ending the Jeroboam dynasty.
Baasha	1 Kings 15:16–16:7	Baasha ruled for 23 years, from about 900 B.C. to about 875 B.C. Noting that Judah's capital of Jerusalem was still a major trade center, Baasha decided to attack the Judean economy by fortifying Ramah, a Northern Kingdom city near the Israel-Judah border, and establishing

Table 11.1 (continued)

King	Verses	Description
		a special trade treaty with Syria. Unfortunately for Baasha, Judah's King Asa was a little too bright for him—bribing Syria's king to declare war on the Northern Kingdom, allowing Judah to take Ramah and a great deal of other territory besides. 1 Kings reports that the prophet Jehu foretold the destruction of his entire dynasty, which had already been threatened by Baasha's failures.
Elah	1 Kings 16:8–14	The son of Baasha, who reigned for about 1 year near 875 B.C. Like his predecessor Nadab, Elah would die at the hands of one of his generals—in this case a charioteer named Zimri.
Zimri	1 Kings 16:9–20	According to 1 Kings, Zimri assassinated the previous king Elah only to die after a 7-day reign. Zimri made the mistake of not securing his military's support *before* assassinating the king, and they quickly selected Elah's second-in-command, Omri, to hold office in his place. Sensing the end was near, Zimri set fire to the palace and burned himself to death.
Omri	1 Kings 16:16–28	Reigned from 875 B.C. or so to the late 860s B.C. Omri conquered the Moabites, established a new Northern Kingdom capital in Samaria, and began erecting monuments throughout Israel that are still being unearthed by archaeologists.
Ahab	1 Kings 16:28–22:40; 2 Chronicles 18:1–34	The son of Omri, who reigned from the late 860s B.C. to about 850 B.C. Although his name inspired the main character in *Moby Dick*, he is not as well known as his wife: Queen Jezebel, a Phoenician princess who convinced him to build a temple to her god, Baal of Tyre, in the Israeli capital of Samaria. This did not sit well with many Jews, and tradition has it that Ahab responded to the controversy very badly by executing prophets. Athaliah, daughter of Ahab and Jezebel, would briefly rule as queen of Judah.
Ahaziah	1 Kings 22:40–53; 2 Kings 1:1–18; 2 Chronicles 20:35–37	The son of Ahab and Jezebel, who reigned for about 1 year at some point near 850 B.C. He is best remembered for falling off the roof of his palace—certainly an unconventional claim to fame. Complications from the resulting injuries killed him.

King	Verses	Description
Joram	2 Kings 8:16–29 and 9:14–26; 2 Chronicles 22:5–9	The brother of Ahaziah, and the final king of the Omri dynasty, Joram (also known as Jehoram) reigned from about 850 B.C. until the early 840s B.C. He was killed at the hands of the reformer Jehu.
Jehu	1 Kings 19:16–17; 2 Kings 9:1–10:36; 2 Chronicles 22:7–9	A conservative religious reformer who ruled Israel from the early 840s B.C. to about 815 B.C. 2 Kings reports that Jehu was anointed king of Israel by the prophet Elisha; he then killed both Joram, King of Israel, and Ahaziah, King of Judah. Next, he worked to purge the Northern Kingdom of foreign religious influences. Ancient inscriptions recovered from nearby empires paint a different picture of Jehu, suggesting that it was their king Hazael, Jehu's most dangerous enemy (2 Kings 10:32), who was actually responsible for the deaths of the two kings. One Assyrian record from the period states that Jehu had actually bowed before and paid tribute to their king, Shalmaneser III, to win his support against the Arameans.
Jehoahaz	2 Kings 13:1–9	The son of Jehu, reigning from about 815 B.C. to about 800 B.C. He was somewhat more lax on religious matters than his father had been. According to 2 Kings, it was on his watch that the Israeli army was almost completely wiped out by a series of costly battles with the Arameans.
Jehoash	2 Kings 13:10–14:16	The son of Jehoahaz, reigning from about 800 B.C. to about 785 B.C. The Bible portrays Jehoash as a complicated figure: willing to tolerate no small number of forbidden practices, including worship of golden calves, but a friend of the prophet Elisha who mourned at his bedside and received his blessing.
Jeroboam II	2 Kings 14:23–29	Jeroboam, son of Jehoash, reigned from about 785 B.C. until about 745 B.C. Like his father, he permitted the worship of golden calves and other forbidden practices. Unlike his father, though, he led the Northern Kingdom through its golden age, during which it pushed back foreign invaders, expanded the realm, and led Israel through a period of astonishing economic growth. On the other hand, it was his reign that inspired Amos and Hosea to condemn the considerable gap between the rich and the poor.

Table 11.1 (continued)

King	Verses	Description
Zachariah	2 Kings 15:8–12	Zachariah, son of Jeroboam II, was the fifth and final king in the Jehu dynasty. He ruled for only 6 months before he was assassinated by Shallum.
Shallum	2 Kings 15:10–16	Shallum assassinated Zachariah to ascend to the throne but served only 1 month before he was assassinated by Menahem.
Menahem	2 Kings 15:14–23	Ruling from about 745 B.C. until the late 730s B.C., Menahem dealt with the insurgency problem the last two kings had faced by violently crushing dissent, "[ripping] open all the pregnant women" in cities where opposition was particularly strong.
Pekahiah	2 Kings 15:22–26	Menahem's son Pekahiah ruled for a mere 2 years before being assassinated by Pekah, one of his generals.
Pekah	2 Kings 15:25–31; 2 Chronicles 28:6	He reigned throughout most of the 730s B.C. Pekah made a fatal error in allying himself with the king of the Arameans to attack Jerusalem, the capital of the Southern Kingdom of Judah, because Judah, as it turned out, had an alliance with the Assyrians. The Assyrian counterattack displaced Israelis, and the destruction of the Northern Kingdom had clearly begun by the time Hoshea assassinated him and took office in about 730 B.C.
Hoshea	2 Kings 15:30, 17:1–6	Hoshea was the final king of the Northern Kingdom of Israel. He was in most respects a puppet of the Assyrians, submitting to the authority of their king and paying substantial tribute. When he held back the tribute and allied himself with the Egyptians, it proved to be a fatal mistake. The Assyrians conquered Samaria and displaced the inhabitants of the Northern Kingdom in 722–721 B.C., repopulating it with immigrants from other regions. The Northern Kingdom had been destroyed.

Judah, the Southern Kingdom, remained intact and stable. Whereas Israel's capital of Samaria was vulnerable to invaders, Jerusalem was more remote and much easier to defend. Whereas Israel's religious tradition gradually disappeared under the influence of Assyrian polytheism, Judah's remained largely intact with the Temple—the center of Jewish worship—located safely in Jerusalem and the Ark of the Covenant of Moses and Joshua safely contained inside. Whereas Israel's kings frequently assassinated each other, Judah's monarchy, as shown in Table 11.2, was remarkably stable according to the biblical account. From the time Solomon's rule passed to his son Rehoboam to the fall of Jerusalem in 586 B.C., the kingdom of Judah remained under the control of David's descendants—seldom falling into the hands of others, and never for long.

Table 11.2 The Kings (and Queen) of Judah (the Southern Kingdom)

King	Verses	Description
Rehoboam	1 Kings 12:1–27, 14:21–31; 2 Chronicles 10:1–12:16	Rehoboam, the son of Solomon, reigned over the Southern Kingdom of Judah from about 930 B.C. until about 915 B.C. It was his decision to retain the strict tax policy of his father that had divided the kingdom in the first place (at some point in the mid-920s B.C.), and he suffered demoralizing defeats at the hands of the Egyptians—most notably the sacking of Jerusalem by the Egyptian king Shishak, who is believed to have taken the Ark of the Covenant.
Abijam	1 Kings 14:31–15:8; 2 Chronicles 12:16–14:1	The son of Rehoboam and the grandson of Solomon, Abijam ruled for 3 years during for the 910s B.C. Abijam is notable primarily his failures to conquer the Northern Kingdom.
Asa	1 Kings 15:8–24; 2 Chronicles 14:1–16:14	Abijam's son Asa, who ruled from about 915 B.C. until about 875 B.C., is remembered for destroying idols, making peace with the Egyptians, and forging a controversial alliance with Syria. According to 2 Chronicles, he died of a foot disease of some kind, probably a foot infection. The text describes this as punishment for his decision to trust his physicians, rather than God, with his care.
Jehoshaphat	2 Kings 3:1–27, 22:1–20; 2 Chronicles 17:1–20:37	Asa's son Jehoshaphat reigned from about 875 B.C. until about 850 B.C. He led the army of Judah to conquer the Moabites but withdrew in horror and disgust when he discovered that King Mesha of Moab had offered his own son as a burnt offering to protect his cities. Jehoshaphat reigned over a period of astonishing economic prosperity and was described by some as the greatest king since Solomon.

Table 11.2 (continued)

King	Verses	Description
Jehoram	2 Kings 8:16–24; 2 Chronicles 21:1–20	Jehoram, son of Jehoshaphat, reigned for 7 years during the 840s B.C. He was regarded as disloyal to the God of Abraham, perhaps because he had married Athaliah (the daughter of King Ahab and Queen Jezebel of the Northern Kingdom), and is best remembered for his misfortunes: the kidnapping of all of his children except for Ahaziah and the painful abdominal infection (probably appendicitis) that killed him soon afterward.
Ahaziah	2 Kings 8:25–9:29; 2 Chronicles 21:17–22:9	Ahaziah reigned for only 1 year during the early 840s B.C. The son of Jehoram and Athaliah, he formed an alliance with his mother's brother—King Joram of Israel, the Northern Kingdom—which cost him his life. It is written that he was killed along with his uncle by the Israeli reformer and future ruler of the Northern Kingdom, Jehu.
Athaliah (queen)	2 Kings 11:1–16; 2 Chronicles 22:2–23:15	The daughter of King Ahab and Queen Jezebel of the Northern Kingdom, Athaliah is the only woman to have functioned as primary ruler of either kingdom in any public capacity. She held power from the early 840s B.C. until about 835 B.C., although she had also played a significant controlling role in the reigns of her husband Jehoram and her son Ahaziah. With no living sons, she attempted to hold onto power by having all possible male successors executed. One, named Jehoash, was kept in hiding by his aunt Jehosheba until he came of age, at which point the priest Jehoiada ordered the queen's death and declared her only surviving grandson king.
Jehoash	2 Kings 11:1–12:31; 2 Chronicles 22:10–24:27	Jehoash reigned from about 835 B.C. (when he would have been about 8 years old) until about 795 B.C. While he was young, the priest Jehoiada essentially reigned over the Southern Kingdom and upheld the religious principles of Judaism; but when Jehoiada died, Jehoash struck out on his own, began to favor the worship of multiple gods, and sometimes ordered the execution of those who protested him (such as Jehoiada's grandson, the prophet Zechariah after whom

King	Verses	Description
		the Book of Zechariah is named). 2 Kings reports that Jehoash was assassinated by his servants after melting down Judah's religious relics to buy the favor of King Hazael of the Arameans.
Amaziah	2 Kings 14:1–29; 2 Chronicles 24:27–25:28	Jehoash's son Amaziah reigned from about 795 B.C. until about 775 B.C. After achieving an important military victory over the Edomites, he began to worship their idols and was soon assassinated.
Uzziah (Azariah)	2 Kings 15:1–7; 2 Chronicles 26:1–23	Uzziah took the throne near 775 B.C. at the age of 16; historians believe he ruled Judah until about 740 B.C., although 2 Kings 15:2 describes a 52-year reign. Most of his reign was perfect—he is remembered, along with Solomon and Jehoshaphat, as one of the greatest kings ever to rule over Judah. Near the end of his life, however, he was stricken with a skin disease by God for marching into the temple and offering a sacrifice on the golden altar himself, using his kingly power to arrogate the position given to priests. In other words, he was punished by God for violating the separation of church and state. Despite his long and majestic reign, his amazing military conquests, and the respect he held with the people, his skin disease rendered his body unclean—necessitating that he be buried away from the other kings of the Judean monarchy and making the statement that even the greatest of kings are subject to God.
Jotham	2 Kings 15:32–38; 2 Chronicles 27:1–9	Jotham, son of Uzziah, reigned over Israel from about 740 B.C. until the early 730s B.C. It is to Jotham that many of the prophecies of Isaiah, Micah, and Hosea are addressed, and by all accounts he did not oppress them for questioning his leadership.
Ahaz	2 Kings 16:1–20; 2 Chronicles 27:9–28:27; Isaiah 7:1–8:19	Ahaz, son of Jotham, reigned from the early 730s B.C. until about 715 B.C. He allied himself with the Assyrians and began to adopt and encourage polytheistic customs, earning the wrath of Isaiah, Micah, and Hosea.
Hezekiah	2 Kings 18:1–20:21; 2 Chronicles 29:1–32:31; Isaiah 36:1–39:8;	Hezekiah, son of Ahaz, most likely reigned from about 715 B.C. until the late 680s B.C. He is remembered as one of the great

Table 11.2 (continued)

King	Verses	Description
	Sirach 48:17–25	reformers of the Jewish tradition and essentially abolished government support of idolatry in Judah.
Manasseh	2 Kings 21:1–18; 2 Chronicles 33:1–20; Prayer of Manasseh	Manasseh, son of Hezekiah, reigned over Judah from about the late 680s B.C. until about 645 B.C. Manasseh was a true rebellious teenager: He took the throne at the age of 12, and during the first 7 or 8 years of his reign, he adopted polytheism, rolled back his father's reforms, and ordered the persecution of the prophets. Tradition has it that it was Manasseh who ordered the death of Isaiah, and it has been speculated that some of the Psalms (49, 73, 77, 140, and 141) were written by those who suffered under his rule. After he was captured and tortured by the Babylonians near 680 B.C., however, he repented and ended his persecution of Jewish traditionalists—although he continued to allow idolatrous practices to flourish. The Song of Manasseh, from the Apocrypha/Pseudepigrapha (see Chapter 18, "Nowhere in the Bible"), is a song of repentance attributed to him after his period of suffering at the hands of the Babylonians.
Amon	2 Kings 21:18–26; 2 Chronicles 33:21–25	Amon, son of Manasseh, reigned for 2 years in the early 640s B.C. He was an outspoken supporter of idolatrous practices, and the prophet Zephaniah (of the Book of Zephaniah) was reportedly one of Amon's fiercest critics.
Josiah	1 Kings 13:2; 2 Kings 21:26–23:30; 1 Chronicles 3:14; 2 Chronicles 34:1–35:27	Reigning from the early 640s B.C. until 609 B.C., Josiah, son of Amon, was the greatest reformer-king in the history of Judah. He completely destroyed every vestige of idolatrous support in Judah, brought back the celebration of Passover, and (according to 2 Chronicles 34:14) oversaw the discovery of the text that became the Book of Deuteronomy. Some scholars believe that the Book of Deuteronomy (along with Joshua and Judges) was written by priests during Josiah's rule.
Jehoahaz	2 Kings 23:31–34; 2 Chronicles 36:1–4	Jehoahaz, son of Josiah, inherited the throne of Judah in 609 B.C. Within a matter of

King	Verses	Description
		months, Jerusalem was attacked by the Egyptians and he was taken abroad to Egypt, much as Manasseh was taken abroad to Babylon. But, unlike Manasseh, he was executed by his captors.
Jehoiakim	2 Kings 23:34–24:6; 2 Chronicles 36:4–8; Jeremiah 22:18–23, 36:1–32; Jeremiah 22:18–23, 36:1–32; Daniel 1:1–2	Jehoiakim, son of Josiah and brother of Jehoahaz, was appointed by the Egyptians in 609 B.C. and reigned until 597 B.C. Initially he lived under the shadow of the Egyptians, but they proved to be less of a problem than Nebuchadnezzar, the warrior-king of the Babylonians, who captured him and carried him off to Babylon (along with the prophet Daniel). At first, the submissive Jehoiakim returned to Judah and ruled it as a province of Babylon, paying annual tribute. But after he gathered his courage and refused to pay, he was killed during a siege of Jerusalem.
Jehoiachin (Coniah)	2 Kings 24:8–25:30; 2 Chronicles 36:8–10; Jeremiah 52:31–34	Jehoiachin, son of Jehoiakim, served for only 3 months in 597 B.C. before he was captured by the Babylonians and imprisoned in Babylon, where he remained for 35 years.
Zedekiah	2 Kings 24:17–25:7; 2 Chronicles 36:10–14; Jeremiah 37:1–39:18, 52:1–11; Lamentations of Jeremiah	Zedekiah, son of Josiah and brother of Jehoahaz and Jehoiakim, was the final king of Judah, ruling from 597 B.C. until its fall in 586 B.C. Appointed to lead Judah by the Babylonians, who essentially controlled it, he made one final attempt to achieve independence by forging an alliance with the Egyptians. This proved hopeless; the Babylonian king Nebuchadnezzar invaded the city and destroyed the temple in 586 B.C., rounding up some 4,600 families of Jerusalem and taking them away to Babylon. They would not be allowed to return for almost 60 years. Zedekiah, too, was taken—the Babylonians gouged his eyes out, after ensuring that the last thing he ever saw was the violent execution of his sons at the hands of his new captors. The price of disobedience was steep.

By the Rivers of Babylon

When Jerusalem fell to the Babylonians in 586 B.C., the Jewish monarchy was destroyed. Israel would never become a fully independent nation again until 1948—and even then, it would do so only as a secular democracy, not as a religious monarchy. The relative security and isolation of Southern Israel had given it about 350 years to build a monarchy, a temple, and a religion. The Babylonians destroyed the monarchy and the Temple and, now that all of Judah's major religious leaders were either slaughtered or exiled and the nation as a whole was less isolated from foreign influence than Northern Israel had been, the religion of Abraham, Isaac, and Jacob did not seem to be long for this world. Judaism, as it was known at the time, had been destroyed. It was no longer a national religion; God did not save Israel; the Babylonians had won, utterly and completely.

But then something amazing happened. The scattered thousands of Jerusalem, who had been exiled to Babylon, preserved their traditions. They held fast to the Sabbath, to circumcision, to the laws of Moses. They changed their faith to create a Judaism that could still survive without the Temple, without the monarchy, without an independent Israel. Facing profound military defeat, incredible societal pressure, and the very real threat of torture and death, they held onto the faith of their fathers, looked on the fall of Jerusalem as a test from God, and prayed for deliverance, certain that God would deliver Jerusalem back into their hands.

And many of the children who had lived to see their fathers and mothers exiled, sometimes massacred, by the Babylonians—the children who lived to see the Temple destroyed, their king blinded and his heirs slaughtered, Israel shattered, and their religious institutions swept away—also lived to see the nightmare end. Because in 539 B.C., Cyrus the Great, king of the Persians—identified in Isaiah 45:1 as the *moschiach* (messiah), the anointed one—defeated the hated Babylonians and

> ## Biblically Speaking
>
> "By the rivers of Babylon—
>
> there we sat down
> and there we wept
>
> when we remembered Zion.
>
> On the willows there
>
> we hung up our harps.
>
> For there our captors
>
> asked us for songs,
>
> and our tormentors asked for mirth,
>
> saying,
>
> 'Sing us one of the songs of Zion!'
>
> How could we sing the LORD's song
>
> in a foreign land?
>
> If I forget you, O Jerusalem,
>
> let my right hand wither!
>
> Let my tongue cling to the roof of my mouth,
>
> if I do not remember you,
>
> if I do not set Jerusalem
>
> above my highest joy."
>
> —Psalm 137:1–6

opened the gates of Jerusalem and let the former inhabitants of Jerusalem return in peace. Their country would now be operated as a semiautonomous province, or *satrapy*, of Persia and they would be completely free to continue to practice their faith. Their first step, as described in the books of Ezra and Nehemiah, was to build a new temple. But their character had changed. No longer were there 12 tribes of Israel. There was only 1: Judah, whose land would later be called Judea. No longer would members of their faith need to live in Judea to practice it. Their religion would become *Judea-ism*—Judaism. And the people of Judea, the people of Judaism, would be known by an abbreviation of the word Judah: They would be known as the *Jews*.

THE ABSOLUTE MINIMUM

- The period of the judges (*shoftim*) ended with the anointing of Saul by the last judge, Samuel.

- King David would later assume power, and his dynasty would control all of Israel until 920 B.C. and all of Judah (Southern Israel) until 586 B.C.

- The fall of Jerusalem in 586 B.C. led to the Babylonian exile, which began with the destruction of the Temple and the exile of Jerusalem's residents to Babylon. It ended with their return in the 530s B.C., after the Babylonian empire fell to the more tolerant Persians.

RESOURCES

- **The Names of the Holy Land (Ontario Consultants)**—www. religioustolerance.org/name_mide.htm
- **David (Wikipedia)**—en.wikipedia.org/wiki/David
- **Solomon (Wikipedia)**—en.wikipedia.org/wiki/Solomon
- **Brief History of Assyria**—www.aina.org/aol/peter/brief.htm

12

The Era Of Prophecy

While Israel was ruled by judges and kings, religious tradition was represented sometimes by the rulers themselves, sometimes by priests, and sometimes by the *nevi'im* (or prophets). A *prophet* is a divine speaker and advocate, one who challenges the existing order, not necessarily a fortuneteller—though most prophets do make predictions about the future.

The Second History

Chapter 11, "The Era of Kings," covered the history of Israel and Judah based on 1 and 2 Samuel, 1 and 2 Kings, 1 and 2 Chronicles, Ezra, and Nehemiah. These books deal, in a fairly straightforward way, with the roughly 300-year history of Israel (1020–721 B.C.) and the roughly 450-year history of Judah (1020–586 B.C.) as independent nations. But there is another history of the two kingdoms given in the Bible, and it is an unapologetically opinionated one. As Figure 12.1 demonstrates, the history of the prophets runs parallel to the history of the kings (described in the previous chapter). However, while the historical books largely reflect the point of view of those recording the history of Israel, the books of the prophets reflect the viewpoints of religious leaders who reaffirmed to the religious traditions of their ancestors.

> **note**
>
> This chapter deals with the prophets as they have been understood on the basis of historical scholarship and as they have been understood in the Jewish tradition. But the prophets also play a central role in the Christian tradition, where their writings are seen as predicting the birth, ministry, death, and resurrection of Jesus Christ. For more on this interpretation, see Chapter 21, "Before He Was Christ."

The prophets (*nevi'im*) were those who spoke on behalf of a deity. The books of God's prophets—Isaiah, Jeremiah, Lamentations, Ezekiel, Daniel, and the 12 "minor" prophets—make up about one third of the Hebrew Bible and include some of its deepest and most challenging passages. They are by and large oriented toward holding the powerful accountable to God, and particularly to God's covenant. (For more on this, refer to Chapter 9, "Covenants Broken and Covenants Renewed.")

There are also other prophets in the Hebrew Bible, as described in Table 12.1—figures such as Elijah, one of the most popular prophets of the Judeo-Christian tradition, and Enoch, the earliest described prophet who enjoyed such intimate friendships with God that they never even had to die. Others, such as Abraham, Moses, and Miriam, were known primarily for qualities other than their prophecy as such.

FIGURE 12.1

When did the
prophets write?

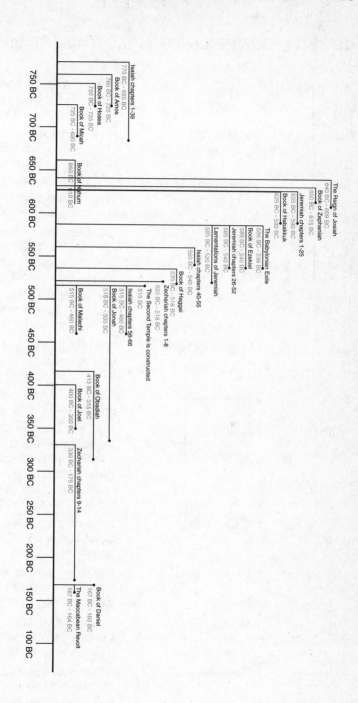

Table 12.1 Other Prophets of the Hebrew Bible

Prophet	Identified in	Description
Abraham	Genesis 20:7	The father of the Jewish people (discussed in greater detail in Chapter 7, "Rise of the Nations") is also identified as a prophet.
Miriam	Exodus 15:20	Moses' elder sister (discussed in greater detail in Chapter 8, "From Slavery to the Promised Land") is described as a prophet.
Moses	Deuteronomy 34:10	Of all the prophets, it is written that Moses (also described in greater detail in Chapter 8) had the closest relationship with God.
Deborah	Judges 4:4	The judge Deborah (described in greater detail in Chapter 10, "Conquests and Chaos") had such great influence as a prophet that entire armies obeyed her command.
Samuel	1 Samuel 3:20	The last of the judges, Samuel (described in greater detail in Chapter 11), was chiefly known as a prophet.
Saul	1 Samuel 10:11	Saul, the first king of Israel (also described in greater detail in Chapter 11), was briefly among the prophets.
Gad	1 Samuel 22:5	Gad, who served as seer under King David, was a prophet.
Nathan	2 Samuel 7:2	Nathan (described in greater detail in Chapter 11) was arguably the most influential of the king's prophets because he announced the Davidic monarchy, exposed King David's murder of Uriah and brought him to repentance, and eased the transition to David's son Solomon.
Ahijah	1 Kings 11:29	It is written that Ahijah foretold the division of Israel into two kingdoms and urged King Jeroboam to repent (refer to Chapter 11).
Old Prophet of Bethel	1 Kings 13:11	The old prophet of Bethel, who is never named, buried an also-unnamed religious figure who spoke out against the excesses of Jeroboam's reign.
Jehu	1 Kings 16:7	A religious reformer and king of Judah (refer to Chapter 11) who was, prior to his ascendancy, a well-known prophet.
Elijah	1 Kings 18:22	Among the best-loved prophets of the entire Hebrew Bible, Elijah is the prophet who is symbolically invited to Passover dinners and was identified as the third figure, with Moses, during the transfiguration of Jesus (see Chapter 22, "The Good Shepherd"). He correctly prophesied a famine in Israel, spoke out against the excesses

Prophet	Identified in	Description
		of King Ahab and Queen Jezebel (refer to Chapter 11), and holds the distinction of being—other than Enoch (see previously)—the only person in the Hebrew Bible who never actually dies. Instead, he is carried off to heaven by God in a whirlwind (2 Kings 2:11).
Elisha	2 Kings 9:1	Elisha, the protégé of Elijah, also advised rulers of the Northern Kingdom.
Huldah	2 Kings 22:14	It is written that the prophet Huldah was an advisor to King Josiah (refer to Chapter 11) and that she predicted that Jerusalem would fall (a reference to the Babylonian Exile) regardless of his reforms.
Iddo	2 Chronicles 13:22	Iddo—variously identified as the grandfather (Zechariah 1:1), father (Ezra 6:14), or son (1 Chronicles 27:21) of Zechariah—was a prophet himself, speaking against the corruption of King Jeroboam (refer to Chapter 11).
Prophet to Amaziah	2 Chronicles 25:15	The anonymous prophet to King Amaziah of the Northern Kingdom (refer to Chapter 11) criticized him for calling on foreign gods in times of trouble.
Oded	2 Chronicles 28:9	The prophet Oded convinced King Ahaz of the Northern Kingdom (refer to Chapter 11) to release hostages he had captured from the Southern Kingdom. Another prophet named Oded is credited with convincing King Asa of the Southern Kingdom to reject idolatry, some 200 years earlier (1 Chronicles 15:8).
Mrs. Isaiah	Isaiah 8:3	The unnamed wife of Isaiah is also identified as a prophet.
Enoch	n/a	Enoch, a seventh-generation descendent of Adam (Genesis 5:18–24) who "walked with God" rather than tasting death, is identified as a prophet in the New Testament (Jude v. 14), in some rabbinic sources, and in the noncanonical Book of Enoch (discussed in Chapter 18, "Nowhere in the Bible").

Conventional wisdom has it that a prophet is a fortuneteller and, in fact, most of the prophets described in this chapter did make predictions about the future. But prophecy is not about mere fortunetelling; it is about warning. It is a sign of the role of the prophet that one of the few false prophets identified as such in the Hebrew Bible was Hananiah (Jeremiah 28:1), who stood up to the gloomy Jeremiah and declared that God had given him word that things were not as bad as they seemed, that all would turn out well for Judah, and that Jerusalem would not fall to Babylonian captivity. For this, the Bible tells us, God struck him dead. Prophets rarely spread good news. They were harbingers of doom, signifying that horrible things were about to occur—that it was time to prepare and repent because the end of the order was near.

Isaiah: The Great Prophet

The Book of Isaiah is the longest of the prophetic books, and one of the most complex. It is also the earliest that we can document; a complete manuscript, dated 250 B.C., has been found. (For more about this and related discoveries, see Chapter 19, "The Dead Sea Scrolls.") The central concern for Isaiah is the future of Jerusalem: its failures, its imminent destruction, and its re-emergence.

It is written that Isaiah prophesied in Judah (the Southern Kingdom) during the reigns of Uzziah, Jotham, Ahaz, Hezekiah, and Manasseh, which suggests at least a 45-year prophetic career spanning the period between 740 B.C. and 695 B.C. (For more on these kings and the history of Israel's two kingdoms, refer to Chapter 11.) According to tradition, he met his end at the hands of Manasseh, who had him sawed in half.

Scholars tend to believe that the original figure of Isaiah did exist, but they do not credit him with authorship of the entire book. Instead, they divide Isaiah into three categories:

- **First Isaiah (chapters 1–39)**—
  Written by the original Isaiah more
  or less during the period attributed to
  him. These chapters address Assyrian conquests of the region, the dangers of associating with the Egyptians, and general concerns regarding non-Jewish practices and care of the oppressed.

- **Deutero-Isaiah (chapters 40–55)**—Written during the Babylonian exile (586–537 B.C.) by a figure who belonged to the prophetic tradition of Isaiah. This new figure expressed hope that Israel would be rescued by a liberator

Biblically Speaking

"Ah, you who make iniquitous decrees,

who write oppressive statutes,

to turn aside the needy from justice

and to rob the poor of my people of their right,

that widows may be your spoil,

and that you may make the orphans your prey!

What will you do on the day of punishment,

in the calamity that will come from far away?

To whom will you flee for help,

and where will you leave your wealth,

so as not to crouch among the prisoners

or fall among the slain?

For all this his anger has not turned away;

his hand is stretched out still."

—Isaiah 10:1–4

(41:1–7), probably the Persian king Cyrus the Great, who would indeed overthrow the Babylonians and allow the Israelites to return home to Jerusalem and rebuild their destroyed temple.

■ **Trito-Isaiah (chapters 56–66)**—Written after the exiled Judeans had returned to Jerusalem and constructed a second Temple (which was completed in 515 B.C.). The third Isaiah figure is concerned with issues of Jewish life under the relatively kind and tolerant rule of the Persians. Those who expected paradise with the construction of the second Temple were disappointed, and in answer to this Isaiah proposes that the sacrifices of the Temple are not adequate; moral behavior is the key (66:1–5).

Jeremiah: The Weeping Prophet

The term *jeremiad*—which refers to a litany of complaints, a long soliloquy expressing suffering—comes from Jeremiah himself, who exemplifies the role of the Jewish prophet. For years he warns that the Babylonians will destroy Jerusalem in response to Judah's failure to fulfill the covenant. When the Babylonians make an initial assault on Jerusalem in 589 B.C. and withdraw, tradition has it that Jeremiah warns his people that they will soon be back to destroy the city. He is imprisoned by King Zedekiah and is still in prison at the time the Babylonians take and raze Jerusalem—at which point he is released and lives in exile from Jerusalem with other devout Jews. While in exile, he might play a role in compiling and/or writing sections of the Hebrew Bible.

As in the case of Isaiah, the Book of Jeremiah seems to be made up of multiple documents. In this case scholars divide Jeremiah into two sections:

■ **First Jeremiah (chapters 1–25)**— Written between 625 B.C. and Jeremiah's imprisonment in 588 or 589 B.C. It is believed that the historical Jeremiah is the principal author of this section.

Biblically Speaking

"As a thief is shamed when caught,

so the house of Israel shall be shamed—

they, their kings, their officials, their priests, and their prophets...For they have turned their backs to me,

And not their faces.

But in the time of their trouble they say,

'Come and save us!'

But where are your gods that you made for yourself?

Let them come, if they can save you,

in your time of trouble;

for you have as many gods as you have towns, O Judah."

—Jeremiah 2:26–28

■ **Deutero-Jeremiah/Baruch (chapters 26–52)**—Written by Jeremiah's scribe Baruch during Babylonian exile (from 586 B.C. to 537 B.C.).

Jeremiah is also credited as the author of the Book of Lamentations, an anonymous poem expressing agony over the destruction of Jerusalem at the hands of the Babylonians. Although Jeremiah witnessed this event as closely as any prophet of the Hebrew Bible and was well known for writing lamentations (tradition has it that he wrote a lengthy poem of grief upon the death of the reformer King Josiah), the oldest Hebrew versions of Lamentations do not credit Jeremiah as author.

Ezekiel: The Visionary Prophet

The prophet Ezekiel wrote his book during the Babylonian exile (from 586 B.C. to 537 B.C.), where he discusses the fall of Jerusalem (the "bloody city") and its eventual resurrection, along with the punishment of the nations that betrayed Judah. Tradition has it that Ezekiel is a wild and somewhat eccentric prophet, making sweeping physical gestures, breaking pottery, and so forth as he prophesies. His prophecies are also much more visual than those of his contemporaries: He begins his prophecy by describing what appears to be God's throne (1:26), seated above a flying dome surrounded by angels, and ends it by describing a new Jerusalem, housing all 12 tribes of Israel (48:1–35).

Daniel: The Prophet-Hero

Daniel was a folk hero in the Canaanite tradition in the ninth century B.C.; stories of Daniel might have been incorporated into those of the Israelites, or the Book of Daniel could refer to a Jewish figure named Daniel. In either case, the Book of

---

Biblically Speaking

"My anguish, my anguish! I writhe in pain!

Oh, the walls of my heart!

My heart is beating wildly;

I cannot keep silent;

for I hear the sound of the trumpet,

the alarm of war.

Disaster overtakes disaster,

the whole land is laid waste."

—Jeremiah 4:19–20

Biblically Speaking

"But you, O LORD, reign forever;

your throne endures to all generations.

Why have you forgotten us completely?

Why have you forsaken us these many days?"

—Lamentations 5:19–20

Daniel stands out from other prophetic books because it is, strictly speaking, more of a story than a prophecy—discussing Daniel, a prophet who had been captured by the Babylonians during an early siege of Jerusalem and his struggles in Jerusalem.

Daniel's experiences are among the most well-known stories of the Bible—his interpretation of King Nebuchadnezzar's dreams (beginning in 2:1–49) predicting the rise of future empires, his ability to read mysterious writing on the palace wall (5:1–30) predicting the fall of Babylon, and his experience in the lion's den (6:18–23). His own prophecies, which foretold the fall of Judah's enemies and the rise of a new kingdom (7:1–12:13), are among the most striking in the Bible. The references to the wicked and oppressive Antiochus IV Epiphanes (11:21–28), the villain of the apocryphal Books of the Maccabees (discussed in Chapter 17, "The Books of Tradition"), date the book with some precision between the years 167 B.C. and 165 B.C.

> **Biblically Speaking**
>
> "Woe to the bloody city,
> the pot whose rust is in it,
> whose rust has not gone out of it!...
> For the blood she shed is inside it;
> she placed it on a bare rock;
> she did not pour it out on the ground,
> to cover it with earth."
>
> —Ezekiel 24:6–7

The 12 "Minor" Prophets

In most Jewish Bibles, all 12 "minor" (meaning small, not unimportant) books of the prophets are classified in a single Book of the Twelve. In Christian Bibles, and in some Jewish Bibles, they are listed separately.

Hosea: The Marrying Prophet

Unlike all the major prophets, Hosea hailed from the Northern Kingdom, Israel. The Northern Kingdom was home to 10 of the 12 tribes of Israel—all Israelites except for the tribes of Judah, Benjamin, and Levi. Yet in 721 B.C., the Northern Kingdom fell to the Assyrians and they made it their duty to expel and scatter the Jewish people, forcing them to assimilate in foreign lands and destroying their cohesiveness. The 10 tribes vanished from history at this point and became known as the "lost tribes of Israel."

> **Biblically Speaking**
>
> "As I watched,
> thrones were set in place,
> and an Ancient One took his throne,
> his clothing was white as snow,
> and the hair of his head like pure wool;
> his throne was fiery flames,
> and its wheels were burning fire."
>
> —Daniel 7:9

The Book of Hosea, which was most likely written sometime between 750 B.C. and 725 B.C., begins with an odd request: "Go, take yourself a wife of whoredom," God commands Hosea," for the land commits great whoredom by forsaking the LORD" (1:2–3). This marriage between a prophet and a prostitute is used to symbolize the marriage between God and the children of Israel. Israel, in the terms of the Book of Hosea, had become a prostitute through the widespread adoption of idolatrous practices.

> **Biblically Speaking**
>
> "The days of punishment have come,
>
> the days of recompense have come;
>
> Israel cries,
>
> 'The prophet is a fool,
>
> the man of the spirit is mad!'
>
> Because of your great iniquity,
>
> your hostility is great."
>
> —Hosea 9:7

Joel: The Locust Prophet

Joel wrote in Judah at some point between 400 B.C. and 350 B.C., citing a recent locust infestation as evidence that God was disappointed with the nation and promising a brighter future to come when Judah obeys its covenant with God.

Amos: The Earthquake Prophet

Amos preached in the last days of the Northern Kingdom, between 760 B.C. and 725 B.C. Much as Joel cited locusts as evidence of God's wrath, Amos cited a recent earthquake (1:1 and 9:1–9). His book is particularly noted for its advocacy on behalf of the poor and oppressed.

Obadiah: The Avenging Prophet

Obadiah is the shortest book of the Hebrew Bible, made up of a single chapter of 21 verses. Written during the Babylonian exile, it promises vengeance against nations that betrayed Judah during its war with Babylon.

Jonah: The Reluctant Prophet

Like Daniel, Jonah is as much a folk hero (of sorts) as he is a prophet. When he refuses to prophesy in Nineveh, the Assyrian capital, he attempts escape—at which point God has a giant fish (which some translators believe was a whale) swallow him (1:4–2:10). When the people of Nineveh do repent, Jonah is frustrated at the apparent injustice of that forgiveness. God urges Jonah to be compassionate, even toward the people of Nineveh.

Although it might be based in part on Northern Kingdom traditions, the Book of Jonah was most likely written by members of the tribe of Judah in the years following the construction of the second Temple.

Micah: The Perceptive Prophet

Micah wrote in Judah during the years 725–690 B.C., when he predicted what would be the fall of Jerusalem more than 100 years later.

Nahum: The Triumphant Prophet

The Southern Kingdom prophet Nahum wrote between the years 660 B.C. and 610 B.C., proclaiming the power of God to overcome any adversary and predicting the fall of Assyria (which would happen not long afterward).

Habakkuk: The Pleading Prophet

Habakkuk wrote in the Southern Kingdom in the years preceding the Babylonian exile (most likely 660–610 B.C.), pleading for assistance from God and predicting the downfall of Israel's enemies.

Zephaniah: The Fiery Prophet

Writing between 630 and 615 B.C. in the Southern Kingdom, Zephaniah predicted that fire would be used as an instrument of God's vengeance just as floods had been in the story of Noah (refer to Chapter 6, "The Creation and the Flood").

> ### Biblically Speaking
>
> "Your eyes are too pure to behold evil,
>
> and you cannot look on wrongdoing;
>
> why do you look on the treacherous,
>
> and are silent when the wicked swallow
>
> those more righteous than they?
>
> You have made people like the fish of the sea,
>
> like crawling things that have no ruler."
>
> —Habakkuk 1:13–14

Haggai: The Temple Prophet

Haggai wrote in the years between 535 B.C. and 518 B.C., when the people of Jerusalem were finally able to return from the Babylonian exile but had not yet finished the second Temple. He urged the Temple's construction, promising that life would be transformed after the project was completed.

Zechariah: The Hopeful Prophet

Like Haggai, Zechariah wrote in the years immediately preceding the construction of the second Temple and predicted that the building of the Temple would transform the entire world.

Malachi: The Justifying Prophet

After the second Temple was constructed, many were disappointed that the promised new age did not come. Malachi attributed this to Judah's lack of faithfulness and promised that God would judge the world in time.

THE ABSOLUTE MINIMUM

- The prophets (*nevi'im*) were responsible for advocating faithfulness to God, most often warning of dire consequences that would occur if faithfulness was not practiced.

- The four major prophets—Isaiah, Jeremiah, Ezekiel, and Daniel— all represent concerns of the Southern Kingdom at various times in history.

- The 12 minor prophets address a wide range of concerns, ranging from the fall of the Northern Kingdom in 721 B.C. to the effects of the rebuilding of the second Temple in 515 B.C. The term *minor* refers only to the length of the books, not to their significance.

RESOURCES

- **Prophets and Prophecy (Judaism 101)**—www.jewfaq.org/prophet.htm
- **Nevi'im (Jewish Virtual Library)**—www.jewishvirtuallibrary.org/ jsource/Bible/Prophetstoc.html
- **Isaiah (Jewish Encyclopedia)**—www.jewishencyclopedia.com/ view.jsp?artid=261&letter=I
- **Habakkuk (Jewish Encyclopedia)**—www.jewishencyclopedia.com/ view.jsp?artid=8&letter=H

13

RUTH AND ESTHER

The books of Ruth and Esther stand out from the rest of the Hebrew Bible, not least of which because they are the only 2 books of the entire Bible named after women —3 books, if you count the deuterocanonical Book of Judith (described in Chapter 17, "The Books of Tradition")— 40 are named after men. They have unconventional heroes—Ruth, a non-Jewish widow, and Esther, the seducer of a Persian king. In addition, rather than emphasizing the issue of God's covenant with Israel, they focus on basic human concerns of love and survival.

The Moabite Widow

The Book of Ruth is set in the era of the *shoftim*, or judges, prior to the rise of Israel's first king. During a famine, a couple named Elimelech and Naomi leave their home in Bethlehem with their sons, Mahlon and Chilion, in search for a better life—or, more to the point, food—among the Moabites, a non-Jewish tribe that had gone to war with the Israelites many times in the past. There in Moab, Naomi's sons inter-marry with local, non-Jewish women. Mahlon marries a young woman named Orpah, and Chilion marries a young woman named Ruth, and they begin to settle down.

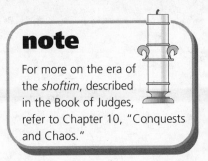

note

For more on the era of the *shoftim*, described in the Book of Judges, refer to Chapter 10, "Conquests and Chaos."

LITERATURE OR HISTORY?

In most Christian editions of the Hebrew Bible, Ruth and Esther are both classified as histori-cal books alongside 1 and 2 Kings, 1 and 2 Chronicles, Ezra, and Nehemiah. But in the Jewish tradition, they make up two of the *Chamesh Megillos*, or Five Scrolls (along with the Song of Songs, Lamentations, and Ecclesiastes), and are used for public readings in synagogues. Although I have classified them with the historical books here for simplicity's sake, most schol-ars believe they are primarily works of literature very loosely based on historical events but of more interest as stories than as history.

Soon, tragedy strikes: All three men die, leaving only Naomi, Orpah, and Ruth as sur-vivors. When the famine in Israel seems to be drawing to a close, Naomi resolves to leave alone and orders her daughters-in-law to remain in Moab, where both food and eligible young Moabite men are likely to be more plentiful. Orpah tearfully agrees, but Ruth insists on following Naomi to Israel in one of the most beautiful passages in the Bible.

Naomi concedes and the two return to Israel, where Ruth does not face a bright future. In the ancient world, women were not generally allowed to provide for themselves. For unmarried women, this generally meant being taken care of by their parents; for mar-ried women, this generally meant being taken care of by their husbands; and for widows without any surviving male relatives, this generally meant stark poverty. For Ruth, finding a man is absolutely essential—and in Israel, where intermarriage with the hated Moabites is frowned upon, Ruth is looking for love in all the wrong places.

Naomi is not much better off. Widows above a certain age were not good candidates for remarriage—"I am too old to have a husband," Naomi laments in 1:12—and with no surviving sons, she cannot rely (as most elderly widows did) on the Mosaic com-mandment ordering children to honor their fathers and mothers (Exodus 20:12).

They arrive in Bethlehem with no money to speak of, no property, and no men to pro-vide for them. Fortunately, Naomi's information is sound—the famine has come to an end—and the two survive on the kindness of strangers. Mosaic law makes special allowances for feeding the hungry (see Leviticus 19:9–10 and Deuteronomy 24:19–22), requiring all farmers to leave a certain portion of their crop alone to be gathered by foreigners, widows, and the poor. And Ruth, as (very bad) luck would have it, falls into all three categories.

Ruth goes out searching for barley to gather and is spotted by a wealthy, middle-aged man named Boaz. He asks one of his servants who she is and is stunned at the answer: She is the Moabite who came back with Naomi. Boaz, as it happens, is a distant relative of Naomi's late husband Elimelech and acquaints himself with the story of how Naomi and Ruth made their way back to Bethlehem. He then approaches Ruth—taboo behavior for many reasons, the fact that she's a Moabite topping the list—and promises to feed and care for her and Naomi as long as they need his aid, so impressed is he with Ruth's loyalty to her mother-in-law.

> ## Biblically Speaking
>
> "But Ruth said,
>
> 'Do not press me to leave you,
>
> or to turn back from following you!
>
> Where you go, I will go ;
>
> where you lodge, I will lodge ;
>
> your people shall be my people,
>
> and your God my God.
>
> Where you die, I will die—
>
> there will I be buried.
>
> May the LORD do thus and so to me,
>
> and more as well,
>
> even if death parts me from you!'"
>
> —Ruth 1:16–17

Ruth and Naomi have achieved economic safety by the standards of their time: They have found a man to take care of them. When Ruth gets home and Naomi asks who the man was, she is as stunned at the unexpected family reunion as Boaz. Boaz provides for Naomi and Ruth for months on end, as Ruth spends many days gathering barley and wheat alongside his wives in the fields. One day, Naomi realizes that Ruth would be a good addition to their ranks. Offering sage advice that only a mother-in-law can give, she tells Ruth to take a bath, put on her best clothes, and follow Boaz to bed after dinner.

"[U]ncover his feet," Naomi suggests, "and lie down; and he will tell you what to do" (Ruth 3:4). Ruth takes her mother-in-law's advice. This brings us to the image that is most closely linked with the Book of Ruth: A young woman lying, humbly and chastely, at the foot of a man's bed. The image is somewhat jarred by the fact that in Hebrew, genitals are often referred to euphemistically as "feet," but because the Hebrew word in this case—*margelah*—means "the place of the feet," it really might refer to the foot of the bed. Either reading works.

Whichever set of feet she uncovers, the strategy works. Boaz is humbled that she chose him over younger men (3:10), and the two are married. The punch line: Their great-grandson will be King David, ruler of Israel and patriarch of the Judean dynasty. Yes, David himself will be one-eighth Moabite—all because of the considerable sacrifices Ruth had made out of loyalty to Naomi.

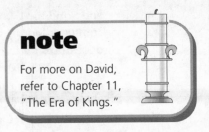

note

For more on David, refer to Chapter 11, "The Era of Kings."

The Book of Ruth is an unusual romance story by modern standards: An impoverished widow goes to bed with an older male relative on the advice of her mother-in-law. Boaz has reason to be astonished at Ruth's interest because he is so much older than she is; Ruth has reason to be astonished at his interest because she hails from a hated foreign country. But in the end, love—and off-the-wall motherly advice—conquers all.

Queen Takes Knight

The Book of Esther is, in essence, a book about court intrigue in the palace of the Persian King Xerxes I (486–465 B.C.), here described under the name Ahasuerus. Ahasuerus and his queen, Vashti, have a strained marriage, living in separate social circles segregated by gender (1:9). When Ahasuerus wants to show off his beautiful queen to his peers, she stands him up. Fearing a worldwide

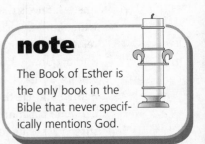

note

The Book of Esther is the only book in the Bible that never specifically mentions God.

revolt of royal wives (1:17–18), Ahasuerus essentially fires her as queen and orders her to stay out of his sight from that point on; then he passes a decree commanding that all women honor their husbands' wishes (1:20). If you think this sounds more like comic relief than a serious statement of ideal gender roles, you're not alone—scholars point out that the Persians were benevolent occupiers of Judah but occupiers nonetheless, and devoted polytheists to boot. Ahasuerus is consistently portrayed throughout the Book of Esther as an essentially goodhearted buffoon with a great love of earthly pleasures, loyal to those who are loyal to him but ultimately clueless and easy to manipulate. This becomes very important later.

Although Ahasuerus has quite an impressive harem, Vashti was his only wife. He isn't happy with "single" life for long. Indeed, he misses Vashti as soon as his anger wears off (2:1). But because he has made the entire situation public by passing national decrees to resolve his own marital issues, he can't very well ask her to come back without losing face. He decides to, in effect, start his own version of *The Bachelor*—inviting beautiful young virgins from all over the Persian territories to his capital, where they can compete for his hand in marriage. After 12 months of beauty regimens, they are ready to compete, by each spending a night with the king (2:14).

Among the contestants is Esther, a young Jewish woman who had been orphaned and raised by her older cousin Mordecai. She spends a night with the king, and he is so impressed with the experience that he makes her queen right away without even asking where she's from. There is only one condition: Queen Esther must come to the king when asked to do so, and only when asked to do so (2:14). In this respect she is more a member of his harem than a full-fledged queen—as, perhaps, Vashti had also been. But in addition to her other

note

Esther actually has two names: Among Persians she is known by her Persian name of Esther, but among Jews she is known by her birth name of Hadassah (2:7).

talents, Esther doubles as a secret service officer. When her cousin Mordecai informs her of a plot against Ahasuerus' life, she informs the king and the would-be assassins are executed. Ahasuerus is happy to be alive but forgets to reward Mordecai. This, too, becomes very important later.

Enter the villain: Haman the Agagite, appointed by Ahasuerus to serve as his second-in-command. Haman is something of a control freak. He demands that all the king's subjects present bow before him, and Mordecai refuses to do so. Seeing Mordecai's refusal to bow as a symbol of the Jewish people's refusal to be assimilated into Persian culture, Haman plots genocide. He convinces Ahasuerus, who ostensibly knows nothing about the Jewish people under his authority, that Jews are a scattered, disobedient lot of ne'er-do-wells and asks for 10,000 talents of silver (several hundred million dollars in modern U.S. currency) that he can use to bribe Persian civilians into doing away with the Jews. Having no real idea of the situation, Ahasuerus agrees to the terms and entrusts Haman to handle the situation in the correct way (3:11). By casting lots (*purim*), Haman selects a day for the annihilation of the Jewish people—the 13th day of the 12th month (the Jewish month of Adar)—and patiently bides his time.

When Mordecai discovers the plot, he alerts Esther. She makes the decision to fast for three days and then violates Ahasuerus' command by visiting him without an invitation. Ahasuerus is gracious, spontaneously offering her half his kingdom (5:3), but she has a much humbler request: She asks that Ahasuerus and Haman attend a banquet together, which she has set up in their honor. The king accepts.

note

Note the situation here: Haman comes in to ask for Mordecai's execution, but before he can get around to it, he is tricked by his own vanity into publicly celebrating Mordecai's accomplishments instead. The humor is intentional.

Meanwhile, Haman crosses paths with Mordecai and notices that the stubborn old man still isn't scared of him. Haman orders gallows built and prepares to ask the king to order Mordecai's execution the next morning. Unfortunately for Haman, the king can't sleep because he has just remembered that he has never rewarded Mordecai for saving his life. That morning, Haman comes to the door and prepares to ask for Mordecai's execution but is interrupted by the king: "What shall be done for the man whom the king wishes to honor?" (6:6). Convinced that Ahasuerus is talking about him, Haman suggests that the honored person be dressed in royal robes and a crown and ridden around town on horseback with a crier shouting, "Thus shall it be done for the man whom the king wishes to honor" (6:9). Ahasuerus thinks this is a splendid idea and orders Haman to implement this decision for Mordecai at once...personally.

The humiliated Haman, having been forced to submit to Mordecai (who has been rendered execution-proof by all the publicity), attends the banquet, where things are about to get much, much worse for him. There Esther tells the king something he has not yet figured out: that she is herself Jewish and that he has inadvertently ordered the execution of her own people by signing Haman's decree. The devastated king leaves the room to think. During his absence, Haman and Esther get into an argument that leads to Haman leaping upon her while she's on the couch—just as the king walks in. Mistaking Haman's aggression as a rape attempt, the king orders him executed at once. One of the king's servants helpfully points out that Haman has himself constructed a new set of gallows, to which the king responds, "Hang him on that" (7:9).

> **note**
>
> To this day, on the 13th day of Adar, Jews celebrate *Purim*—Haman's casting of the lots. The holiday is marked by singing, noisemaking, over-the-top humor and practical jokes, heavy drinking, the eating of little triangular cookies called *haman-taschen* (which, tradition says, resemble Haman's hat), and of course a public reading of the Book of Esther.

But the Jewish people are not yet safe because the king cannot reverse his own decree. To make the situation more fair, he introduces a new, second decree—yes, the Persians can freely attack Jews on the 13th day of Adar, but they will encounter a heavily armed Jewish population, bolstered by the Persian army, if they do. Those crazy enough to follow Haman's original decree are slaughtered in battle, and the Jewish people are safe once more.

THE ABSOLUTE MINIMUM

- The books of Ruth and Esther are classified among the five *megillot*, scrolls of high literary value often read during synagogue services. (The other three *megillot* are the Song of Songs, Lamentations, and Ecclesiastes.)

- In the Book of Ruth, Ruth is a Moabite widow who converts to Judaism and later falls in love with an older Jewish man.

- Set about 800 years later, the story of Esther describes the king of Persia's Jewish wife, whose courage and craftiness save the Jewish people from slaughter.

RESOURCES

- **The Status of Women in the Bible (Ontario Consultants)**—www.religioustolerance.org/fem_bibl.htm

- **Interracial Marriage and the Bible**—www.christiananswers.net/q-sum/sum-g003.html

- **The Conversion to Judaism Home Page**—www.convert.org

- **Purim on the Net**—www.holidays.net/purim

PART IV

POETRY AND WISDOM LITERATURE

14

BIBLICAL POETRY AND WISDOM LITERATURE

The five literary books of the Hebrew Bible—Job, Psalms, Proverbs, Ecclesiastes, and the Song of Solomon—would be regarded as masterpieces even outside the context of the Bible. They are the pinnacle of ancient Near Eastern literature, charged with power, meaning, and a profound sense of the human experience.

The Books of Wisdom

For the most part, the books of the Hebrew Bible are organized around one topic: God's relationship with the children of Abraham and Sarah. The books of Job, Proverbs, Ecclesiastes, and the Song of Solomon stand out because they focus on more general issues facing humanity: practical advice, erotic love, unjust suffering, and the stark reality of death. They fall into the category of *Wisdom literature*, a type of Near Eastern writing that attempts to answer human questions and doubts through reason, aphorisms, and parables.

In Christian Bibles, these books are often set aside, along with Psalms (and, in Roman Catholic and Orthodox Bibles, the Wisdom of Solomon and the Book of Sirach), under a heading such as "Literary and Poetic Books of the Bible." In the Hebrew Bible, they form—along with certain historical books—the *Kethuvim* ("writings"), or the final third of the Hebrew Bible.

The most famous Near Eastern wisdom literature is found in the Bible, but the genre as a whole was very healthy, and countless examples of wisdom literature can be found in other ancient Near Eastern traditions. A few of the better-known classics of wisdom literature are described in Table 14.1.

> **Biblically Speaking**
>
> "Wisdom cries out in the street;
>
> in the squares she raises her voice.
>
> At the busiest corner she cries out;
>
> At the entrance of the city gates she speaks…"
>
> —Proverbs 1:20

> **note**
>
> For more on the Wisdom of Solomon and the Book of Sirach, see Chapter 17, "The Books of Tradition."
>
> For more on the *Kethuvim* and the structure of the Jewish Bible, refer to Chapter 4, "The Meaning of Torah in Judaism."

Table 14.1   Wisdom Literature in Other Traditions

Title	Origin	Description
The Wisdom of Ahiqar	Babylonian	Miscellaneous literature attributed to, or dealing with, the Babylonian sage Ahiqar.
A Dialogue About Human Misery	Babylonian	A conversation between a suffering man and his friend; reminiscent of sections from the Book of Job.
Dispute Between the Date Palm Tree and the Tamarisk	Sumerian	Two trees argue over which is the greatest.

Title	Origin	Description
The Instructions of Suruppak	Babylonian	The wisdom that Suruppak passed on to his son Ziusudra, who (according to Babylonian myth) was the lone survivor of a great flood.
Pessimistic Dialogue Between Master and Servant	Babylonian	A debate between a master and his servant about the meaning of life. Reminiscent of the first two chapters of Ecclesiastes.
I Will Praise the Lord of Wisdom	Akkadian	Reflections on the nature of suffering.
The Instructions of Amenemope	Egyptian	A collection of proverbs credited to a high-ranking agriculture official.
The Man Who Was Tired of Life	Egyptian	The lamentations of a suffering soul who waits for death to take him.
The Instructions of Ptatohep	Egyptian	Advice from an Egyptian city official. Reminiscent, in places, of Machiavelli's *The Prince*.
The Oracles of Ashurbanipal	Assyrian	Various documents associated with the Assyrian ruler Ashurbanipal, best known for building a massive library at Nineveh.
The Oracles of Esarhaddon	Assyrian	Wit and wisdom credited to another seventh-century Assyrian king.

Scholars have noted parallels between the Bible's Wisdom books and the literature of other traditions. Most scholars believe that Proverbs 22:17–24:34 is adapted from the Instructions of Amenemope, for example. Each contains 30 instructions, many of them worded in almost exactly the same way. This is consistent with what historians believe the Wisdom tradition to be: an accumulated collection of wisdom, passed along through the centuries, attributed each time to a culture's wisest leader, the one trusted with the duty of carrying on instructions for the next generation.

The Biblical Voice

In English, poetry often rhymes or follows a set meter. This is not generally true of ancient Near Eastern poetry, which is marked by a poetry of rhetoric—the use of phrases that interact, reflecting each other and charging the work with meaning.

A good example is Ecclesiastes 3:1–8:

> For everything there is a season, and a time for every matter under heaven:
>
> a time to be born, and a time to die;
>
> a time to plant, and a time to pluck up what is planted;
>
> a time to kill, and a time to heal;

a time to break down, and a time to build up;

a time to weep, and a time to laugh;

a time to mourn, and a time to dance;

a time to throw away stones, and a time to gather stones together;

a time to embrace, and a time to refrain from embracing;

a time to seek, and a time to lose;

a time to keep, and a time to throw away;

a time to tear, and a time to sew;

a time to keep silence, and a time to speak;

a time to love, and a time to hate;

a time for war, and a time for peace.

Note the overall balance of these verses—the repetition of "a time...and a time...," which gives it the force of a chant. Each verse also has a sense of balance; the opposing pairs of statements create a rhythm of words and ideas, and it is very easy to come away from these verses feeling that they flawlessly describe human life in all its complexity, even thousands of years later.

Martin Luther King, Jr.'s "I Have a Dream" speech is a more recent masterpiece of the biblical voice:

> I have a dream that one day this nation will rise up and live out the true meaning of its creed.... I have a dream that one day on the red hills of Georgia the sons of former slaves and the sons of former slaveowners will be able to sit down together at a table of brotherhood. I have a dream that one day even the state of Mississippi...will be transformed into an oasis of freedom and justice. I have a dream that my four children will one day live in a nation where they will not be judged by the color of their skin but by the content of their character. I have a dream today.

Dr. King was an ordained Baptist minister, and his mastery of the biblical voice is unparalleled in modern times. Each

Biblically Speaking

"Give your ears and hear what is said,

Give your mind over to their interpretation...

Mark for yourself these thirty chapters:

They please, they instruct."

—From the Instructions of Amenemope

"Incline your ear and hear my words,

and apply your mind to my teaching...

Have I not written for you thirty sayings

of admonition and knowledge...?"

—Proverbs 22:17

statement begins with "I have a dream," creating a chant effect. The intricate balance of ideas in each statement ("the sons of former slaves and the sons of former slaveowners"; "not by the color of their skin but by the content of their character") creates the same sense of balance, of wholeness, that we see in the verses quoted from Ecclesiastes.

But sometimes the biblical voice is less dramatic. For example, Ecclesiastes 1:18 reads:

> For in much wisdom is much vexation,
>
> and those who increase wisdom increase sorrow.

If the verse were rephrased to read:

> For there is vexation in wisdom,
>
> and sorrow in the process of gaining wisdom.

Then the meaning would be more or less retained, but the poetry—the contrasts between *much* wisdom and *much* vexation, between *increasing* wisdom and *increasing* sorrow—would be lost.

The biblical voice is difficult to describe but easy to recognize. As you read the Bible with an eye for what it accomplishes as a work of poetry and a work of literature, you will be able to spot more and more examples of the biblical voice—both inside and outside the Bible.

THE ABSOLUTE MINIMUM

- The Wisdom books—Job, Proverbs, Ecclesiastes, and the Song of Solomon—differ from all other books of the Hebrew Bible in that they focus on general human experience rather than the covenant between God and Israel.

- Hebrew poetic literature, like most great literature of the ancient Near East, is not marked by rhyme or meter. Instead, it is a way of writing and speaking that relies on repetition and balance to create a distinctive rhetorical effect.

RESOURCES

- **Writings (Kethuvim)**—www.hope.edu/academic/religion/bandstra/RTOT/PART3/PT3_0.HTM

- **The Wisdom Literature (EWTN)**—www.ewtn.com/library/SCRIPTUR/WISINTRO.TXT

- **Biblical Poetry (Wikipedia)**—en.wikipedia.org/wiki/Biblical_poetry

- **The Key to Biblical Poetry**—www.wcg.org/lit/bible/poet/poetry.htm

15

PSALMS AND PROVERBS

Only two books of the Hebrew Bible are obvious compilations: Psalms is a collection of hymns, and Proverbs is a collection of ancient Near Eastern aphorisms. These revered anthologies, in use for millennia, connect readers with the culture of the ancient Jewish people in a deep, meaningful way.

Hymns of Ancient Israel

The Book of Psalms, the longest book in the Bible, is made up of Hebrew hymns that were originally written to be sung, sometimes with musical accompaniment. These hymns express the religious experience of ancient Israel—its hopes, fears, histories, and rituals. In many ways, the Psalms are a summary of the entire Hebrew Bible and of the Bible as a whole. In this book, containing both the longest chapter in the Bible (Psalm 119) and the shortest (Psalm 117), you will find the full range of religious life—almost every conceivable response to God, from the saintly to the horrific, from the desperate to the joyous, from the gutter to the stars.

> **note**
>
> A *psalm* was an ancient stringed instrument, similar to a harp or lyre. Over time, the word was also used to describe songs accompanied by a psalm.

Traditionally, the Book of Psalms (sometimes referred to as the *Psalter*) has been organized into five books (Psalms 1–41, Psalms 42–72, Psalms 73–89, Psalms 90–106, and Psalms 107 and onward). The Jewish and Protestant versions of the Book of Psalms, based on the Masoretic Text, contain 150 psalms; but a 151st psalm (a royal psalm on the life of David) can be found in Roman Catholic and Orthodox Bibles as part of the Deuterocanon. (For more information on the Deuterocanon, see Chapter 17, "The Books of Tradition.")

A PSALM GLOSSARY

Depending on which translation of the Psalms you use, you might run across these Hebrew notations:

almot	Plural of *almah* ("maiden"), it can indicate that the psalm was originally intended to be sung by young women. The word *almah* has historically been translated as "virgin" in Isaiah 7:14, which many Christians believe prophesies the Virgin Birth.
higgaion	The meaning of this word is unclear, but it could refer to a pause in the recitation of the psalm. Example: Psalm 9.
Jeduthun	The house of Jeduthun, a musician hired by King David (1 Chronicles 16:41–42). Example: Psalm 77.
maskil	"Instruction." A thoughtful, contemplative psalm. Example: Psalm 88.
miktam	Meaning uncertain; the authors of the Septuagint (the ancient Greek translation of the Bible) translated the word as "engraved," and it has been associated with *kethem* ("the thing that is set apart," sometimes translated as "gold"). Example: Psalm 56.
mizmor	A psalm to be sung with musical accompaniment.
neginoth	A song to be sung with the accompaniment of stringed instruments. Example: Psalm 4.

nehiloth	Means "perforation," and—as used in Psalm 5—probably means that the psalm should be sung with the accompaniment of wind instruments. Example: Psalm 5.
selah	The meaning of this word is unclear, but some traditions hold that it was originally intended to mark a pause or moment of silence in the psalm. Example: Psalm 24.
sheminith	"Eight." Refers either to the lowest vocal octave or to an eight-stringed musical instrument. Example: Psalm 12.
shiggaion	Nobody is quite sure what this (the title of Psalm 7) means. Its root is *shagah*, which translates loosely as "to reel about drunkenly."
tehillah	"Praise."
tephillah	"Prayer."

Today, the Book of Psalms is more commonly organized by type. Psalms fall into one or more of the following categories:

- Hymns of praise
- Psalms of trust
- Thanksgiving psalms
- Laments
- Royal psalms
- Wisdom psalms
- Liturgical psalms
- Historical psalms

Controversy

Although individual psalms are attributed to a variety of authors—David, Solomon, Moses, Jeremiah, Asaph, Heman, Ethan, and the sons of Korach—scholars tend to believe that these attributions are essentially dedications and provide no indication of who actually wrote the psalm.

In Table 15.1, I've classified each of the 151 psalms into one or more of the Psalter categories as laid out in the *New Jerome Biblical Commentary*.

Table 15.1   Psalms for Every Occasion

Type	Examples
Hymns of praise	8, 19, 24, 29, 33, 36, 46, 47, 48, 66, 68, 76, 87, 90, 93, 95, 96, 97, 98, 99, 100, 104, 105, 111, 113, 115, 117, 119, 122, 133, 134, 135, 136, 139, 145, 146, 147, 148, 149, 150
Psalms of trust	11, 16, 23, 27, 41, 62, 63, 64, 82, 84, 91, 112, 121, 123, 125, 131
Thanksgiving psalms	9, 18, 21, 30, 32, 34, 40, 66, 67, 75, 92, 103, 107, 108, 109, 116, 118, 124, 129, 138
Laments	3, 4, 5, 6, 7, 10, 12, 13, 14, 17, 22, 25, 26, 27, 28, 31, 35, 36, 38, 39, 40, 41, 42, 43, 44, 51, 52, 53, 54, 55, 56, 57, 58, 59, 60, 61, 64, 69, 70, 71, 74, 77, 79, 80, 83, 85, 86, 88, 89, 90, 94, 102, 106, 109,

Table 15.1 (continued)

Type	Examples
	115, 119, 120, 125, 126, 129, 130, 137, 139, 140, 141, 142, 143, 144
Royal psalms	2, 18, 20, 21, 35, 45, 59, 61, 66, 72, 89, 101, 110, 132, 144, 151
Wisdom psalms	1, 19, 32, 36, 37, 39, 41, 49, 111, 119, 127, 128, 141
Liturgical psalms	15, 24, 45, 46, 47, 50, 65, 73, 75, 81, 82, 85, 95, 134
Historical psalms	46, 48, 77, 78, 105, 106, 114, 135, 136

Psalm types are not always very distinct, but they go a long way toward explaining the breadth and character of individual psalms. Sorting psalms by type also allows us to find psalms suitable for specific occasions, which is much nicer than finding psalms unsuitable for specific occasions.

Hymns of Praise

Hymns of praise generally consist of two parts: an introduction praising God or calling for God's praise and an explanation detailing the reasons for praise. Some also feature a conclusion. Hymns of praise are what most of us imagine when we think of the Psalms, but only slightly more than one quarter of the psalms are hymns of praise.

PSALM 100:1–5

"Make a joyful noise to the LORD, all the earth.

Worship the LORD with gladness;

come into his presence with singing.

Know that the LORD is God.

It is he that made us, and we are his;

we are his people, the sheep of his pasture.

Enter his gates with thanksgiving

and his courts with praise.

Give thanks to him, bless his name.

For the LORD is good;

his steadfast love endures forever,

and his faithfulness to all generations."

In the short example given here the structure of the hymn of praise is in place: an introduction (1–4) exhorting all people to praise God and an explanation (5) emphasizing God's goodness, faithfulness, and love of humanity.

Psalms of Trust

About 10% of the psalms emphasize faith itself, promoting trust in God. Some psalms of trust (such as Psalm 23) focus on personal faith, whereas others (such as Psalm 115) call more attention to the faith of the religious community as a whole.

PSALM 23:1–6

"The LORD is my shepherd, I shall not want.

He makes me lie down in green pastures;

he leads me beside still waters;

he restores my soul.

He leads me in paths of righteousness

for his name's sake.

Even though I walk through the valley of the shadow of death,

I fear no evil;

For you are with me,

your rod and your staff—

they comfort me.

You prepare a table before me

in the presence of my enemies;

you anoint my head with oil;

my cup overflows.

Surely goodness and mercy shall follow me

all the days of my life

and I shall dwell in the house of the LORD

my whole life long."

The 23rd psalm is the most widely known psalm of all and, in the opinion of many, also the most beautiful. Written from the perspective of the shepherd David, the psalm is a serene statement of faith and comfort.

Thanksgiving Psalms

Twenty psalms are songs of thanksgiving, expressing gratitude to God for what He has already done. In the example given here, the author justifies the existence of the psalm itself as a musical statement of overwhelming joy.

PSALM 92:1–4

"It is good to give thanks to the LORD,

to sing praises to your name, O Most High;

to declare your steadfast love in the morning,

and your faithfulness by night,

to the music of the lute and the harp,

to the melody of the lyre.

For you, O LORD, have made me glad by your work;

at the works of your hands I sing for joy."

Laments

Over one third of psalms are laments, the most common category of psalm. Laments call on God for aid and generally follow a specific literary formula: a complaint (usually preceded by praise or some other form of address directed toward God), a prayer for aid, a justifying statement of why God would want to help (either because of the qualities He has demonstrated or because of a prior covenant), a guarantee of further prayer or sacrifice, and concluding praise.

PSALM 22:1–2, 4–6, 9–11

"My God, my God, why have you forsaken me?

Why are you so far from helping me,

from the words of my groaning?

O my God, I cry by day, but you do not answer;

and by night, but find no rest…

In you our ancestors trusted;

they trusted, and you delivered them.

To you they cried, and were saved;

in you they trusted, and were not put to shame.

But I am a worm, and not human;

scorned by others, and despised by the people…

Yet it was you who took me from the womb;

you kept me safe on my mother's breast.

On you I was cast from my birth,

and since my mother bore me you have been my God.

Do not be far from me,

for trouble is near,

and there is no one to help."

Psalm 22 is probably the best-known lament. It's the psalm Jesus recited while suffering on the cross (Matthew 27:46): "O God, O God, why have you forsaken me?" translating into his native Aramaic as *"Eli, Eli, lama sabachthani?"* Although the psalm is too long to include in its entirety here, the basic structure is apparent: verses addressing God, a complaint ("For I am a worm, and not human...") that segues into the abuse the petitioner has suffered at the hands of his enemies, and a justifying statement ("Yet it was you who took me from the womb...").

Royal Psalms

A royal psalm is any psalm in which the author or the subject is a king. It can be a historical psalm, a lament, or any other type of psalm, but it is its royal nature that gives it special distinction.

PSALM 132:11–12

"The LORD swore to David a sure oath

from which he will not turn back:

'One of the sons of your body

I will set on your throne.

If your sons keep my covenant

and my decrees that I shall teach them,

their sons also, forevermore,

shall sit on your throne.'"

This psalm focuses on the preservation of the Davidic kingship, which was often disrupted by invaders.

Wisdom Psalms

Wisdom psalms are written in the style of biblical wisdom literature and were probably intended for use in private instruction rather than public worship or performance. They generally offer advice and draw distinctions between righteous and wicked behavior.

PSALM 37:5–9

"Commit your way to the LORD;

trust in him, and he will act.

He will make your vindication shine like the light,

and the justice of your cause like the noonday.

Be still before the LORD, and wait patiently for him;

do not fret over those who prosper in their way,

over those who carry out evil devices.

Refrain from anger, and forsake wrath.

Do not fret—it leads only to evil.

For the wicked shall be cut off,

but those who wait for the LORD shall inherit the land."

This psalm follows that formula perfectly by calling on its audience to follow God without anger or fear, seeking his vindication without falling prey to the wickedness that can result from these temptations.

Liturgical Psalms

Liturgical psalms were used for specific religious services. (A *liturgy* is a religious ritual.) The two most common were Temple entrance rites (psalms stating who was worthy to enter the Temple) and processional hymns.

PSALM 15:1–5

"O LORD, who may abide in your tent?

Who may dwell on your holy hill?

Those who walk blamelessly, and do what is right,

and speak the truth from their heart;

who do not slander with their tongue,

and do no evil to their friends,

nor take up a reproach against their neighbors;

in whose eyes the wicked are despised,

but who honor those who fear the LORD;

who stand by their oath even to their hurt;

who do not lend money at interest,

and do not take a bribe against the innocent.

Those who do these things shall never be moved."

Psalm 15 is almost certainly a Temple entrance rite, recited before congregants were admitted to the Temple. It encourages obedience of Jewish law and calls those who disobey it to repent.

Historical Psalms

Any hymn that focuses on recounting the history of God's people is a historical psalm, although it can fall into other categories as well. The goal of a historical psalm is to connect the reader or listener with a sense of history, which is central to both the Jewish and Christian traditions and particularly central to the Bible. Both Judaism and Christianity are, to a great extent, about remembering—remembering the covenant of Abraham, remembering the flight from Egypt, remembering the Last Supper of Jesus. Historical psalms connect to this aspect of Judeo-Christian religious life.

PSALM 78:1–4

"Give ear, O my people, to my teaching;

incline your ears to the words of my mouth.

I will open my mouth in a parable;

I will utter dark sayings from of old,

things that we have heard and known,

that our ancestors have told us.

We will not hide them from their children;

we will tell to the coming generation

the glorious deeds of the LORD, and his might,

and the wonders that he has done."

This historical psalm recalls the experience of the author's ancestors (focusing on Moses and Jacob) and calls on future generations to remember their experiences.

Speaking of Wisdom

The Proverbs are unique among the books of the Hebrew Bible in that they contain only sayings, and sayings on a diverse range of topics at that. They reflect the best of ancient Jewish wisdom, focusing on how to live a wise life relatively free of sin, unhappiness, and unnecessary personal conflict.

note

Most scholars believe that Proverbs represents a long, multicultural oral tradition of ancient wisdom sayings. To support this claim, they cite similarities between the Book of Proverbs and ancient Egyptian sources such as the *Proverbs of Ahiqar* and the *Instruction of Amenemope*.

Proverbs is made up of material that falls into three categories: verses in praise of wisdom, lengthy meditations, and short aphorisms. Verses praising wisdom identify her (wisdom is always female) as a mediator between God and humanity, a means by which life can be lived in harmony with the divine.

Among the lengthy meditations the most well known is the meditation on the good wife (Proverbs 31:10–31), which concludes the Book of Proverbs. Attributed to King Lemuel, it suggests that strong, assertive, and generous women who proactively take on the role of wife make for better companions than beautiful but otherwise unremarkable women who do not. It was, by the standards of its time, an astonishing feminist statement.

PROVERBS 31:17–20

"She girds herself with strength,

and makes her arms strong.

She perceives that her merchandise is profitable.

Her lamp does not go out at night.

She puts her hands to the distaff,

and her hands hold the spindle.

She opens her hand to the poor,

and reaches out her hands to the needy."

But Proverbs is best known for its shorter aphorisms, which are easily quoted and remembered. With its practical advice on matters relevant to everyday life ("Prepare your work outside, get everything ready for you in the field; and after that build your house."—Proverbs 24:27), Proverbs is in some ways one of the most approachable books of the entire Bible.

WHAT KIND OF FOOL DO YOU THINK I AM?

"How long, O simple ones, will you love being simple?

How long will scoffers delight in their scoffing

and fools hate knowledge?"

—Proverbs 1:22

If you're looking for a word to the wise, Proverbs might not be your cup of tea: the 31 chapters of Proverbs refer to various types of fools a grand total of 64 times. Here are the three kinds of fools you'll find described in

note

According to the Gnostic tradition, Sophia (wisdom) is the cosmic sister of Christ, responsible for bringing *pneuma* (spiritual essence) into the world. She is also revered as the personification of wisdom in Eastern Orthodox traditions. According to the Deuterocanonical book titled the Wisdom of Solomon (see Chapter 17), she is identified as the wife of Solomon and the person responsible for teaching him how to build the temple.

Proverbs, loosely based on the three categories of Proverbial foolishness described by Jason Jackson of *The Christian Courier*:

- **The simple one (phethaim)**—Simple fools aren't exactly stupid; they're just uneducated, naive, or both. With a little instruction, simple fools can become wise and call other people simple fools. Or not. Example: "The simple believe everything, but the clever consider their steps." (Proverbs 14:15)

- **The scoffer (letz)**—Likes to start trouble. Scoffers are arrogant hecklers, sophists, loudmouths, and generally unpleasant people to be around. They find great joy in disrupting other people's conversations and bringing as much attention as possible to themselves. Example: "Scoffers do not like to be rebuked; they will not go to the wise." (Proverbs 15:12)

- **The outright fool (ewil, or "thick," and kesil, or "stupid")**—Is pathologically stubborn. The outright fool is angry, argumentative, slanderous, and intellectually lazy. The outright fool won't listen to anybody, living life from bad decision to bad decision. Proverbs actually describes stubborn fools as followers of evil (13:22) and is generally harder on this kind of fool than any other. Example: "Better to confront a she-bear robbed of its cubs than to confront a fool immersed in folly." (Proverbs 17:12)

THE ABSOLUTE MINIMUM

- The Book of Psalms, the oldest book in the Hebrew Bible, is made up of either 150 or 151 hymns (depending on which edition of the Bible you use).
- Each hymn falls into one or more categories: hymns of praise, psalms of trust, thanksgiving psalms, laments, royal psalms, wisdom psalms, liturgical psalms, or historical psalms.
- The Book of Proverbs is a compilation of ancient wisdom, celebrating the virtues of a wise life and urging the simple to become educated.

RESOURCES

- **Hebrew Psalms Radio**—www.hebrewpsalms.org
- **Introducing the Psalm**—www.cresourcei.org/psalmsintro.html
- **Proverbs (*Catholic Encyclopedia*)**—www.newadvent.org/cathen/12505b.htm
- **Psalms (Catholic Encyclopedia)**—www.newadvent.org/cathen/12533a.htm

16

MORTAL QUESTIONS

The books of Job, Ecclesiastes, and the Song of Solomon address some of the most fundamental issues humanity faces: the suffering of the innocent, the cause of evil, the apparent purposelessness of human existence, and the incomparable thrill of falling in love. From a strictly literary perspective, these three books are often regarded as the finest in the Bible.

And You Think *You've* Got Problems?

The Book of Job begins like a bad joke: God is sitting in heaven, Satan shows up, and they have a conversation about the faithfulness of one of God's favorite servants. God says Job is faithful; Satan says Job is just comfortable; and to settle the bet, God gives Satan free rein to test the man. From this strange beginning emerges one of the most powerful and provocative books of the entire Bible—a lengthy dialogue on the nature of God, suffering, and evil.

According to the story, Job is an extremely wealthy Arabian landowner—"the greatest of all the people of the east" (Job 1:3)—with 10 children and a passionate devotion to God. It is logical for Satan to ask whether Job's devotion has more to do with gratitude and an overall sense of well-being than with a deep and meaningful faith. Satan wants to know whether a cursed Job will rail against God just as readily as a blessed Job will worship, so he and God make a bet: God thinks Job will stand firm, and Satan thinks he'll buckle. Satan takes away virtually everything Job has—depriving him of his livestock (the core of his assets) and his servants, killing his 10 children, and afflicting him with horribly painful and disfiguring sores. His wife lovingly suggests that he "curse God and die" (Job 2:9), and things go downhill from there.

THE DEVIL YOU KNOW

According to Christian tradition, Satan (Hebrew: *the opponent*) was originally Lucifer—the morning star, the Angel of Light—but he challenged God and fell, with other angels who had taken his cause, to the depths of hell. From hell he is bent on destroying humanity by separating people from God. Satan is, in contemporary terms, evil incarnate—the Prince of Darkness and the Father of Lies, who will finally be overthrown by Jesus Christ at the end of the world. This is similar to the Islamic tradition of Iblis, or *shaytan*, a being made of fire who was cast down into hell for refusing to serve humanity.

In the Hebrew Bible, however, Satan's role is less clear. The Hebrew word is usually translated as "adversary," as for example in 1 Kings 11:14: "Then the LORD raised up an adversary [Hebrew: *satan*] against Solomon, Hadad the Edomite...." But in the Book of Job, and in at least two other verses (1 Chronicles 21:1, in which Satan tempts David, and Zechariah 3:1–2, in which Satan accosts Joshua before God), the word *Satan* is intended to refer to a specific being—an angel or other celestial entity who really dislikes human beings. It is important to note that in the Hebrew Bible, this Satan is never explicitly described as an enemy of God; the Book of Job places Satan in heaven and on speaking terms with the Lord of Hosts. The Satan of the Hebrew Bible is only described as being the adversary of *humanity*. He is the prosecutor in the heavenly court, where God sits in judgment. For this reason, some theologians suspect that the Satan of the Hebrew Bible might refer to a different being than the Satan of the New Testament, who is an enemy of both God *and* humanity.

Interestingly, the serpent in Genesis 3 who tempts Adam and Eve is never explicitly identified as Satan. Most scholars suspect that the use of the serpent was meant to be a jab at the pagan religions of the time, which regarded the serpent as wise. The story also functions as a folk tale by explaining why serpents don't have legs.

But Jewish and Christian theologians have traditionally identified Satan with the serpent—he presumably had motive and opportunity, and who better than Satan to drive the first wedge between God and humanity?

The New Testament goes into more detail about the nature of Satan—identifying him as the lord of the demons (Mark 3:23–27) who fell down from heaven (Luke 10:18). By the time of the Middle Ages, the view of Satan as God's adversary had been accepted by the vast majority of Jewish and Christian theologians. This is partly because the New Testament clearly establishes Satan as God's opponent and partly because the serpent in the garden, the tempter of David, and the prosecutor of Job all seem to share a similar role—they all work to undermine humanity's relationship with God.

The nature of Satan was explored in even greater detail in John Milton's epic poems *Paradise Lost* and *Paradise Regained*, which expanded the traditional view of Satan as a fallen angel by giving him clearer motives. Milton's Satan is a clever, charming being with complex, albeit thoroughly selfish, motives—in many ways a reflection of the worst that humanity has to offer.

Job is essentially made up of three parts, beginning with a short prologue (chapters 1–2) and ending with an even shorter epilogue (chapter 42, verses 7–17). The 40 chapters in between make up the heart of the book, consisting of Job's laments and lengthy monologues from three friends of dubious wisdom:

> **note**
>
> Although "the patience of Job" often refers to the ability to bear suffering without complaint, the reference doesn't quite fit—Job actually complains at great length. His saving grace is his refusal to curse God in these complaints.

- **Eliphaz the Temanite (4:1–5:27, 15:1–35, 22:1–30)**—Eliphaz believes that suffering is due to divine punishment, suggesting that Job must have done something to warrant what has happened to him.

- **Bildad the Shuhite (8:1–22, 18:1–21, 25:1–6)**—Bildad argues that perhaps Job's children sinned, causing their own death, and that Job (being blameless) can appeal to God for mercy, as he would in a court of law.

- **Zophar the Naamathite (11:1–20, 20:1–29)**—Zophar claims that Job is unwise and ill-equipped to understand the nature and depth of his own guilt. By learning wisdom, Zophar claims, Job can overcome his suffering.

Job's response to the three friends forces him into a tricky situation: How can he affirm his own innocence without denying God's justice? He could only express his confusion—stating that he was sure of his own moral character ("[Job] was righteous in his own eyes," reads verse 32:1) but equally sure of God's majesty and justice. At this point a young man named Elihu—not mentioned anywhere else in the text—speaks up (32:1–37:24). Many contemporary scholars believe that Elihu's discourse, a lengthy monologue on the nature of divine justice, was inserted later—particularly because he is never answered by Job. Although Elihu suggests that God rewards the good and punishes the wicked, he also claims that moral behavior is always justified, regardless of any reward or punishment, because of the positive effects it has on other human beings (35:1–8).

> ## Biblically Speaking
>
> "Then Job answered:
> 'I have heard many such things;
> miserable comforters are you all.
> Have windy words no limit?
>   Or what provokes you that you keep on talking?
> I also could talk as you do,
>   if you were in my place;
> I could join words together against you,
>   and shake my head at you.'"
>
> —Job 16:1–4

The most authoritative response, however, comes from God himself (38:1–41:34, 42:7–8). God reminds Job that he is too powerful and too mysterious for his purposes to be understood by human beings and states that, in effect, Job's complaints are accurate—he remains God's innocent servant and yet was punished. God chides Eliphaz, Bildad, and Zophar for attacking Job's character and states that he will forgive them if Job chooses to pray on their behalf, which he does.

In the epilogue (42:9–17), Job's fortunes are increased and he has 10 new children— 7 more sons and 3 more daughters. He lives for another 140 years, during which time his wife presumably did not tell him to curse God and die quite as often. And in the Book of Job, as in the real world, the problem of why human beings must suffer remains a mystery. What is clear, however, is that Job's ability to bear suffering without cursing God—to humbly recognize that life is sometimes not fair—is as an admirable quality. Job rejects hostile self-pity in favor of a clear-eyed understanding of the situation, recognizing his own suffering without letting it cloud his judgment. In this respect, the benefit of Job is not so much that it solves the problem of evil; it is that it explains how an innocent person can respond to suffering without losing dignity.

The Problem of Evil

The world can be a horribly unjust place. If God is all-powerful and loving, why does it have to be so? This question always seems to come up when a society experiences extreme trauma, but tragedy surrounds all of us every day. A recent newspaper story tells of an 11-year-old child who got into his parents' car and inadvertently ran over his 2-year-old brother. Where was God? An 8-year old girl was recently discovered alive in a landfill, the victim of rape and torture. For her—and for those children who are less lucky and do not even survive their ordeals—where was God?

Theologians have grappled with this question for as long as there have been theologians. Some ancient systems sidestep this problem by making their gods selfish, malevolent, or just plain uncaring, but the Judeo-Christian tradition affirms a *loving* God—and this creates a problem. Job (and, as we discuss in the following, Ecclesiastes) wrestles with this problem.

The branch of theology concerned with solving this problem is called *theodicy* (literally "a just God"). Job's theodicy states that you are not obligated to lock yourself into a permanent answer on the problem of evil. This is the central message of the text: that the problem of suffering can't simply be reasoned away. The book's approach is less about confronting and dissolving the problem of evil than it is about acknowledging it within the context of a life of faith, as Job did.

Biblical Existentialism

The Book of Ecclesiastes (Greek: "the speaker") is unique among all Bible books in that it suggests that death will inevitably destroy every human being. Judging our success by human standards is a waste of time because such human standards—whether you measure success by accumulated wisdom, wealth, power, or magnitude of effort—are rendered

Biblically Speaking

[And Job said:]

"If I have withheld anything that the poor desired,

or caused the eyes of the widow to fail,

or have eaten my morsel alone, and the orphan has not eaten from it—

for from my youth I reared the orphan like a father,

and from my mother's womb I guided the widow—

if I have seen anyone perish for lack of clothing,

or a poor person without covering, whose loins have not blessed me,

and who was not warmed with the fleece of my sheep;

if I have raised my hand against the orphan,

because I saw I had supporters at the gate;

then let my shoulder blade fall from my shoulder,

and let my arm be broken from its socket.

For I was in terror of calamity from God,

And I could not have faced his majesty."

—Job 31:16–23

irrelevant by the brutal fact of our inevitable extinction. If death awaits all of us, according to Ecclesiastes, then the sensible thing is to find meaningful work and try to live a happy life as God intends (2:24–26).

Attributed to a kingly "son of David, king of Jerusalem" whom readers have traditionally assumed to be Solomon (who reigned during the tenth century B.C.), Ecclesiastes contains references to Persian and Aramaic terms that suggest a much

note

The word translated as "vanity" (*hebel*) actually means vapor, breath, or a puff of wind; it refers to the impermanence of all things.

later date—most likely near 250 B.C. The book might have been attributed to Solomon in his honor (a common practice at the time), or it could be attributed to another figure referred to as a "son of David" (just as the term *ben*, translated as "son," can also refer in a more general sense to descendants). However, Solomon is the only likely candidate who would have actually served as king of Jerusalem.

Whoever the narrator is, he is identified as a teacher of wisdom (12:9–14), essentially an ancient philosopher of the region. He is somewhat suspicious of scholarship, writing that "Of making many books there is no end, and much study is a weariness of the flesh" (12:12); instead he takes on students and instructs them verbally, much as Socrates did in the Greek world.

His emphasis on the futility of human goals in the face of death is reminiscent of a much later philosophical movement called *existentialism*, most prominently represented in the twentieth century by the French philosophers Albert Camus, Simone de Beauvoir, and Jean-Paul Sartre. Existentialism teaches that existence precedes essence—in other words, that reality is a brutal fact without any purpose backing it up. Life, according to existentialism, is absurd and death robs it of its meaning and robs us of our dignity. The author of Ecclesiastes seems to agree, but at the same time affirms the sovereignty of God (12:13–14)—a tension that acknowledges the difficulty and suffering that comes with life without abandoning faith in a just God.

Sex and the Single Bible

Most people don't associate the Bible with erotic poetry, but the Song of Solomon—also called the Song of Songs or the Canticle of Canticles—is as much a part of the Hebrew Bible as any other book. Fully accepted by the Jewish tradition and every major Christian denomination, this sexually explicit love poem stands in sharp relief against Ecclesiastes, the book that precedes it.

Like Ecclesiastes, it is generally attributed to Solomon; also like Ecclesiastes, it contains loan words from Persian and Aramaic that suggest a later date of composition near 250 B.C. It can be read in two ways: On the surface, it's an exceptionally solid love poem, although it appeals to imagery that is perhaps not as timeless as in other biblical metaphors ("Your teeth are like a flock of shorn ewes that have come up from the washing," exclaims the lovesick gentleman in verse 4:5). It is sometimes jarringly graphic (it doesn't take much imagination to see the double entendres in verses 5:4–6) and sometimes astonishingly superficial (as when the female narrator taunts her less well-endowed sister in verses 8:8–9). Sex is certainly not a taboo subject in the Hebrew Bible, as Table 16.1 demonstrates—and the Song of Solomon, the only book of the Bible dedicated to sex, portrays it in a very positive light.

> ## Biblically Speaking
>
> "For everything there is a season, and a time for every matter under heaven:
>
> a time to be born, and a time to die;
>
> a time to plant, and a time to pluck up what is planted;
>
> a time to kill, and a time to heal;
>
> a time to break down, and a time to build up;
>
> a time to weep, and a time to laugh;
>
> a time to mourn, and a time to dance;
>
> a time to throw away stones, and a time to gather stones
>
>   together;
>
> a time to embrace, and a time to refrain from embracing;
>
> a time to seek, and a time to lose;
>
> a time to keep, and a time to throw away;
>
> a time to tear, and a time to sew;
>
> a time to keep silence, and a time to speak;
>
> a time to love, and a time to hate;
>
> a time for war, and a time for peace."
>
> —Ecclesiastes 3:1–8

TABLE 16.1   Sex in the Hebrew Bible

Genesis 4:1	Adam and Eve have sexual relations, the first mention of such in the Bible.
Genesis 6:4	Angels come to Earth and impregnate human women, producing a race of giants called *nephilim*. This is the primary reason given for the Flood.
Genesis 16:1–4	When Sarah is unable to conceive children, she suggests that her husband Abram produce an heir by using their slave, Hagar, as a surrogate mother. (In Genesis 30, Jacob's wives will suggest the same approach.)
Genesis 29:23–25	Jacob enters a tent to sleep with his new wife, Rachel, but is tricked into having sex with her older sister Leah instead.

TABLE 16.1 (continued)

Genesis 38:8–10	Onan, commanded by God to impregnate his brother's wife, practices *coitus interruptus*—coining the term "*Onanism,*" a euphemism for masturbation.
Ruth 3	Ruth asks Boaz to be her husband by following him to bed and then uncovering his feet. This sounds chaste enough (if a little odd), but if we read "feet" as a euphemism for genitals—as it often is in the Hebrew Bible—then the account becomes much more risqué.
1 Kings 11:1–3	King Solomon, David's son, has some 1,000 sexual partners—700 wives and 300 concubines.

But the Song of Solomon didn't just make it into the canon to spice things up; in the earliest Aramaic commentaries on the Hebrew Bible, and perhaps earlier, the Song is considered a metaphor for God's relationship with humanity—particularly God's relationship with Israel. The use of sexual metaphors to describe the God-Israel relationship is not unheard of (see Ezekiel 16:6–8), and many commentaries have been written on the book's possible religious symbolism.

Whichever interpretation you use, it is helpful to remember—because many translations do not make this clear—that the Song alternates between its male and female narrators. It is generally easy to tell which is speaking at a given time by watching for personal pronouns and other cues.

THE ABSOLUTE MINIMUM

- The Book of Job is the story of a good man who experiences tremendous suffering at God's hand. The first book of the Bible to explicitly mention Satan, it is an allegory dealing with the problem of evil, or the question of why an almighty and loving God would allow so much suffering in the world. The branch of theology concerned with addressing the problem of evil is called *theodicy*.

- The longest treatment of Satan in the Hebrew Bible is found in Job, which establishes him as a member of the heavenly court and the being responsible for prosecuting humanity. Later, rabbinic authors—and the New Testament—would describe Satan in more detail, generally presenting him as the primordial force of evil.

- Ecclesiastes is a highly readable monologue that combines wise aphorisms with a lengthier discussion of the meaning of life. The author argues that human life is without meaning and that human philosophy can provide no adequate consolation without the presence of God.

- The Song of Solomon (also called the Song of Songs) celebrates human love and sexuality and has traditionally been interpreted as an effective metaphor of God's love for his people. Although it is the only erotic poem in the Bible, it is far from being the only reference to sex.

RESOURCES

- **And Adam Knew Eve: A Dictionary of Sex in the Bible**—www.hobrad.com/and.htm

- **Satan (Ontario Consultants)**—www.religioustolerance.org/chr_sat1.htm

- **Satan (Wikipedia)**—en.wikipedia.org/wiki/Satan

- **The Song of Songs**—ccat.sas.upenn.edu/~jtreat/song

- **Theodicy (Wikipedia)**—en.wikipedia.org/wiki/Theodicy

PART V

BEYOND THE BIBLE

IN THIS CHAPTER

- An explanation of how Catholic and Eastern Orthodox Bibles differ from Protestant Bibles

- A brief history and overview of the Deuterocanonical Books (sometimes called the Apocrypha), extra books and verses that are not included in most Protestant Bibles

17

THE BOOKS OF TRADITION

The 13 books and miscellaneous additional verses making up the *Deuterocanonical* ("added to the canons") Books, referred to by Protestants as the *Apocrypha* ("hidden teachings"), tell stories that are not recorded in the traditional Jewish Hebrew Bible or the New Testament. Most are accepted as authoritative by the Roman Catholic and Eastern Orthodox churches, but even in those traditions they remain some of the most neglected texts in the Bible. Some are also among the most fascinating.

Fired from the Canons

Although many of these stories are central to the Jewish religion (1 and 2 Maccabees, for example, provide the basis for Hanukkah), none of these additional passages (described in Table 17.1) or books (described in Table 17.2) are included in the Hebrew Bible. They are later compositions included in early Greek editions of the Bible, accepted as canonical at the earliest church councils but not found in the original Hebrew. Their status was secure until the Protestant Reformation, when some theologians critical of the Roman Catholic Church noticed that the Deuterocanonical books and passages did not appear in the early, Jewish editions of Scripture and decided that they could not be trusted. In the King James Version of 1611, the Apocrypha was set aside in a special section between the Old and New Testaments—to be studied, but not to be revered.

Table 17.1 Longer Versions of Existing Books

Book	New Content
Esther	In Catholic and Eastern Orthodox Bibles: Mordecai dreams (10:4–13, 11:2–12, 12:1–6); more on Haman's treachery (13:1–7, 16:1–24); new prayers (13:8–18, 14:1–19); Esther faints in front of the king (15:4–19).
Daniel	In Catholic and Eastern Orthodox Bibles: Azariah's prayer (3:24–45); the song of Shadrach, Mesach, and Abednego (3:46–90); Daniel acts as defense attorney for Susanna, a woman falsely accused of adultery (13:1–64); Daniel discredits an idol (14:1–42).
Psalms	In Russian Orthodox Bibles: A final Psalm (151:1–7) retells the story of David's early life.

The Apocrypha, or Deuterocanon, has largely been ignored by Protestants, but in recent years, it has attracted a new following. Many of the factors that made these books seem subversive and strange in earlier centuries (such as the depiction of a femme fatale seductress-assassin Bible heroine in the Book of Judith) now appear edgy and thought-provoking. For Roman Catholics and Eastern Orthodox Christians, the Deuterocanonical books have always been a valued part of the Bible. For others, their relative obscurity has given them gravity and mystique, aging them like fine wine.

Table 17.2 Church Recognition of the Deuterocanon

Book	Roman Catholic?	Greek Orthodox?	Russian Orthodox?
Tobit	Yes	Yes	Yes
Judith	Yes	Yes	Yes
Wisdom of Solomon	Yes	Yes	Yes
Ecclesiasticus (Sirach)	Yes	Yes	Yes
Baruch	Yes	Yes	Yes

Book	Roman Catholic?	Greek Orthodox?	Russian Orthodox?
The Letter of Jeremiah	Yes	Yes	Yes
1 Esdras	No	Yes	Yes
2 Esdras	No	No	Yes
Prayer of Manasseh	No	Yes	No
1 Maccabees	Yes	Yes	Yes
2 Maccabees	Yes	Yes	Yes
3 Maccabees	No	Yes	Yes
4 Maccabees	No	No	No

The Incredible Shrinking Bible

They tell stories of oppression and revolution, angels battling demons, and a defense attorney (the Prophet Daniel, no less) defending a client who had been falsely accused of a capital crime. They are the 13 books and scattered chapters of what Protestants call the *Apocrypha*, or the hidden teachings of the Bible. To Roman Catholic and Eastern Orthodox readers, however, they are the *Deuterocanon* ("added to the canons"), bridging the gulf between the Hebrew Bible and the New Testament.

If you're not familiar with the Deuterocanonical Books, you don't know what you're missing. Full of excitement, intrigue, and wisdom from the biblical era, they add richness and depth to the story of the Jewish faith and, by extension, to the story of the Christian faith as well. Table 17.3 summarizes the plot of each Deuterocanonical Book; if you're not sure where to start, I recommend Tobit, Judith, or one of the Maccabees.

Table 17.3 The Deuterocanonical Books

Book	Summary
Tobit	A saga of good versus evil, recounting the angel Raphael's battle with the demon Asmodeus over the life of a young woman.
Judith	The story of the assassin Judith, who saves the tiny Jewish city of Bethulia from occupation at the hands of the brutal Assyrians.
Wisdom of Solomon	A defense of Judaism, written for Jews living under Greco-Roman occupation.
Ecclesiasticus (Sirach)	A lengthy commentary on wisdom, virtues, and the meaning of life.
Baruch	Prayers, reflections on the nature of Wisdom, and visions of a restored Israel.

Table 17.3 (continued)

Book	Summary
The Letter of Jeremiah	An exhortation against polytheism and idol worship.
1 Esdras	Further adventures of the prophet Ezra, who also has his own book in the Hebrew Bible.
2 Esdras	Describes the destruction of the Second Temple at the hands of the Romans in 70 A.D. It also examines the problem of evil and includes a mystical vision of the Apocalypse.
Prayer of Manasseh	A prayer of repentance, attributed to the formerly idolatrous king Manasseh (described in 2 Chronicles).
1 Maccabees	The story of Hanukkah, a holiday that has its origins in the successful revolt, led by Judas Maccabaeus, against the oppressive ruler Antiochus (second century B.C.).
2 Maccabees	Another account of the Maccabean revolt, this time including mention of the new holiday of Hanukkah and meditations on the nature of the afterlife.
3 Maccabees	An account of the persecution of Jews under the Egyptian ruler Ptolemy IV (third century B.C.), a predecessor to Antiochus.
4 Maccabees	A defense of Judaism provided in the mode of Greek philosophy, followed by an account of the martyrdom of a family of devout Jews at the hands of Antiochus.

THE ABSOLUTE MINIMUM

- The Roman Catholic and Eastern Orthodox Bibles include special Old Testament books and extra verses of existing Old Testament books, which are collectively referred to as the Apocrypha or Deuterocanonical Books. These additional books and verses are not included in the Jewish Bible or most Protestant Bibles.

- Most of the Deuterocanonical Books were compiled later than the books of the Hebrew Bible. Most of them were also written in Greek rather than Hebrew.

- The Deuterocanonical Books were included in all Bibles until the time of the Protestant Reformation, when Protestant leaders rejected them as nonauthoritative.

RESOURCES

- **Deuterocanonical Books Referred to in the New Testament—** www.scripturecatholic.com/deuterocanon.html

- **Early Jewish Writings—**www.earlyjewishwritings.com

- **The Maccabees (from the Catholic Encyclopedia)—**www. newadvent.org/cathen/09493b.htm

- **What are the Deuterocanonical Books?—**www.bluffton.edu/~bergerd/ deutero.html

In This Chapter

- A brief discussion of the pseudepigrapha ("falsely attributed writings") and other unauthorized texts, books that have not historically been included in Catholic or Protestant Bibles

- A summary of five unauthorized texts that tell stories about Hebrew Bible characters

- A summary of five unauthorized texts that tell stories about New Testament characters

18

Nowhere in the Bible

In addition to the 66 books that make up the Protestant Bible and the 13 books that make up the Apocrypha or Deuterocanonical Books, there are literally hundreds of unauthorized texts about Bible characters that appear nowhere in the Biblical canon. These texts vary widely in quality and credibility, but some—such as the Book of Enoch (recognized by the Ethiopian Orthodox Church) and the Gospel of Thomas (published in a recent British edition of the New Testament)—are important to the Jewish and Christian traditions in their own right.

The Second Place Finish

The Bible is the ultimate prestigious anthology. The books selected for inclusion have been endorsed as representing the will of God, a standard most writers wouldn't even try to meet. (Some writers think they *are* God, but that's a different issue entirely.) When books surfaced that clashed with the rest of the Bible, or came from an obviously suspicious source, they were rejected as strictly human products.

Unauthorized books that are named for biblical figures are sometimes referred to as *pseudepigrapha* (falsely attributed writings), but the term is something of a misnomer because most so-called pseudepigrapha do not identify an author at all. As a general rule, the more widely read unauthorized books tend to reflect oral traditions that held less credibility at the time the canon was compiled than the traditions later reflected in the text. They are a diverse assortment of mostly unconnected texts. Though dismissed from the Bible and often kept out of public view in the past, they have since been published and made easily accessible to anybody with access to a good bookstore, the Internet, or a public library system.

Lost Books of the Bible

At some point thousands of years ago, books referred to in the Hebrew Bible—books that almost certainly existed at one point—simply vanished from history and never became part of the biblical canon. Some of the books cited here might have been incorporated into other Bible books—the Acts of Solomon, for instance, might be a reference to texts describing the life of Solomon that were later incorporated into 1 Kings—and many were probably destroyed by invaders. But in some cases, if you listen really hard, you might still be able to hear a scribe cursing in ancient Hebrew, furiously trying to dab spilled ink from an old scroll:

- **The Book of the Wars of the Lord** (Numbers 21:14)
- **The Book of Jashar** (Joshua 10:13)
- **The Acts of Solomon** (1 Kings 11:41)
- **The Book of David** (1 Chronicles 27:24)
- **The Book of Nathan** (1 Chronicles 29:29, 2 Chronicles 9:29)
- **The Book of Gad** (1 Chronicles 29:29)
- **The Book of Ahijah** (2 Chronicles 9:29)
- **The Book of Iddo** (2 Chronicles 13:22)
- **The Annals of Jehu** (2 Chronicles 20:34)
- **The Book of the Kings** (2 Chronicles 24:27)
- **The Book of Hozai** (2 Chronicles 33:19)
- **The Chronicles of Ahasuerus** (Esther 2:23, 6:1)

10 Important Extrabiblical Texts

Frankly, most unauthorized books are so bizarre and poorly written that it's hard not to suspect that church fathers who kept them out of the canon had quality control in mind. It's worth mentioning, though, that a few are really quite good, or (when not so good) at least important enough to justify a quick read.

Five Books Connected to the Hebrew Bible

Made up of a series of long, epic sagas swarming with fascinating characters, the Hebrew Bible is ripe for storytellers. Many *midrashim* (Jewish commentaries) tell new stories about characters from the Hebrew Bible, but they are usually treated as part of the rabbinic tradition and not as part of Scripture itself. Longer, self-contained works tend to be the products of later Christian authors, who retell Hebrew Bible stories in a way that explicitly asserts Christian doctrine, but there are some notable exceptions.

The Book of Enoch

Enoch, the father of Methuselah, is the only figure in the entire Hebrew Bible, other than Elijah, who ascends into heaven rather than facing death (Genesis 5:18–24). The Book of Enoch describes him as a prophet to fallen angels, hints at the origins of Satan, and provides a vision of the end of the world.

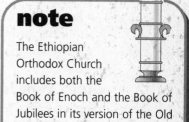

note

The Ethiopian Orthodox Church includes both the Book of Enoch and the Book of Jubilees in its version of the Old Testament.

The Book of Jubilees

The Book of Jubilees suggests that while Moses was on Mt. Sinai, the Angel of the Presence (a messenger angel) delivered a revelation to him in which he retold the entire story of the Torah—from the moment of Creation to Moses' ascension to Sinai—and placed new emphasis on the unique character of the Jewish people.

The Life of Adam and Eve

The Life of Adam and Eve is a midrash on the first four chapters of Genesis. It provides a detailed biography of the first family, tells the story of Cain and Abel, and describes the fall of Satan.

The Testament of Abraham

A midrashic account of the death and ascension of Abraham, it provides a description of heaven, answering the question: Do angels eat?

The Testament of Solomon

On his deathbed, Solomon describes the powers of individual demons and the names of angel-protectors. The document was originally a Jewish source, but Christian references were later added.

Five Books Connected to the New Testament

Perhaps no life has ever been as widely reflected upon as that of Jesus Christ. Although the number of Gospels written near Jesus' lifetime seems to be low, later Gospels—some of them relying, perhaps, on reliable oral traditions—are easily found.

The Gospel of Thomas

Sometimes described as the fifth Gospel, the Gospel of Thomas retells the story of Jesus from a Gnostic, almost Buddhist perspective. According to Thomas, Jesus' private teachings placed a great deal of emphasis on personal enlightenment and spiritual growth. Some consider Thomas to be the most accurate Gospel of all—and it was recently anthologized as part of the New Testament in *Good as New*, a popular British paraphrase of the New Testament—but most historians believe that it was written later than Matthew, Mark, and Luke.

The Gospel of Mary

Almost completely ignored for thousands of years, the Gospel of Mary has recently attracted attention from feminist theologians because of the prominent role it grants to Mary Magdálene, Jesus' closest female disciple. It suggests that she received secret teachings from him that other disciples were not privy to and that the 12 apostles reacted with moderate skepticism when she attempted to pass the teachings along.

The Shepherd of Hermas

This is an early Christian text describing the slave Hermas and the series of complex visions he received from the Angel of Repentance ("the Shepherd"). The Shepherd of Hermas was widely used during the early years of the Christian church but was later banned for suggesting that the earthly Jesus Christ was not the original Son of God.

The Gospel of Barnabas

This retelling of the life of Jesus denies the existence of the Trinity and argues that Jesus did not die on the cross or claim to be the Messiah. Although references to the text date as far back as the fifth century A.D., no pre-Renaissance manuscripts of the Gospel exist. For this reason, and because the document affirms the Islamic tradition that Jesus did not die by crucifixion, most historians believe that it was either written or modified by Muslim scholars.

The Acts of Peter

Peter, the "Prince of the Apostles" and the first Bishop of Rome (later known as the Pope), was a highly regarded figure in his own right. The Acts of Peter expands his legend by telling of a supernatural duel he fought with the Gnostic mystic Simon Magus, and by providing an account of Peter's eventual death at the hands of the Romans.

THE ABSOLUTE MINIMUM

■ The *pseudepigrapha* (falsely attributed writings) is a term used to describe the hundreds of miscellaneous books about Bible characters written during the history of the Jewish and Christian traditions that have never been widely accepted as part of the Bible.

■ Many books referred to in the Bible itself have vanished and might have been lost or destroyed.

■ In the Jewish rabbinic tradition, extrabiblical stories about Bible characters are extremely common. They are regarded as commentaries and parables, not forgeries.

RESOURCES

■ **Early Christian Writings**—www.earlychristianwritings.com

■ **Early Jewish Writings**—www.earlyjewishwritings.com

■ **The Nag Hammadi Library**—www.gnosis.org/naghamm/nhl.html

19

THE DEAD SEA SCROLLS

For more than 50 years, the field of biblical archaeology has fed on a collection of documents called the Dead Sea Scrolls. But what are they, exactly, and what is their relevance to the Bible?

11 Caves

In 1947, a 15-year-old Palestinian shepherd named Muhammed edh-Dibh was tending to his herd near Qumran, located on the northwestern shore of the Dead Sea east of Jerusalem. When a goat wandered into a cave, he threw rocks in the cave to drive the animal out and was surprised at the sound the rock made when it hit. Investigating further, he found that the stone had ricocheted off some old pottery.

Archaeologists were mesmerized by what they found in the pottery: ancient manuscripts dating back thousands of years. Realizing that the nearby abandoned fortress of Qumran was a haven to religious groups in the centuries before Christ, they began searching nearby caves. Between 1947 and 1956, local and international researchers found a total of 11 caves containing more than 900 documents dating between 150 B.C. and 70 A.D.

Scholars believe the documents were concealed by a Jewish religious sect hiding in the Qumran fortress, but there is a great deal of disagreement regarding what sort of religious group it was. Certain documents suggest that it was a messianic group dissatisfied with the status quo of Judaism under the yoke of Roman occupation.

Among the scrolls are documents and fragments of documents making up the Hebrew Bible, with the exception of the Book of Esther, which predate any other manuscripts of comparable length. A complete Hebrew edition of the Book of Isaiah, more than 99% identical to the version accepted by Jews and most Christians today, was among the scrolls, lending credence to the theory that scribes were generally faithful in their reproductions of ancient manuscripts.

Biblically Speaking

"On the day when the [Mediterranean invaders] fall there shall be a battle and horrible carnage before the God of Israel, for it is a day appointed by Him from ancient times as a battle of annihilation for the Sons of Darkness.... The Sons of Light and the forces of Darkness shall fight together to show the strength of God with the roar of a great multitude and the shouts of gods and men; a day of disaster.... In three lots the Sons of Light shall stand firm so as to strike a blow at wickedness, and in three the army of [the fallen angel] Belial shall strengthen themselves so as to force the retreat of the forces of Light.... In the seventh lot the great hand of God shall overcome [Belial and all] the angels of his dominion...."

—*The War Scroll*, column 1. From Michael Wise, Martin Abegg Jr., and Edward Cook (ed. trans.), *The Dead Sea Scrolls: A New Translation* (1995), pp. 151–152.

New Life by the Dead Sea

But the vast majority of Dead Sea Scroll documents are not biblical; there are several examples of pseudepigrapha (discussed in the previous chapter), such as the Book of Enoch, and hundreds of original documents—in fragmentary form—that scholars had never seen before. Here are just a few:

- **The Book of Giants**—Tells the story of giants who walked the earth prior to the Great Flood

- **The Copper Scroll**—A document written on copper, giving the location of various ancient buried treasures

- **A Vision of the Son of God**—A prophecy of a coming messiah who "will be called the Son of God, they will call him the son of the Most High"

- **The War of the Messiah**—Predicts that the coming messiah will take up arms against enemy forces

- **The War Scroll**—An account of the Apocalypse, the final battle between those to whom the scroll refers as the Sons of Light and the Sons of Darkness

Very few of the Dead Sea Scroll documents were fully intact at the time of their discovery, so English translations tend to feature plenty of brackets and ellipses denoting garbled or missing text. But for scholars, and for many nonscholars, the brackets and ellipses are a small price to pay.

THE ABSOLUTE MINIMUM

- The Dead Sea Scrolls are a collection of more than 900 manuscripts and partial manuscripts excavated east of Jerusalem between 1947 and 1956.

- Among the scrolls are fragments of every Hebrew Bible book except the Book of Esther, including a complete Book of Isaiah—the earliest original copy ever found.

- The Dead Sea Scrolls were written by an unknown messianic sect that used the nearby Qumran fortress to hide out from hostile authorities.

Resources

- **The Dead Sea Scrolls (Brigham Young University)**—farms.byu.edu/dss/index.html
- **The Dead Sea Scrolls (Virtual Religion Network)**—virtualreligion.net/iho/dss.html
- **The Dead Sea Scrolls Collection (Gnostic Society Library)**—www.gnosis.org/library/dss/dss.htm
- **Basic Facts About the Dead Sea Scrolls (University of North Carolina)**—www.religiousstudies.uncc.edu/jdtabor/dssfacts.html

PART VI

THE LIFE OF CHRIST

20

THE SEARCH FOR THE HISTORICAL JESUS

For centuries, scholars have attempted to construct a reliable biography of Jesus Christ as a historical figure. By using the New Testament alongside secular historical sources, it is possible to gain a more well-rounded understanding of Jesus and the time in which he lived than the Bible alone can provide. Nevertheless, the four Gospels remain the oldest, most extensive, and most widely read biographies of Jesus Christ.

Jesus, We Hardly Knew Ye

If you glance through the biography shelves at your local library, you will see frighteningly thick biographies of people from many walks of life: actors, writers, politicians, social reformers, war heroes, criminals, and many others, all described in great detail. More often than not you will learn their parents' names and occupations, their childhood experiences, their education and coming of age, and the events that made them famous. You might learn about their hobbies, their favorite foods, and how they spent their leisure time. But if you want information on the life and ministry of Jesus Christ, you have only four overlapping biographies—all of them written more to spread the message of Christianity than provide a complete historical biography of Jesus, and none of them longer than a detailed encyclopedia entry.

We don't even know with any confidence what Jesus looked like, although we can safely assume that (classical Renaissance paintings aside) an impoverished itinerant rabbi in Roman-occupied Palestine probably would not have had silky blond hair and flowing, unstained white robes. He was Middle Eastern, not western European, and was (unless he suffered from a skin disorder) very well tanned—and probably very calloused as well. Men living in that region during that period also tended to be short. He might or might not have had long hair and a beard; most Jews of the time probably did have beards, but short hair was more common and those who had been influenced by Greek culture were often clean-shaven. The hair he did have would have been black and curly, and quite possibly thinning. The fact that the Bible makes a point of stating that Jesus wore white robes after his resurrection suggests that he probably didn't usually wear white robes before he died—a sensible decision because white cloth stains easily.

These statements might sound controversial, but there is absolutely no biblical or theological basis for the popular portrait of Jesus Christ. It is based on cultural, rather than historical, priorities. Jesus is painted as white by white artists, often wearing luxurious clothing because it looks better on canvas. He is usually tall because height suggests gravitas, his hair is almost unfailingly clean and perfectly conditioned because in the human mind cleanliness really is next to godliness. But if Jesus really were as odd-looking by first-century Middle Eastern standards as popular portraits suggest, then his strange appearance would have been the first thing people noticed about him—and the Gospels make no mention of his appearance.

It isn't terribly important to know what Jesus looked like, but it's reasonable to ask the following: If cultural biases have led many contemporary artists to depict Jesus as a bearded European superhunk, could our understanding of Jesus be flawed in other ways? The purpose of the Gospels was most likely to spread the Christian faith, not to provide a secular, historical biography of Jesus. That task falls on those of us of every generation who try to scrape together the available historical information on Jesus and personally confront the question he asked his disciples: "Who do you say that I am?"

Jesus in the Bible

The best biographies of Jesus available to us are those in the New Testament. All the noncanonical gospels we have discovered so far—such as the Gospel of Thomas—were composed at a later date, and the references to Jesus made by Roman historians (discussed in the next section, "Roman Historians on the Life of Jesus") are brief and sketchy. For this reason, historical Jesus scholarship begins with the four Gospels: Matthew, Mark, Luke, and John, summarized in Table 20.1.

Table 20.1 The Four Gospels

Gospel	Date	Likely Intended Audience
Mark	About 65 A.D.	Gentile Christians, especially those living in Rome
Matthew	About 85 A.D.	Fairly traditional Jewish Christians
Luke	About 85 A.D.	Non-Jewish Christians and Jewish Christians on the margins of society (especially women)
John	About 95 A.D.	Christians already familiar with the stories of Jesus' life and teachings

Or maybe we should say Mark first, *then* Matthew, Luke, and John. The reason Matthew always appears first in the New Testament is because, for most of Christian history, people believed that he wrote the earliest Gospel. Scholars now believe that this honor belongs to Mark. Although 1 of the original 12 apostles was in fact the penitent Roman tax collector Matthew, the name was fairly common in Jesus' day—and even if the original Matthew had been the source of the information, it would have been common practice for a later student to write down the account and credit it to his teacher as a sign of respect.

The case for Mark as the earliest Gospel is strong. For starters, we can be fairly confident about who Mark was thanks to the work of a second-century church father named Papias of Hierapolis, who described Mark as "Peter's interpreter" (yes, that Peter) who, for the benefit of the new Christian community in Rome, "wrote down accurately whatever [Peter] remembered of what was said or done by the Lord, however not in order." For various historical reasons, we have good reason to believe that Mark was composed before 70 A.D.

Careful study has shown that Matthew and Luke quote certain portions of Mark word for word, but that they also rely on a third Greek source for Jesus' teachings. Although it is possible that one account was simply copied from the other, it is far more likely that an older written record of Jesus' teachings formed the basis of Matthew and Luke. This is borne out by Papias' description of the Gospel of Matthew: "Matthew compiled the *Sayings* in the Aramaic language [the language Jesus spoke], and everyone translated them [into Greek] as well as he could." This suggests that there were earlier Aramaic and Greek sources that consisted entirely of Jesus' teachings and predated the Gospel accounts. Biblical scholars are particularly enthusiastic about the possibility of one day finding a Greek document that they refer to as the Q Source or the Sayings Gospel Q, which they believe to be the primary source used by the authors of Matthew and Luke. If this document is ever found, then we will have access to an entirely new account of Jesus' teachings, older than that provided in any of the canonical Gospels. Until that day comes, Mark remains the oldest biography of Jesus, and Matthew and Luke remain the oldest detailed accounts of his teachings.

Roman Historians on the Life of Jesus

Although the Gospels are necessarily the starting point for any research into the historical Jesus, they are not the only contemporaneous accounts of Jesus' life. We also have the work of two Roman secular historians: Flavius Josephus (37–100 A.D.) and Cornelius Tacitus (55–120 A.D.). Josephus mentions Jesus twice in his *Antiquities of the Jews* (completed in 93 A.D.). The briefest reference—and the one that historians believe Josephus actually wrote—appears in Book XX, chapter 9, paragraph 1, where Josephus refers to an illegal trial conducted by a figure named Ananus, who had ordered the execution of James (identified as "the brother of Jesus, who was called Christ").

The more controversial reference appears earlier in the text, in Book XVIII, chapter 3, paragraph 3. Referred to as the *Testimonium Flavium*, this paragraph asserts that Jesus is "the Christ" and vouches for his miracles and character. There are several serious problems with this passage, however, the most serious being that the Greek phraseology is not the sort that Josephus uses elsewhere in the text. In addition, later references indicate that Josephus still considered himself a traditional Jew, not a Christian. For these reasons and for others, scholars believe that the *Testimonium Flavium* was added by Christian monks reproducing Josephus' work in the third or fourth century. It was not typical of monks to insert positive Christian references into classical texts at random, however, and that fact—combined with the fact that the paragraph occurs exactly where one would expect to see Jesus mentioned—suggests that perhaps Josephus had made a neutral or derogatory reference, which was then "corrected" a bit by later editors with a notably higher opinion of Jesus.

The possibility of a derogatory reference seems even more likely alongside the reference made by Josephus' contemporary, Cornelius Tacitus. Tacitus, a Roman pagan, was not terribly impressed with Christianity but was offended by the extreme measures that the Roman emperor Nero had taken against its followers (writing that "there arose a feeling of compassion; for it was...to glut one man's cruelty, that they were being destroyed"). His reference to Christianity in the *Annals* (distributed in 115 A.D.) says more about the early church than it does about Jesus himself, but a historian of Tacitus' caliber would have been in a position to say whether Jesus had been crucified by Pontius Pilate—and he wrote that he had. He would not, however, have been in a position to say much about the highly secretive Christian rituals of his time, which is likely why he refers to them as "abominations." Romans not personally familiar with the sacrament of the Lord's Supper—where participants eat bread and wine identified with the body and blood of Christ—often suspected that Christians practiced cannibalism.

JOSEPHUS AND TACITUS WRITE ABOUT JESUS

"Now there was about this time Jesus, a wise man, if it be lawful to call him a man; for he was a doer of wonderful works, a teacher of such men as receive the truth with pleasure. He drew over to him both many of the Jews and many of the Gentiles. He was [the] Christ. And when Pilate, at the suggestion of the principal men amongst us, had condemned him to the cross, those that loved him at the first did not forsake him; for he appeared to them alive again the third day; as the divine prophets had foretold these and ten thousand other wonderful things concerning him. And the tribe of Christians, so named from him, is not extinct at this day."

—The *Testimonium Flavium*, a heavily Christianized paraphrase of a reference to Jesus from Flavius Josephus, *The Antiquities of the Jews*, Section 18.3.3.

"[Ananus] assembled the sanhedrim of judges, and brought before them the brother of Jesus, who was called Christ, whose name was James, and some others, [or, some of his companions]..."

—Flavius Josephus, *The Antiquities of the Jews*, Section 20.9.1

"Nero...inflicted the most exquisite tortures on a class hated for their abominations, called Christians by the populace. Christus, from whom the name had its origin, suffered the extreme penalty during the reign of Tiberius at the hands of one of our procurators, Pontius Pilatus, and a most mischievous superstition, thus checked for the moment, again broke out not only in Judaea, the first source of the evil, but even in Rome, where all things hideous and shameful from every part of the world find their centre and become popular."

—Cornelius Tacitus, *The Annals*, Section 15.44

Although Josephus' and Tacitus' references to Jesus are brief, they are important because they provide secular historians' perspectives on the story told by the Gospels. For purposes of faith, of course, such references might or might not be useful—but they are immensely valuable as historical documents, providing the only known contemporaneous accounts of Jesus' life as seen by outsiders.

The Absolute Minimum

- The historical Jesus movement incorporates both secular and religious sources to study Jesus Christ as a historical figure.
- The four Gospels of the New Testament are the oldest written accounts of the life of Jesus available to us, but historians believe that they are themselves based in part on even older accounts that have been lost or destroyed.
- The Roman historians Flavius Josephus (37–100 A.D.) and Cornelius Tacitus (55–118 A.D.) refer to Jesus in their works.

Resources

- **Early Christian Writings**—www.earlychristianwritings.com
- **Into His Own: Perspective on the World of Jesus**—www.virtualreligion.net/iho
- **The Jesus Seminar at the Westar Institute**—www.westarinstitute.org
- **A Portrait of Jesus: From Galilean Jew to the Face of God**—www.united.edu/portrait

In This Chapter

- The birth of Jesus
- Jesus' missing years and the origins of the Holy Grail myth
- John the Baptist and prophecies pertaining to the life of Jesus

21

Before He Was Christ

In the same way that the Hebrew Bible is about the covenant between God and Israel, the New Testament is about one person: Jesus Christ. The Gospels tell the story of a life with a mysterious beginning and a tragic end—the life of one who lived the prophecies of the Hebrew Bible and, more than that, became known as the Son of God.

But by the time his public ministry had begun, He was in His mid-30s. Before He began traveling and preaching, before He began to gather disciples, who was Jesus of Nazareth?

Away in a Manger

In the year we now call A.D. 525, a Romanian monk named Dionysius Exiguus had been assigned by Pope John I to deal with issues pertaining to the church calendar. One of the things he took it upon himself to do was calculate the birth year of Jesus, which he reasoned to be December 25 in the Roman year 753. He called the Roman year 754 the first *anno Domini nostri Iesu Christi* ("the year of our Lord Jesus Christ")—or, as we call it today, A.D. 1. Dionysius' estimate turned out to be off by a few years, as both Matthew and Luke state that Jesus was born before the death of King Herod the Great (which took place in 4 B.C.), but the basic idea stands. To this day, Dionysius' estimated year of Jesus' birth remains the standard by which nearly everyone in the Western world measures time.

The story of Jesus' birth, told in Matthew (2:1–12) and Luke (2:1–7) but not in the other two Gospels, has been enshrined in our culture thanks in large part to Christmas, which began as a somewhat low-key church holiday celebrating Jesus' birth. However, it has taken on substantial religious and secular importance over the past century. Jesus is born of the union between his mother, a young Jewish woman named Mary, and the Holy Spirit (Luke 1:35).

According to Matthew and Luke, no biological father is involved; the only physical, gene-producing person for Jesus is His mother. This is in accord with the prophecy in Isaiah 7:14, which predicts that a messiah (savior) will be born of an *almah*—a young unmarried woman, presumably a virgin. Mary fits the bill. Matthew reports that Joseph is

Biblically Speaking

"In those days a decree went out from Emperor Augustus that all the world should be registered.... All went to their own towns to be registered. Joseph also went from the town of Nazareth in Galilee to Judea, to the city of David called Bethlehem, because he was descended from the house and family of David. He went to be registered with Mary, to whom he was engaged and who was expecting a child. While they were there, the time came for her to deliver her child. And she gave birth to her firstborn son and wrapped him in bands of cloth, and laid him in a manger, because there was no place for them at the inn."

—Luke 2:1, 3–7

note

Contrary to popular belief, the phrase *Immaculate Conception* does not refer to the Virgin Birth. It instead refers to the belief that Mary *herself* was conceived without inheriting original sin—allowing Jesus, too, to be born without this legacy.

understandably concerned about his allegedly virginal fiancée's pregnancy, but he comes to believe her story after an angel explains the situation to him in a dream (Matthew 1:18–25).

And Mary is a remarkable figure. In many circles, and especially in the Roman Catholic Church, she is revered as the mother of God—the woman who quite literally gave birth to, nursed, and raised God. The prayer for Mary's intercession, the Hail Mary (*Ave Maria*), is based on Luke 1:28 and Luke 1:42 ("Hail Mary, full of grace. Blessed art thou among women, and blessed is the fruit of thy womb, Jesus"). It acknowledges the influence that she would logically have in the world to come. She continues to play a prominent role in Jesus' ministry, such as when she persuades him to perform his first public miracle (John 2:1–12) and when she joins in prayer with the apostles after Jesus' Ascension (Acts 1:14).

As shown in Table 21.1, the virgin birth is only one of many Hebrew Bible prophecies that the birth story of Matthew and Luke fulfills. Those who believe that the story is accurate cite this as evidence that Jesus was in fact the promised messiah, while critics argue that Matthew and Luke wrote the story around existing Hebrew Bible prophecies as a means of emphasizing that Jesus was in fact who they believed him to be. (This would not necessarily be dishonest; if they already believed he was the promised messiah, the prophecies would have been seen as existing testimonies of Jesus' life and appropriate sources of biographical evidence.)

note

Joseph plays no role in Jesus' public ministry and vanishes from the story entirely after Jesus' childhood (Luke 2:41–51). Because he was not present with Mary when she attended the wedding in Cana where Jesus performed His first public miracle (John 2:1–12) and was not present to care for Jesus' body after the crucifixion, tradition has historically taught that Joseph died while Jesus was young. In some traditions, he is even portrayed as the patron saint of good deaths, dying with total faith in his son's ability to care for him in the world to come.

TABLE 21.1   Prophecies Associated with Jesus' Birth and Early Life

Prophecy	Verses	Description
Descendant of David	Isaiah 11:1, 22:22; Jeremiah 23:5, 33:14–15; Ezekiel 17:22–24, 34:23–24; **Luke 3:23–31**	The Hebrew Bible prophecies speak of a new king from the lineage of David. This is not a name chosen at random. David reigned over a united Israel (which would split into Israel and Judah only two generations later) and over the original 12 tribes of Israel (11 of which had been dispersed and assimilated into other cultures). David's dynasty was also the only

TABLE 21.1 (continued)

Prophecy	Verses	Description
		dynasty that survived for a significant length of time, lasting from his anointment near 1000 B.C. to the fall of Jerusalem in 586 B.C.
Born to unmarried woman; will be called Immanuel	Isaiah 7:14; Jeremiah 31:22; **Matthew 1:18–23**	Isaiah 7:14 states that the messiah will be born to an *almah*; the word can mean "young woman" or "virgin," but the overall connotation is that of a woman who has not yet taken on the role of a married woman.
Comes from Bethlehem	Micah 5:2; **Matthew 2:1–2**	It is not clear that Micah 5:2 specifies that the future leader will be born in the *city* of Bethlehem; most scholars suspect that the verse is a reference to the dynasty of David, which came from Bethlehem (the city of his father, Jesse).
Death of the holy innocents	Jeremiah 31:15; **Matthew 2:16**	Jeremiah's verse, on the atrocities that the Babylonians inflicted against Judean infants (through both violence and starvation), also applies to the story of King Herod's slaughter of the Judean infants. Scholars tend to be extremely skeptical that Herod ever slaughtered infants on the scale described in the Gospel of Matthew because no other sources from the period (including Jewish sources such as Josephus) reported this atrocity, which would not have gone unnoticed.
Called out of Egypt	Hosea 11:1; **Matthew 2:13–15**	This obvious parallel with Moses is satisfied by the verses pointing out Mary and Joseph's journey into Egypt to save Jesus from Herod's raids.
Childhood wisdom	Isaiah 7:15, 11:3; **Luke 2:40–51**	It would be very strange for a child to speak with authority in the Temple, in a society where age was valued and children were encouraged to be humble and listen to their elders. When Jesus did, the priests who happened to be standing by realized that they were witnessing something special.

Prophecy	Verses	Description
John the Baptist	Isaiah 40:3; **Matthew 3:1–12, 4:12, 11:2–19; Mark 1:7–14,** 6:14–29, 9:11–13; **Luke 1:1–80, 3:15–18,** 7:18–35, 9:7–9; **John 1:6–35,** 3:27–30, 5:33–36	Jesus' cousin John the Baptist (discussed later in this chapter) is identified with the "voice crying out in the wilderness" described by Isaiah. He is what Christian theologians have called the *forerunner*, the person whose prophetic role is to announce the coming of Jesus.

After Jesus and His family return to Nazareth, the story as told in Matthew in Luke gets somewhat quiet. The Gospel of Luke makes brief mention of an incident where Jesus, at age 12, wanders into the Temple of Jerusalem and has friendly, sophisticated conversations about scripture with the religious leaders there (2:41–51). Luke then proceeds to say that "Jesus increased in wisdom and in years, and in divine and human favor" (2:52), but offers no details. If we estimate that Jesus was born in 6 B.C. or 4 B.C. and was crucified in or around A.D. 33, then we know that He was in his late 30s when He died. This leaves more than 20 years unaccounted for. What did Jesus do before He began His public ministry?

The Missing Years

According to Matthew 13:55, Jesus' father Joseph was described as a craftsman. Most biblical translations define the word as *carpenter*, but the truth is that the Greek word *tekton* can refer to any skilled laborer. Some have suggested that Joseph would have been a stonemason, but he could just as easily have been an architect or a shipbuilder. Whatever his occupation, it is likely that Jesus worked as his apprentice and learned the trade. In Nazareth, He could have whiled away many happy years simply living a normal life, perhaps in anticipation of the public ministry that would require Him to give that normal life away.

But there is still the question of His religious life. The Gospels make it clear that Jesus had an impressive, even encyclopedic, knowledge of the scriptures—which indicates that He most likely also received some kind of religious training, and most likely not at the hands of the Pharisees or Sadducees (Matthew 3:7). It seems most likely that He was a follower of John the Baptist, a major religious figure in Roman-occupied Judea who was described by the Roman historian Josephus in even greater detail than Jesus had been (refer to Chapter 20, "The Search for the Historical Jesus"). Josephus tells us that John the Baptist was killed by Herod Antipas (governor of two provinces and son of King Herod the Great) because Antipas:

> "...feared lest the great influence John had over the people might put into his
> power and inclination to raise a rebellion (for they seemed ready to do anything

he should advise), thought it best, by putting him to death, to prevent any mis-chief he might cause, and not bring himself into difficulties, by sparing a man who might make him repent of it when it was too late."

John was, according to the Gospels, an eccentric prophet who lived in the wilder-ness and survived on locusts and wild honey. Subversive and with little respect for the traditional religious establishment, he preached a strict moral code that bore a strong resemblance to the one later taught by Jesus. Josephus had this to say about John ("who was called the Baptist"):

"[He was a] good man, who had commanded the Jews to exercise virtue, right-eousness towards one another and piety towards God. For only thus, in John's opinion, would the baptism he administered be acceptable to God, namely, if they used it to obtain not pardon for some sins but rather the cleansing of their bodies, inasmuch as it was taken for granted that their souls had already been purified by justice."

Both Jesus and John the Baptist could have been associated with the *Essenes* (from the Aramaic word *Issim*, or "holy"), a group of monastic Jews who lived outside Jerusalem and were suspicious of its religious authorities. Most in this group held that the Temple should not be at the center of religious life, and many also practiced other disciplines such as vegetarianism—which would explain John's unusual diet.

If we accept that Jesus worked as a craftsman and was initially a follower of John the Baptist, then that may well address the most essential details of His missing years. But other, more exotic theories have also been suggested on how Jesus spent at least some of this undocumented time.

Jesus and the Holy Grail

The English poet William Blake once wrote a piece called "Jerusalem" that was later adapted into a hymn. It begins:

"And did those feet in ancient times

walk upon England's mountains green?

And was the holy Lamb of God

on England's pleasant pastures seen?

And did the countenance divine

shine forth upon our clouded hills?

And was Jerusalem builded here

among these dark satanic mills?"

Blake is referring to a tradition that Jesus traveled as a child with Joseph of Arimathea, a rich merchant and member of the Sanhedrin who might also have been brother of the Virgin Mary. There is no evidence of this in the Bible, but the fact that he pays for Jesus' tomb in Matthew 27:57–61—something that an older male relative would have been expected to do—is significant. Joseph of Arimathea, this tradition argues, spent a great deal of time in England with Jesus. At Jesus' death, it is said that Joseph of Arimathea used the cup Jesus had drunk from at the Last Supper to catch His blood while preparing the body for burial and then hid this relic—the Holy Grail—in England for safekeeping.

The Prophet Isa

Other legends hold that Jesus traveled to India and Tibet during His missing years and spent 17 years there studying under—and, later, instructing—Hindu and Buddhist holy men. Numerous documents of the region do in fact refer to a "Prophet Isa" who preached ideas similar to those of Jesus, though there is (as of yet) no indication that any of these documents can be traced to any period close to Jesus' lifetime.

THE ABSOLUTE MINIMUM

- The birth of Jesus probably happened between 6 and 4 B.C. Although the Gospels specify Bethlehem as the city of Jesus' birth, scholars have several reasons to suspect that Jesus was actually born in Nazareth. One compromise view suggests that Jesus was born in a small village near Nazareth that was sometimes referred to as Bethlehem, rather than the larger Bethlehem associated with David.

- Very little is known about what Jesus did before He began His public ministry, by which point He was well into His 30s. The simplest theory connects Him to unorthodox Jewish religious movements, such as that of John the Baptist. Jesus and/or John might have been associated with the Essenes, a group of Jewish sects that rejected the authority of Jerusalem's religious leaders.

- John the Baptist, who inaugurated Jesus' public ministry, was in many ways a more famous figure during his lifetime than Jesus was. The Jewish historian Josephus wrote a fairly detailed description of his life and beliefs, and his death was said to have provoked widespread outrage in the region.

RESOURCES

- **The Birth of Jesus (*Newsweek*)**—www.msnbc.msn.com/id/6653824/site/newsweek/
- **The Mary Page**—www.udayton.edu/mary
- **Christmas (Wikipedia)**—en.wikipedia.org/wiki/Christmas
- **Joseph of Arimathea (britannia.com)**—www.britannia.com/history/biographies/joseph.html

22

THE GOOD SHEPHERD

The public ministry of Jesus Christ, which lasted about 3 years, is the part of His life that we remember. His miracles, from walking on water to feeding the 5,000 with loaves and fishes, have become part of our cultural memory. His teachings, centering on the importance of love and humility and the radical concept of the Kingdom of God, make up the core religious teachings of some 2.1 billion people. His parables, such as the Good Samaritan and the Prodigal Son, still inspire today. Jesus' public ministry, as described in the four canonical Gospels, are the nucleus of all Christian teaching.

The Power and the Glory

According to the Gospel of John, Jesus' first recorded miracle—performed at the very beginning of his public ministry—was rather unconventional: He made sure there was plenty of liquor on tap at a party, and it was His mother who talked Him into it. The scene is a wedding in Cana, a city just north of Nazareth. Jesus, His mother, and some disciples He had gathered are in attendance when Mary points out that the wine has run out and subtly suggests that He do something about it. Jesus resists at first (John 2:4) but quickly gives in: He notices six 20- or 30-gallon jars and instructs the servants to fill them with water. When someone tries the water, the verdict is in: It isn't just wine; it's really *good* wine (2:10). The party continues, and Jesus' reputation as a miracle-worker is born.

The miracles described in the Gospels always served at least one of two purposes:

- They validated Jesus' claims to authority, making it more likely that the people would listen to His teachings.

- They were acts of kindness. Running out of wine may not have created a life-and-death situation, but—wine being the crucial party drink that it was in first-century Palestine——it would have certainly ruined the party.

But most of Jesus' miracles, as shown in Table 22.1, did deal with life-and-death issues. Not counting the many times in the Gospels where Jesus is credited for healing a crowd of people, the ailments suffered by Jesus' patients reads like a list of prescription drug side effects: leprosy, blindness, deafness, muteness, withered hand, paralysis, fever, demonic possession, and occasional death. Okay, so no drugs resulting in demonic possession have actually gotten FDA approval yet—but that's still a pretty diverse list. The bottom line: Jesus was a healer who occasionally worked other miracles, not a stage magician.

TABLE 22.1   The Miracles of Jesus

Miracle	Verses	Description
Turns water into wine	John 2:1–11	Jesus' first miracle. While He is attending a wedding, the hosts run out of wine. Jesus' mother talks Him into remedying the problem in a somewhat unconventional way.
Heals the Roman official's son	John 4:43–54	By healing the official's son, the Jesus of the Gospels is shown to be more than a military revolutionary; He is as willing to help supposed enemies as He is members of His own community.
Performs an exorcism in a synagogue	Mark 1:21–28; Luke 4:31–37	Jesus' exorcism, performed in a synagogue, is presented as a public confrontation between good and evil, with an audience of

Miracle	Verses	Description
		devout worshippers who had come to hear Jesus preach but expected nothing so dramatic.
Heals Simon Peter's mother-in-law	Matthew 8:14–17; Mark 1:29–34; Luke 4:38–41	
Miraculously catches fish	Luke 5:4–10	Although Jesus and Simon Peter are already well acquainted by this point in the story, it is Jesus' ability to fill Simon's nets with fish that convinces Simon Peter that Jesus is the real deal. "From now on," Jesus tells him, "you will be catching people."
Heals the leper	Matthew 8:1–4; Mark 1:40–45; Luke 5:12–16	In Jesus' time, lepers (a term used to describe anyone who suffered from a severe skin disease) were regarded as unclean. Touching them was forbidden. So when Jesus heals the leper with His touch, it is both a miraculous healing and a bold display of human solidarity.
Calms the storm	Matthew 8:23–27; Mark 4:35–41; Luke 8:22–25	As Mark tells it, Jesus is asleep on a boat as the disciples are awake. Suddenly the boat is in the midst of a terrible storm. The disciples wake Jesus up: "Teacher, do you not care that we are perishing?" An annoyed Jesus tells the wind to be quiet and then perhaps goes back to sleep.
Heals the paralyzed man	Matthew 9:1–8; Mark 2:1–12; Luke 5:17–26	
Heals the invalid at the healing pool	John 5:1–15	According to John, the man sits by the Bethzatha healing pool in Jerusalem waiting for someone to put him in the water. Nobody will oblige. Then Jesus arrives and gives him what must seem like a ridiculous instruction: Get up. Perhaps to his own surprise, the man obliges.
Heals the man with the shriveled hand	Matthew 12:9–14; Mark 3:1–6; Luke 6:6–11	
Heals the centurion's servant	Matthew 8:5–13; Luke 7:1–10	The centurion, as a Roman soldier, is more strongly identified with violence and oppression than any other class—and yet Jesus is willing to give him a miracle.

TABLE 22.1 (continued)

Miracle	Verses	Description
		In some ways, this story is more radical than the healing of the leper.
Raises the widow's only son from the dead	Luke 7:11–17	
Heals the blind and mute man	Matthew 12:22–23; Luke 11:14	
Casts out demons and sends them into the bodies of pigs	Matthew 8:28–34; Mark 5:1–20; Luke 8:26–39	
Heals the bleeding woman and raises a little girl from the dead	Matthew 9:18–26; Mark 5:21–43; Luke 8:40–56	According to Mark and Luke, Jesus is en route to heal the dying daughter of a temple official when a woman, rendered unclean by 12 years of hemorrhages, sneaks up on Him and touches the edge of His clothes in hopes of being healed. She is indeed healed with a blessing, but the little girl dies before Jesus arrives. Without missing a beat, He goes in and brings her back from the dead. (In Matthew, the story is the same except that the little girl has already died by the time Jesus hears she needs help.)
Heals the two blind men and the mute man	Matthew 9:27–34	
Feeds the five thousand	Matthew 14:13–21; Mark 6:30–44; Luke 9:10–17; John 6:1–15	This is the only miracle described in all four Gospels. According to Matthew, Mark, and Luke, this miracle comes about on a very bad day for Jesus. He has just heard about the horrible death of John the Baptist and leaves to mourn in solitude, but His followers walk on right behind Him. Jesus gives up on solitude, turns back around, and spends the day preaching and healing the sick. As it becomes clear that His followers are growing hungry, Jesus takes five loaves and two fish and begins to break them, giving a piece to each person walking by. Before long, He has fed 5,000 people on that small amount of food alone, with 12 baskets left over.

Miracle	Verses	Description
Walks on water	Matthew 14:22–27; Mark 6:45–52; John 6:16–24	According to Matthew, Jesus tells the disciples to get into their boat and cross the river while He dismisses the crowd of 5,000. They oblige, no doubt wondering how Jesus plans to reach the other side. The next morning, they see Jesus slowly and disconcertingly walking toward them on the surface of the water.... Calling to His shocked disciples, He asks Peter to join Him. Peter obliges but has some difficulty staying on the surface of the water due to his weak faith.
Heals the Canaanite woman's daughter	Matthew 15:21–28; Mark 7:24–30	A Canaanite woman pleads with Jesus to exorcise her daughter, who is possessed by a demon. Although Jesus expresses initial reservations about healing a Canaanite (the traditional enemy of the Jewish people), she talks Him into it and He enthusiastically complies.
Heals the deaf and mute man	Mark 7:31–37	In the Book of Mark, Jesus' healings tend to be more physical and ritualistic than in Matthew, Luke, or John. Here, Jesus spits on His finger, sticks it in the deaf-mute man's ear, and says "Ephphatha," meaning "Be opened."
Heals the blind man	Mark 8:22–26; John 9:1–41	Both of these accounts run more-or-less parallel in that Jesus heals a blind man by using His own saliva as a kind of salve. In the Book of John, He mixes it with dirt to form mud, which He then uses to coat the man's eyes. John is also remarkable because it is there that Jesus addresses the cause of suffering. His disciples ask Him: Did the blind man sin, or did his parents? Jesus answers that his blindness is not the result of sin, but rather the opportunity to show God's work (9:2–3).
Feeds a second, slightly smaller crowd	Matthew 15:29–39; Mark 8:1–10	
Heals the epileptic boy	Matthew 17:14–21; Mark 9:14–29; Luke 9:37–43	In Matthew, Jesus is extremely frustrated at His disciples' inability to heal an epileptic child, calling them a "faithless and perverse generation" (17:17).

TABLE 22.1 (continued)

Miracle	Verses	Description
Pays the temple tax with a fish	Matthew 17:24–27	Every March, Jews were obligated to give a half-shekel to support the Temple. Jesus is not particularly fond of the mandatory nature of the tax but tells Simon Peter to go fishing and he'll find the money inside the mouth of the first fish he catches. It's a full shekel, enough to pay the Temple tax for both Jesus and Simon Peter.
Heals the 10 lepers	Luke 17:11–19	
Heals the man with edema	Luke 14:1–6	
Heals two blind men by the road	Matthew 20:29–34	
Heals the blind beggar	Mark 10:46–52; Luke 18:35–43	
Curses the fig tree	Matthew 21:18–22; Mark 11:12–14, 20–26	This is the only point in the Gospels where Jesus actually kills anything, and the meaning of the text is not immediately clear. It does not seem likely that Jesus would be furious at a fig tree for not bearing fruit out of season. Some see these verses as a prophecy of the Temple's destruction in 70 A.D.
Raises Lazarus from the dead	John 11:1–44	Jesus receives word from His friends, Mary and Martha of Bethany, that their brother Lazarus is ill. Facing angry mobs in the region, Jesus waits 2 days; then, realizing that Lazarus is already dead, He begins the march. According to the Gospel of John, it is the very public healing of Lazarus that makes Jesus so much of a celebrity in the region that He and His disciples can no longer travel there safely. He will make only one more public stand: in Jerusalem, where He faces death at the hands of the Romans.
Heals the ear of His persecutor	Luke 22:49–51	When the Romans arrive to arrest Jesus, one of His disciples—whom John identifies as Simon Peter (18:10)—draws his sword and prepares to fight them, cutting off the ear of the high priest's slave. But Jesus orders Simon Peter to put his sword away and heals the slave's ear for good measure.

Miracle	Verses	Description
Makes a second miraculous catch of fish	John 21:1–11	After He comes back from the dead, Jesus appears on the shore, some distance away, while His disciples are fishing. He shouts out that they should cast their nets on the right side of the boat—and the nets miraculously fill up with fish, cluing them in to the fact that the stranger on the shore is none other than Jesus.

In the Gospels, Jesus' healing miracles persistently run afoul of local religious authorities. When He tells the invalid at the pool of Bethzatha to pick up his mat and walk (John 5:15), for instance, a few busybodies standing by criticize the guy for carrying his mat on the Sabbath (which technically qualifies as work). And the Gospel of John has it that when Jesus raises Lazarus, He draws so much attention to Himself that He contributes to His own condemnation and death. Not that His teachings weren't already moving Him in that direction, and fast.

THIS SPACE FOR LENT

According to the synoptic Gospels (Matthew 4:1–11, Mark 1:12–13, and Luke 4:1–13), Jesus began His public ministry by fasting in the wilderness, during which time He was tempted by Satan. Every year, many Christians—especially Roman Catholics—observe 40 days of penitence, called the season of *Lent*, which are patterned after Jesus' 40 days of temptation. (The number 40 is reminiscent of the 40 years the Israelites wandered in the desert under Moses—refer to Chapter 8, "From Slavery to the Promised Land"—and, in Jewish tradition, 40 represents a large but indefinite number.) The three temptations were

- **Food**—After all that fasting, Jesus was hungry. Satan goaded Him to turn stones into bread.

- **Safety**—Satan stuck Jesus on top of the spire of the Temple in Jerusalem and urged Him to jump down, knowing angels would catch Him.

- **Power**—Satan offered Jesus all the world, if only He would switch sides and worship the devil.

Jesus, of course, rejected all three—the Gospels would make for mighty strange reading if He hadn't.

The Good News

Jesus' teachings are fairly complex in some ways, but extremely simple in others. If we summarize the core teachings, they can be divided into three categories:

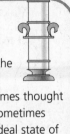

note

A central theme in Jesus' teachings is the Kingdom of God. While this is sometimes thought of as heaven and sometimes thought of as the ideal state of things on earth, the more literal meaning is the King-*ship* of God—the Reign of God, wherever it takes place. It is, in other words, God's way of doing things—regardless of whether God happens to be doing them on earth or in Heaven.

- **The Greatest Commandment**—Two statements that form the core of Jesus' teachings.
- **The Sermon on the Mount**—A summary of Jesus' approach to God, humanity, and faith.
- **The Parables**—Most of these stories appear simple at first, but they contain profound truths and difficult, ambiguous theological concepts.

The Greatest Commandment (Matthew 7:12 and 22:36–38; Luke 10:26–28)

The core of Jesus' teachings is very simple: Love God and love every other human being. All other teachings hang on these principles, which Jesus described as the greatest commandments. Both come from the Torah: Deuteronomy 6:5 ("You shall love the LORD your God with all your heart, and with all your soul, and with all your might") and Leviticus 19:18 ("[Y]ou shall love your neighbor as yourself"). It is worth mentioning that other faiths also tend to emphasize these commandments, the latter of which is often called the *Golden Rule*:

- **Rabbinic Judaism**—"That which is hateful to you, do not do to your neighbor. That is the whole Torah; the rest is commentary. Go and study it." (Rabbi Hillel [ca. 60 B.C.–10 A.D.], as quoted in the *Babylonian Talmud*)
- **Islam**—"Not one of you truly believes until you wish for others that which you wish for yourself." (The Prophet Muhammad [ca. 570–632 A.D.], as quoted in *Hadith an-Nawawi*.)
- **Zoroastrianism**—"That nature only is good when it shall not do unto another whatever is not good for its own self." (From the *Dadistan-i-Dinik* [ca. 700 B.C.])
- **Hinduism**—"This is the sum of duty: Do naught unto others which would cause you pain if done to you." (Krishna, as quoted in Book Five of the *Mahabharata*)

- **Buddhism**—"Hurt not others in ways that you yourself would find hurtful." (Siddhartha Gautama, the Buddha [ca. 563–485 B.C.], from the *Udana-Varga*)

- **Confucianism**—"What you do not want done to yourself, do not do to others." (Kong Qiu Fu-tze, a.k.a. Confucius [ca. 551–479 B.C.], from the *Analects*)

> **Biblically Speaking**
>
> "[A] lawyer asked [Jesus] a question to test him. 'Teacher, which commandment in the law is the greatest?' He said to him, 'You shall love the Lord your God with all your heart, and with all your soul, and with all your mind.' This is the greatest and first commandment. And the second is like it: 'You shall love your neighbor as yourself.' On these two commandments hang all the law and the prophets."
>
> —Matthew 22:35–40

The Sermon on the Mount (Matthew 5:1–7:27; Luke 6:17–49)

The Sermon on the Mount is the core of Jesus' teachings, summarizing His philosophy and exactly how it differed from the Judaism of His time. In Matthew, it is described as a secret teaching given to the 12 apostles (5:1); in Luke, it's a public teaching given to a large crowd (6:17). Conservative scholars have historically said that this means the verses refer to two separate sermons, the private Sermon on the Mount (Matthew) and the more public Sermon on the Plain (Luke).

Wherever and whenever the teachings were delivered, they stand out due to their emphasis on nonviolence, the poor and marginalized, and the primacy of love. The longer version of the Sermon, in Matthew, can be broken down into the following parts.

The Beatitudes (Matthew 5:1–12)

Reprinted in Appendix B, "Great Quotations from the Bible," the *Beatitudes* ("blessings")—which begin "Blessed are the poor in spirit, for theirs is the kingdom of heaven"—are among the most beautiful and frequently cited passages of scripture. They promise blessings to the poor in spirit, the grieving, the meek, the just, the merciful, the pure in heart, the peacemakers, and the righteous persecuted. But this paragraph doesn't do them justice, so if you're not familiar with the Beatitudes, feel free to peek at Appendix B—I'll wait for you.

The Role of the Disciple (5:13–16)

This is where Jesus tells His followers that they are the "salt of the earth" and the "light of the world"; their duty is to be visible signs of God's love, even if they face persecution for it.

Reflections on the Law of Moses (5:17–48)

Jesus had the following thoughts to offer on Jewish law:

- He has no intention of abolishing Jewish law; He has come to fulfill it (5:17). The meaning of this statement has been debated for many centuries, but it probably refers to the new covenant established by Jesus' life and sacrifice— the New *Testament* ("covenant").

- The prohibition against murder (Exodus 20:13) also applies to anger and hatred, which are destructive to the soul even if no physical violence actually results. Grudges should be resolved quickly. (5:21–26)

> **note**
>
> For more on Jewish law, refer to Chapter 8.

- The prohibition against adultery (Exodus 20:14) also applies to lust. Married men who lust after women, or men who lust after married women, have already committed adultery of the heart. (5:27–30)

- Remarriage after divorce (Deuteronomy 24:1–4) is not necessarily permitted. The primary effect of these verses has to do with the protection of women, as men were permitted to divorce their wives without mutual consent—and, since women weren't really given the option of holding down jobs, this often allowed husbands to impoverish their wives at will. (5:31–32)

CASTING THE FIRST STONE (JOHN 8:3–11)

"The scribes and the Pharisees brought a woman who had been caught in adultery; and making her stand before all of them, they said to him, 'Teacher, this woman was caught in the very act of committing adultery. Now in the law Moses commanded us to stone such women. Now what do you say?' They said this to test him, so that they might have some charge to bring against him. Jesus bent down and wrote with his finger on the ground. When they kept on questioning him, he straightened up and said to them, 'Let anyone among you who is without sin be the first to throw a stone at her.' When they heard it, they went away, one by one, beginning with the elders; and Jesus was left alone with the woman standing before him. Jesus straightened up and said to her, 'Woman, where are they? Has no one condemned you?' She said, 'No one, sir.' And Jesus said, 'Neither do I condemn you. Go your way, and from now on do not sin again.'"

This story—one of the best-known passages in the Gospels—was almost left out entirely. Appearing only in later manuscripts of the Gospel of John, it tells a story of Jesus that is entirely consistent with His teachings—teachings that rejected the authority of religious leaders, defended the worth and dignity of those who did not follow the law, and (perhaps most surprisingly, to modern readers) defended women against the sexist social conventions of their time.

The question of what Jesus was writing on the ground is an open one, debated by many scholars—but one possibility half-seriously suggested by feminist theologians is that He was writing, "Where is the man?" In nations where adultery is still punishable by death, the scenario is identical to that of the Gospel of John: The woman is brought before a group of men, who throw rocks at her until she is beaten to death. The man goes unpunished. Punishing adultery by death is a way for husbands to protect their property rights over their wives. Jesus rejected this code.

Jesus also rejected much of the artificial separation between women and men that was regarded as necessary during His era. Many of His most prominent disciples—His mother Mary, the apostle Mary Magdalene, and the sisters Mary and Martha of Bethany, to name a few—were women. When Jesus had a lengthy religious discussion with a Samaritan woman at a well (John 4:7–42), His disciples "were astonished that he was speaking to a woman" (7:27). And Jesus' respect for women did not extend only to mere tolerance. Only two people in the Gospels ever won an argument against Jesus: His mother, who convinced Him against His better judgment to perform His first public miracle (John 2:1–11), and a Samaritan woman, who convinced Jesus to heal her daughter (Matthew 15:21–28 and Mark 7:24–30). There is no indication that Jesus ever distinguished women from men in His teachings; as far as the specific records of the Gospels are concerned, He treated men and women as equals—something that very, very few religious leaders in Jesus' time did.

- The prohibition against false oaths (Leviticus 19:12) applies to all oaths. Swearing oaths is arrogant because it implies power over the thing sworn by. An honest answer—yes or no—is enough. (5:33–37)

- Practice nonviolence. Love your enemies, and strive to love everyone perfectly. (5:43–48)

Faith and Piety (Matthew 6:1–34)

Jesus was particularly frustrated with the prominent "respectable" religious men in His community who made great shows of their religious devotion. More at home with prostitutes and ethnic outcasts than priests and socialites, He affirmed a theology that condemned self-righteousness and encouraged simplicity, humility, and self-criticism:

- If you pray or give to charity in a public way, then it has no spiritual value. Do both humbly and in secret. (6:1–8)

- The Lord's Prayer was intended to function as a substitute for the vain, public prayers that many reputably pious people used at the time. (6:9–13)

- God's forgiveness of your sins is contingent upon your willingness to forgive others. (6:14–15)

- If you fast in a public way, then it has no spiritual value. Fast humbly and in secret. (6:16–18)

- "Where your treasure is, your heart will be also." Do not become attached to your material possessions. (6:19–24)

- Don't worry about your fate. Strive for the Kingdom of God. (6:25–34)

Conclusion (Matthew 7:1–27)

The Sermon on the Mount ends with a series of statements on a variety of issues affecting His followers:

- "Do not judge, so that you may not be judged." Only God is fit to judge. Be tolerant of one another. (7:1–5)

- Preaching to people who express outright hostility to the teachings of Jesus is ineffective. (7:6)

- God does answer prayers, so by all means pray. (7:7–11)

- The Golden Rule: Do unto others as you would have them do unto you. "This is the law and the prophets." (7:12) (This is discussed earlier in this chapter in the section "The Greatest Commandment.")

- Don't be forced into conformity. Be true to your convictions. (7:13–14)

- Beware of those who claim to receive messages from God, but who are preaching evil. (7:15–20)

- Professing belief in Jesus is not the same thing as actually participating in the Kingdom of God. (7:21–23)

- Act based on these teachings and your ministry will be secure; ignore them at your peril. (7:24–27)

> ## Biblically Speaking
>
> "Our father in heaven,
> hallowed be your name.
> Your kingdom come.
> Your will be done,
> on earth as it is in heaven.
> Give us this day our daily bread.
> And forgive us our debts,
> as we also have forgiven our debtors.
> And do not bring us into temptation,
> but rescue us from evil."
>
> —Matthew 6:9–13

The Parables

Most of Jesus' teachings are not explicit statements; rather they are *parables*, metaphorical stories that one reflects on and tries to interpret. As shown in Table 22.2, these stories are spread throughout the four Gospels (though the Gospel of John has only two, and they are two that do not appear in any of the other Gospels). Sometimes obvious and sometimes cryptic, these parables form the larger framework of Jesus' teachings.

The Good Samaritan (Luke 10:30–37)

The story of the good Samaritan is the best-known and best-loved of Jesus' parables. The Samaritans were residents of Samaria, the capital of the Northern Kingdom of Israel (discussed in Chapter 11, "The Era of Kings"). Because they intermarried with Assyrians and did not adopt the reforms of the Southern Kingdom Jews who returned after the Babylonian exile to rebuild the Temple, they were not considered Jews in any meaningful religious sense and were treated as heretical outsiders by the mainstream Jewish community in Jerusalem in the time of Jesus. Levites and priests, on the other hand, were seen as holy and righteous—quite the opposite of a Samaritan.

The story is a familiar one: A man is beaten, robbed, and left for dead. A priest and Levite passing by avoid him, for reasons not specified in the text—maybe they're afraid of touching a corpse (which would render them ritually unclean), maybe they're concerned that the robbers could still be lurking and don't want to fall prey themselves, or maybe they're just coldhearted. The Samaritan, in contrast, takes the riskier, costlier, more compassionate route: He puts himself at risk and then spends an afternoon and a significant amount of money nursing this complete stranger back to health. By using a Samaritan as an example, Jesus suggests that being a good neighbor is not contingent on outward signs of faith and piety; it is instead based on love and compassion.

LUKE 10:25–37

"Just then a lawyer stood up to test Jesus. 'Teacher,' he said, 'what must I do to inherit eternal life?' [Jesus] said to him, 'What is written in the law? What do you read there?' [The lawyer] answered, 'You shall love the Lord your God with all your heart, and with all your soul, and with all your strength, and with all your mind; and your neighbor as yourself.' And [Jesus] said to him, 'You have given the right answer; do this, and you will live.'

But wanting to justify himself, he asked Jesus, 'And who is my neighbor?' Jesus replied, 'A man was going down from Jerusalem to Jericho, and fell into the hands of robbers, who stripped him, beat him, and went away, leaving him half dead. Now by chance a priest was going down that road; and when he saw him, he passed by on the other side. So likewise a Levite, when he came to the place and saw him, passed by the other side.

But a Samaritan while traveling came near him; and when he saw him, he was moved with pity. He went to him and bandaged his wounds, having poured oil and wine on them. Then he put him on his own animal, brought him to an inn, and took care of him. The next day he took out two denarii, gave them to the innkeeper, and said, "Take care of him; and when I come back, I will repay you whatever more you spend." Which of these three, do you think, was the neighbor to the man who fell into the hands of the robbers?' [The lawyer] said, 'The one who showed him mercy.' Jesus said to him, 'Go and do likewise.'"

Table 22.2 The Parables of Jesus

Parable	Verses	One Interpretation
Houses on rock and sand	Matthew 7:24–27	Those who heed Jesus' words will be well-prepared, but those who ignore His words will not.
The sower	Matthew 13:3–23; Mark 4:1–20; Luke 8:5–15	The sower is the evangelist for the Kingdom of God. Only by casting seeds with wild abandon, without watching to see which ones grow and which ones don't, can she produce an adequate crop.
The weeds	Matthew 13:24–30	Rather than passing judgment on others and attempting to separate the wheat from the weeds ourselves, we should acknowledge that we are not qualified to tell the difference between the two and that the decision is out of our hands.
The mustard seed	Matthew 13:31–32; Mark 4:30–32; Luke 13:18–19	The Kingdom of Heaven often works through small groups of people who are weak, are marginalized, or have no credibility. But it is impossible to judge the fruits of their work based on whether or not the seed looks impressive.
The flour and the yeast	Matthew 13:33; Luke 13:20–21	Those small groups of people who are doing the work of the Kingdom of God can have a profound effect on others, disproportionate to their numbers.
The hidden treasure	Matthew 13:44	The kingdom of heaven is worth more than all of a person's material possessions.
The pearl of great price	Matthew 13:45–46	Essentially the same message as the previous parable.

Parable	Verses	One Interpretation
The good and bad fish	Matthew 13:47–50	The message seems to be similar to that of the parable of the weeds—that the duty of those who work for the Kingdom is to catch fish, not to judge the good fish from the bad.
The lost sheep	Matthew 18:10–14; Luke 14:3–7	God does not abandon people who seem least likely to be salvageable, and He is very pleased when they repent and come back.
The debtors	Matthew 18:23–35	A parable in the spirit of the verse from the Lord's Prayer: "And forgive us our debts, as we have also forgiven our debtors" (Matthew 6:11).
The laborers	Matthew 20:1–16	The Kingdom of God is not restricted by earthly standards of justice. It is based on grace and mercy, not fairness and compensation. It is scandalously, exuberantly generous and does not necessarily yield special rewards for the righteous, or those who consider themselves to be so.
The two sons	Matthew 21:28–32	Those who appear to be the most pious and moral may in fact be further from the Kingdom of God than those who appear to be faithless and immoral.
The wicked tenants	Matthew 21:33–44; Mark 12:1–12; Luke 20:9–18	Those who appear to be commissioned to do the work of God on earth often kill God's prophets.
The wedding feast	Matthew 22:1–14	God's invitation is not to any special segment of humanity—it is to the world as a whole.
The fig tree	Matthew 24:32; Mark 13:28–29	When the world comes to an end (see Chapter 27, "The End of the World"), the event will be preceded by dramatic signs.
The wise and foolish virgins	Matthew 25:1–13	Always be prepared for the coming of Jesus.
The stern master	Matthew 25:14–30	Those who do God's work will be rewarded with more of God's work to do.
The seed growing mysteriously	Mark 4:26	The Kingdom of God will be fully realized on earth, but nobody will be able to recognize it until it happens.
The master going on a journey	Mark 13:34–37	Jesus will leave His disciples in charge of His ministry, but they had better do their jobs because He could return at any time.

Table 22.2   (continued)

Parable	Verses	One Interpretation
The greater debt	Luke 7:36–47	Those who have been forgiven for many sins are more likely to love God than those who have been forgiven for few.
The good Samaritan	Luke 10:30–37	Discussed earlier in the chapter.
The persistent friend	Luke 11:5–8	Persistent prayer works.
The rich fool	Luke 12:16–21	You can't take it with you.
The watchful servants	Luke 12:35–48	Be prepared for the return of Jesus.
The barren fig tree	Luke 13:6–9	A landowner has a fig tree that has not borne fruit in 3 years. He wants to chop it down, but his gardener convinces him to let it stay for 1 more year to see if it bears any fruit. The landowner has generally been interpreted as being God, and the fig tree the second Temple in Jerusalem—which was destroyed by the Romans in 70 A.D.
The great dinner	Luke 14:15–24	A wealthy man has planned a massive dinner but discovers at the last minute that everyone he has invited has come up with an excuse not to attend. So he invites the poor, the lame, the crippled, and the blind—and, when there is still room, he invites everyone else. The Kingdom of God, Jesus says, is like this: The outcast and suffering are given first dibs and everyone is invited, but the people we think of as most exalted in this world will have trouble finding a seat in the next.
The lost coin	Luke 15:8–10	Just as a woman who has lost money rejoices when she finds it, so do the angels rejoice whenever anyone repents.
The prodigal son	Luke 15:11–32	The message of this parable seems to mirror the message of the parable of the laborers, which teaches that the Kingdom of God is based on grace rather than fair compensation, and the message of the parable of the lost sheep, which teaches that God is delighted when lost sheep return to the fold.

Parable	Verses	One Interpretation
The dishonest manager	Luke 16:1–9	Telling others that God forgives them is commendable, even if we do not seem to have the authority to do so.
The rich man and the beggar	Luke 16:19–31	A rich man lives in abundant wealth and comfort and despises the poor man, Lazarus, suffering outside his door. But in the world to come, Lazarus faces a far more pleasant fate. (This is not the same Lazarus whom Jesus raises in John, chapters 11–12.)
The persistent widow	Luke 18:1–8	A widow continually pleads to a judge for justice. Like the parable of the persistent friend (see the previous), this parable affirms the value of prayer.
The Pharisee and the tax collector	Luke 18:9–14	A prominent, respectable religious man goes to the Temple and prays to God with gratitude that he is such a holy and moral person. A Roman tax collector, one of the most despised occupations in Judaea, goes to the Temple and humbly prays for forgiveness. The tax collector is the only one of the two who actually benefits from the prayer; self-righteousness has no spiritual value whatsoever.
The stern king	Luke 19:11–27	The Gospel of Luke's version of the parable of the stern master (see previous).
The good shepherd	John 10:11–18	Like a good shepherd, Jesus is willing to lay down His life for the sake of His flock.
The vine	John 15:1–11	Jesus is like a vine grown by God, and His followers are like that vine's branches.

THE ABSOLUTE MINIMUM

■ Jesus' public ministry began with His baptism at the hands of the unorthodox prophet John the Baptist.

■ The miracles of Jesus were not mere displays of power; nearly all of them had positive, practical effects on others. They were means by which He healed the sick and fed the hungry.

continues

- Facing a society segregated by ethnicity, gender, and cultural norms, Jesus preached a gospel of radical love that challenged, and continues to challenge, social order and popular concepts of justice and fairness.

- Central to Jesus' teachings was the concept of the Kingdom of God, or God's sovereignty over all things. It refers neither to a future heaven nor to an earthly paradise; instead, it refers to God's way of doing things, as opposed to humanity's way of doing things.

RESOURCES

- **Rejesus**—www.rejesus.co.uk

- **Yeshua of Nazareth (Ontario Consultants)**—www.religioustolerance.org/chr_je.htm

- **Jesus Christ (Catholic Encyclopedia)**—www.newadvent.org/cathen/08374c.htm

- **Jesus Christ (Wikipedia)**—en.wikipedia.org/wiki/Jesus_Christ

- **The Jesus Seminar at the Westar Institute**—www.westarinstitute.org

- **A Portrait of Jesus: From Galilean Jew to the Face of God**—www.united.edu/portrait

IN THIS CHAPTER

- Jesus' final days on earth
- The stations of the cross
- Different views on the meaning of Jesus' sacrifice

23

THIS IS MY BODY

The Mystery of Faith (*Mysterium Fidei*), as expressed in the religious services of the Roman Catholic Church, is made up of three simple statements: "Christ has died. Christ is risen. Christ will come again." The final chapters of the Gospels and the first few verses of Acts tell the stories behind these three statements, upon which the entire Christian faith has historically rested.

Into Jerusalem

According to the Gospels, Jesus' last days are a whirlwind of doubt, confusion, and agony. Facing certain death at the hands of the Romans, He defies earthly authority with unearthly courage, He defies violence with nonviolence, and—the Christian tradition teaches us—He defies death with resurrection. Although arrested, beaten, stripped, and executed, presumably to be driven into oblivion by the most powerful government on earth, He conquers the grave and with it the world. Two millennia later, nearly everyone on earth knows the story of Jesus Christ—and, even after these millennia, after these countless ages of empires and kings, nearly two billion people still proclaim Him ruler of the universe.

This chapter is about what most at the time probably would have presumed to be the last chapter of the story of Jesus Christ—the crucifixion of the "King of the Jews," the end of the Jesus movement, and the reassertion of Roman authority. What it demonstrates instead is the weakness of empires and the power of ideas. The most famous man on earth at the time of Jesus Christ's execution was Emperor Tiberius Caesar Augustus of Rome, who ruled the closest thing to a globe-spanning empire that the world had ever seen; statues were built in his honor, armies fought at his command, and people like Jesus were crucified for defying his authority. But, aside from students of history, who remembers Tiberius?

> ## Biblically Speaking
>
> "While they were eating, Jesus took a loaf of bread, and after blessing it he broke it, and gave it to the disciples, and said, 'Take, eat; this is my body.' Then he took a cup, and after giving thanks he gave it to them, saying, 'Drink from it, all of you; for this is my blood of the covenant, which is poured out for many for the forgiveness of sins. I tell you, I will never again drink of this fruit of the vine until that day when I drink it new with you in my Father's kingdom.'"
>
> —Matthew 26:26–29

The following are the major events of Jesus' last days:

- **Jesus rides into Jerusalem on a donkey during Passover (Matthew 21:1–9; Mark 11:2–10; Luke 19:29–38; John 12:12–15)**—This is to fulfill a prophecy. In this case, Zechariah has predicted that the messiah will arrive riding a donkey—a sign that he is not there to wage war (as donkeys are not generally considered effective for that purpose—who ever heard of a "war donkey"?). Having already been threatened in Jerusalem, He knows that His decision to return in such a public way will guarantee His death.

- **Jesus has one final Passover supper with the apostles (Matthew 26:17–30; Mark 14:12–26; Luke 22:7–38)**—Jesus identifies the bread and wine of Passover with His own body and blood, establishing what many Christians call the Communion, or the *Eucharist*—the ritual by which Christians consume bread and wine that represent the flesh and blood of Jesus, identifying with His suffering and death in the hope of sharing in His resurrection.

- **Jesus experiences a crisis of faith at Gethsemane (Matthew 26:36–46; Mark 14:32–42; Luke 22:40–46)**—Jesus faces the prospect of His own death at the Garden of Gethsemane, near the Mount of Olives. With resolve, He stands to meet His fate.

- **Jesus is arrested (Matthew 26:47–56; Mark 14:43–50; Luke 22:47–53; John 18:1–12)**—Jesus' trusted disciple Judas Iscariot betrays Him to the Romans, who prepare to put Him on trial.

It might seem a little strange that Jesus goes out of His way to do such dangerous things. Why go back to Jerusalem when there are plenty of other, less dangerous cities to visit? Why offend the Romans? Why not resist arrest? But Jesus has decided, by this point, to fulfill the prophecies about the death of the Messiah (as shown in Table 23.1)—He is ready to die and deliberately takes steps He knows will kill Him.

Table 23.1 Prophecies About Jesus' Trial and Death

	Verses
Rides donkey into Jerusalem	Zechariah 9:9; **Matthew 21:6–9**
Back will be struck	Isaiah 50:6; **Matthew 27:26**
Face will be spat upon	Isaiah 50:6; **Matthew 26:67**
Marks on the palms	Isaiah 49:16; **John 20:25–28**
Despised and rejected	Isaiah 53:3; Zechariah 13:7; **Matthew 27:21–23; Luke 4:28–29**
Deserted by his followers	Zechariah 13:7; **Matthew 26:31–56, 69–75**
Buried in a rich man's tomb	Isaiah 53:9; **Matthew 27:57**

Stations of the Cross

In the Roman Catholic tradition, and in some other denominations, meditations on Jesus' crucifixion and death are organized around 14 events described as the *stations of the cross*. Ordinarily, these events are depicted on sculptures or other images hung in sequence in a church. At each station worshippers stand together, recite prayers, listen to the appropriate Gospel reading, and then walk together to the next station.

note

Mel Gibson's 2004 film *The Passion of the Christ* is organized around the stations of the cross and is loosely based on passages from the Gospel of John.

The 14 stations show the points in the story at which

- **Jesus is condemned to death (Matthew 27:11–26; Mark 15:2–15; Luke 23:2–25; John 18:29–19:16)**—Encouraged by an angry crowd, the Roman governor Pontius Pilate orders the crucifixion of Jesus.

JESUS AND "THE JEWS"

For most of its 2,000-year history, the Christian church as a whole has been brutally anti-Semitic. The tendency has been to view "the Jews" as responsible for Jesus' death and the innocent Romans as mere pawns. But most Christian leaders now recognize that this interpretation of Jesus' trial and execution simply doesn't make sense.

The most obvious sign that Jewish authorities were not responsible for Jesus' death was the means of execution: crucifixion. Roman authorities routinely used crucifixion as a means to punish devout Jews who railed against Roman paganism; its grotesquely violent and very public nature sent a message to Jews that the Romans would not tolerate rebels. While traveling through certain sections of town, Jews would see naked corpses hanging on crosses, rotting, half-eaten by birds. (Jesus' case was unusual; most victims of crucifixion were not buried so quickly.) This was a symbol of Roman power, of Roman authority—it was a form of state-endorsed terrorism directed against the Jewish people. After a certain point, it didn't really matter *who* was crucified; crucifixion rendered most of its victims unrecognizable anyway. It would have been unthinkable for Jewish religious authorities to endorse crucifixion, much less demand it, particularly since the practice is never authorized in Jewish religious texts. The "crowd" mentioned in Matthew 27, Mark 15, Luke 23, and John 18–19 did not represent all the Jews of Jerusalem—the Greek word translated as "crowd," *ochlos*, refers to any disorganized gathering of people of any size. The "crowd" of the Gospels could have been a dozen people.

Much of the Gospel of John includes verses holding "the Jews" accountable for various acts leading to Jesus' crucifixion, but it is important to remember that John was writing the gospel of a Jewish man born of a Jewish woman, whose 12 apostles, all of them Jews, had been subjected to Roman persecution (and often death) by the time the Gospel was written. John was writing for an audience of Christians that included both Jews and gentiles and was most likely skewed toward Jewish Christians; his criticism of "the Jews" had to do with not blaming "the gentiles," but was certainly not directed at all Jews (who still made up the core of the Christian community at the time).

- **The cross is laid upon Him (John 19:16–17)**—Jesus carries His cross through the streets of Jerusalem. The cross one generally carried was the heavy top beam, slung across the shoulders.

- **Jesus falls**—Jesus is clearly struggling with the cross after suffering numerous beatings; later He will hand it over to Simon of Cyrene (see the following).

- **Jesus meets His mother (John 19:25–27)**—Jesus' mother encounters Him as He is walking toward His own place of execution.

- **Simon of Cyrene bears the cross (Matthew 27:32; Mark 15:21; Luke 23:26)**—Jesus is unable to bear the cross alone, so a man named Simon of Cyrene is recruited to help Him.

- **Veronica wipes Jesus' face**—According to a medieval tradition, a young Jewish woman named Veronica wiped Jesus' face with her handkerchief. When she looked at the cloth, she noticed that the face of Jesus had miraculously appeared on it. The legend is based on the Veil of Veronica, a relic that pilgrims flocked to see from about 1300 until about 1600, when it was lost during the remodeling of St. Peter's Basilica.

- **Jesus falls again**—The Gospels never specifically record that Jesus fell while carrying the cross, but it seems consistent—perhaps inevitable—given His battered state and His need of help carrying it.

- **Jesus meets the women of Jerusalem (Luke 23:27–31)**—Women of Jerusalem lament Jesus' horrible state, but He urges them not to cry for Him—but to cry for themselves and their children because of the torment and persecution to come. (The Romans clashed fiercely with Jewish rebels in the years following Jesus' crucifixion, destroying the Temple entirely in 70 A.D.)

- **Jesus falls once more**—Jesus falls again, near the foot of the post upon which the cross will be hung.

- **Jesus is stripped (Matthew 27:28–29; Mark 15:24; Luke 23:34; John 19:23–25)**—Jesus is stripped, and the Roman soldiers gamble for his clothes.

- **Jesus is nailed to the cross (Matthew 27:35; Mark 15:25; Luke 23:33; John 19:18)**—As a means of both mocking Jesus and intimidating the surrounding Jewish community, the Romans write an inscription on the cross: "Jesus Christ, King of the Jews."

> ## Biblically Speaking
>
> "A great number of the people followed [Jesus], and among them were women who were beating their breasts and wailing for him. But Jesus turned to them and said, 'Daughters of Jerusalem, do not weep for me, but weep for your children. For the days are surely coming when they will say, "Blessed are the barren, and the wombs that never bore, and the breasts that never nursed." Then they will begin to say to the mountains, "Fall on us"; and to the hills, "Cover us." For if they do this when the wood is green, what will happen when it is dry?'"
>
> —Luke 23:27–31

- **Jesus dies on the cross (Matthew 27:45–50; Mark 15:33–37; Luke 23:44–46; John 19:28–30)**—According to the Gospels, the sky went dark, the Temple curtain separating the priests from the people was torn in two, earthquakes ravaged the land, and some dead rose from their graves at the moment of Jesus' death.

■ **Jesus' body is taken down from the cross (Mark 15:46; Luke 23:53; John 19:38)**—Jesus' lifeless body is taken down from the cross and wrapped in burial linens.

■ **Jesus' body is placed in the tomb (Matthew 27:60–61; Mark 15:46–47; Luke 23:50–56; John 19:38–42)**—Jesus is placed in the expensive tomb purchased by Joseph of Arimathea, who has courageously approached Pilate to ask for the body.

He Is Risen

On the third day after Jesus' death, something amazing happens: According to the Gospels, the humiliating execution that the Romans have inflicted upon Jesus doesn't stick. Jesus returns from the tomb and, for a short time, resumes His ministry.

THREE VIEWS ON THE RESURRECTION

Beliefs about Jesus' resurrection tend to fall into three categories:

■ **Bodily resurrection**—On the third day, Jesus physically rises from the grave. This is the most traditional of the three views and the one generally affirmed by the early Christian church.

■ **Spiritual resurrection**—Jesus transcends his human body and appears to his disciples from a higher plane of existence. This interpretation was popular among those who believed, as some ancient philosophers did, that the spirit is the pure and the flesh is corrupt.

■ **Metaphorical resurrection**—Resurrection is a way of describing the continuing influence Jesus continues to have on the world after His death. This interpretation is especially popular among Christians who find it difficult to accept the idea that Jesus literally came back from the dead but still find the resurrection to be a meaningful concept.

After His death, Jesus meets...

■ **At the tomb (Matthew 28:8; Mark 16:1; John 20:11)**—Women—described alternatively as Mary Magdalene alone, Mary Magdalene and Mary mother of James, and a larger group of women—discover that Jesus has risen from the dead. They run to tell the apostles, who—according to Luke—ignore them at first.

- **On the road to Emmaus (Luke 24:13–35)**—A disguised Jesus joins two of His disciples on the road, who bemoan their Lord's death until they realize who they have seen.

- **In the apostles' house (Mark 24:36–53; John 20:19–29)**—Jesus appears before the 11 remaining apostles.

- **To the apostles fishing in Galilee (John 21:1–23)**—Jesus helps Peter catch a miraculous number of fish once more and sits down to meet with his apostles. "Feed my lambs," Jesus tells Peter. "Tend my sheep" (21:15 and 17). According to John (21:18–19), he also warns Peter of his own crucifixion, which will take place more than 30 years later.

- **Ascending on the Mount of Olives (Acts 1:1–11)**—Here the story of the Gospels ends and the Book of Acts begins with Jesus' return to heaven.

THE ABSOLUTE MINIMUM

- By all accounts, Jesus knew in advance that He faced death at the hands of the Romans. In the Garden of Gethsemane, the night before He was betrayed by His apostle Judas Iscariot, He cried, sweated blood, and pleaded with His Father—but when the guards came to arrest Him, He faced His fate with courage and resolve.

- In addition to being one of the most painful forms of execution ever invented, crucifixion was a form of state terrorism. The torn, naked bodies of the condemned were left on crosses to be picked apart by crows as a warning to the rest of the population.

- According to the Gospels, Jesus rose from the dead on the third day after He was crucified. After spending a short time on earth, He ascended into heaven.

RESOURCES

- **The Catholic Sacrament of Eucharist**—www.americancatholic.org/Features/Sacraments/Eucharist.asp

- **On the Physical Death of Jesus Christ**—www.frugalsites.net/jesus

- **The Shroud of Turin (Ontario Consultants)**—www.religioustolerance.org/chr_shro.htm

- **Resurrection of Jesus (Wikipedia)**—en.wikipedia.org/wiki/Resurrection_of_Jesus_Christ

PART VII

THE NEW COVENANT

IN THIS CHAPTER

- Biographies of the 12 apostles
- Women in the early church
- The Holy Spirit
- The Pentecost event and the birth of the Christian church

24

THE FIRST CHRISTIANS

The Book of Acts tells the story of how the Christian church emerged in the months and years following Jesus Christ's death. The 12 apostles who had followed Jesus became leaders themselves, and His presence was replaced by the presence of the *paraclete* ("helper") He had promised to send them—the Holy Spirit.

The Magnificent 12

The 12 apostles were crucial to the development of early Christianity. According to the first two chapters of Acts, they were Jesus' representatives on earth—the vessels of the Holy Spirit, the heirs to His church. Today, in most Christian traditions, ordained religious leaders are seen as the successors to these 12, filling the roles the apostles created nearly 2,000 years ago.

Little is known for certain about the 12, but a great deal is known with less certainty. Where the Bible is silent, other ancient texts fill in gaps. Any fair biography of the 12 apostles must incorporate the two dimensions of their lives—the historical facts we can verify and what the church came to believe about them over time—because, in the final analysis, that is who they are to us: children of history and legend.

Simon Peter, the First Pope

When Jesus began His ministry, Simon was a fisherman living with his wife and her mother in Nahum, a small town known primarily for its 70-foot tall synagogue (massive by the standards of its time). While much has been made of Simon being a poor, simple fisherman, fishing is a lucrative and challenging line of work—and it was especially exciting in Simon's day because he had to catch a satisfactory amount of fish every day without the benefit of modern technology.

Simon and his brother, Andrew, worked together as fishermen as they dreamed of a messiah who would overthrow their Roman oppressors. Both devout Jews, they were followers of the charismatic but highly eccentric John the Baptist, who railed against the Romans and proclaimed that God's day of judgment was near.

Andrew's life changed forever when his teacher, the Baptist, pointed to a wandering rabbi named Joshua of Nazareth and shouted, "Look, here is the Lamb of God" (John 1:35–36). Andrew introduced Simon to Joshua, who, according to John, greeted him in an unusual way, "You are Simon son of John. You are to be called Cephas" (John 1:42). (Other Gospels have Jesus referring to Simon as *Peter* or *Cephas* after he identified Jesus as the son of God.) Cephas isn't just a clever nickname; it is a form of the Aramaic word *kepha*, meaning "rock." The Greek synonym for *rock* is *petra*; just as the Gospels speak of Joshua as Jesus, using the Greek form of his name, they refer to Cephas as Peter.

> **note**
>
> Peter's wife is never named, but one apocryphal story has it that she converted with him to Christianity and was later executed by the Romans.

> **note**
>
> For more on John the Baptist, refer to Chapter 21, "Before He Was Christ."

Throughout the Gospels and the Book of Acts, Simon Peter is identified as the head of the apostles and the figure Jesus trusted to lead the church after His death. According to Matthew (16:19), Jesus also gave Simon Peter the keys to heaven and immense power over heaven and earth. It is for this reason that the popular Christian image of heaven involves meeting St. Peter at the pearly gates, where he literally holds the keys to heaven. For the rest of Jesus' public ministry as described in the Gospels, he was the apostle Jesus spoke to most often, acting as an intermediary at times between Jesus and the others.

Yet Simon Peter was not perfect. He holds the dubious distinction of being, as far as we know, the only apostle Jesus ever compared to Satan (in Matthew 16:23, after he asked Jesus not to give Himself over to be crucified).

When a guard came up to arrest Jesus, Simon Peter drew a sword and cut off a chunk of the attacker's ear—and was chided for it. Worst of all, Jesus correctly predicted that Peter would deny knowing Him three times on the night of his trial.

But Jesus forgave Peter, who would go on to serve as the first bishop of Rome and, as discussed in the next chapter, clash with a new disciple named Paul of Tarsus over the issue of kosher law. As we meet him again in the Book of Acts, his role is clear and his authority is unchallenged. He is the undisputed leader of the Christian faith—the Prince of the Apostles and the man whose successors would be called Pope (from the Greek *papas*, or "father").

He dedicated the next 30 years of his life to spreading the Christian message, tirelessly and quietly traveling from city to city throughout the Roman Empire. In 64 or 67 A.D., after a 30-year ministry as the leader of the Christian faith, he was finally captured by representatives of the insane Emperor Nero and ordered to be crucified. Feeling that he was not worthy of sharing Jesus' mode of

> ## Biblically Speaking
>
> "[And Jesus said] 'you are Peter [*Petros*], and on this rock [*petra*] I will build my church, and the gates of Hades will not prevail against it.'"
>
> —Matthew 16:18

> ## note
>
> John Mark—author of the Gospel of Mark— was the protégé of Simon Peter. According to tradition, Peter's recollections were the primary basis of Mark's Gospel.

> ## Biblically Speaking
>
> "[And Jesus said to Peter] 'Very truly, I tell you, when you were younger, you used to fasten your own belt and to go wherever you wished. But when you grow old, you will stretch out your hands, and someone else will fasten a belt around you and take you where you do not wish to go.'"
>
> —John 21:18

death, he asked to be crucified upside down—and was obliged. He is remembered today as the central symbol of stability for the early church—a "rock," exactly as his name attests.

Andrew, the First Patriarch of Constantinople

Far less is known about Andrew than his brother Peter; he almost disappears from the Bible following Jesus' crucifixion, his name appearing only once in Acts. This might be because he traveled east to spread Christianity, becoming the first Bishop of Byzantium—later the Patriarch of Constantinople, the Eastern Orthodox Church's equivalent to a pope. Legend has it that Roman authorities captured him in Greece and crucified him on an X-shaped cross, known to this day as St. Andrew's Cross.

Andrew is the patron saint of Romania, Russia, and Scotland.

James the Great

According to the Gospel of Luke, James and his brother John (later known as the Beloved Disciple) were fishing in a boat next to the one that Simon (Peter) and Jesus were fishing in. Astonished by the miraculous amount of fish Jesus had given Simon, James and John—whom Jesus nicknamed the "Sons of Thunder"—left their father's fishing business and became disciples.

James was the first of the 12 apostles martyred after Jesus' death. In 44 A.D., barely a decade after the crucifixion of Jesus, he was killed by Roman oppressors.

note

According to one story, Simon Peter fled Rome to avoid execution and met Jesus going the other way. *"Domine, Quo Vadis?"* ("Lord, where are you going?"), he asked. "I am going to Rome to be crucified again," Jesus answered. At this point, legend has it that Peter turned on his heels and went to Rome to meet his own fate.

note

The inverted crucifix—known as St. Peter's Cross—appears on many Vatican City monuments as a symbol of Simon Peter's crucifixion, an example of courage, humility, and fortitude that all popes are expected to follow. It should not be confused with the inverted crucifix sometimes used as a symbol by Satanists and others hostile to Christianity.

WOMEN WHO LED THE EARLY CHURCH

The 12 apostles have something in common: They're all men. Some theologians take this as a sign that Jesus favored men over women for leadership positions, but it could also be a sign that the culture of the time was not as receptive toward women as it was toward men and that Jesus, in recognition of this fact, chose as his earliest apostles those whose opinions would be respected. Or, as some historians have suggested, it could be a sign that Jesus' female apostles—such as Mary Magdalene, Mary of Bethany, and Martha—were considered by Jesus to have been on equal par with the 12 but were relegated to a less central role by the authors of the Gospels. Regardless, the early church as a whole was not a boy's club, and many of its first leaders had two X chromosomes:

- **The Virgin Mary**—Jesus' mother and only human parent, who talked Him into performing His first miracle (turning water into wine at a wedding). Later she would witness His crucifixion and join His disciples in their evangelism work. (For more on the Virgin Mary, refer to Chapter 21.)

- **Mary of Bethany**—The sister of Martha and Lazarus and one of the first people to see Jesus after His resurrection. Some scholars believe that Mary of Bethany and Mary Magdalene were the same person.

- **Martha**—The sister of Mary and Lazarus and one of the first disciples to witness Jesus' resurrection.

- **Priscilla**—An educated friend of Paul, noted for her sharp intellect and knowledge of Torah. She is best known for the instrumental role she played in converting Apollos, a prominent Jewish leader, to Christianity.

- **Phoebe**—An ordained deacon praised by Paul as "a benefactor of many" in his Epistle to the Romans (16:1).

- **Junia**—A leader of the church and a Jewish convert to Christianity who was briefly imprisoned with Paul.

- **Chloe**—A leader of the early Christian church in Corinth who was held in high esteem by Paul.

- **Tryphaena, Tryphosa, Julia, the unidentified mother of Rufus, and the unidentified sister of Nereus**—Women whose leadership was praised by Paul in his letter to the Romans (16:1–16).

John the Beloved

While Simon Peter was the ranking apostle, the Gospel of John suggests that Jesus had a much closer relationship with its author—identified as the Beloved Disciple. It is the Beloved Disciple who was asked to look after Jesus' mother (John 19:26–27), who sat next to Jesus (13:23) at the last supper, who—one rumor had it—would not die until Jesus came again (21:20–23), and who at least first told the stories of Jesus' life recorded in the fourth Gospel (21:24).

Tradition has it that, after Jesus' death, John was exiled to the island of Patmos where he wrote the book of Revelation (also known as the Apocalypse of St. John). In later years, it is said that he retired to Ephesus (in what is now known as Turkey), where he took care of the aging Virgin Mary and led a growing Christian community. It was there, it is said, that John wrote the three epistles that bear his name—and even the most skeptical of secular scholars tend to allow for the possibility that he wrote or dictated at least two of them. John was never martyred, and it is believed that he outlived all the other apostles; as he lay dying, his last words to his followers were, "Little children, love one another."

Controversy

Scholars strongly disagree about the identity of the Beloved Disciple, as well as the identity of the author of the Gospel of John, the three epistles attributed to John, and Revelation. This biography of John presents the most commonly accepted version of his life but certainly not the only version. For more on the authorship of books attributed to John, see Chapters 27 and 28.

Philip the Serpent-Slayer

The Bible says very little about the apostle Philip, but what it does have to say is interesting. He is the disciple who recruits Bartholomew (also known as Nathanael) in John 1:43, and yet he is—other than Thomas—the greatest skeptic of the 12. It is Philip who tells Jesus that 6 months' wages would buy only appetizers for the crowd of 5,000 that Jesus would later feed with only a basket of bread and fish (John 6:5–7), and it is Philip who asks Jesus at the Last Supper to "Show us the Father, and we will be satisfied" (John 14:8).

Most of Philip's story is drawn from extrabiblical sources. It is in the writings of the early Christian historians that we hear that Philip was married with three daughters and became the first Bishop of Narcissos in Greece. His death was an interesting one: According to legend, he and the apostle Bartholomew had attempted to establish a church in Phrygia (now part of Turkey), home to a snake cult. In the cult's temple was a large snake; Philip and Bartholomew killed the snake through prayer and then healed various locals of snake bites. Roman authorities, already suspicious of the Christian church and eager to keep peace with the local cult, ordered Philip and Bartholomew to be crucified. During the crucifixion, an earthquake ensued.

Biblically Speaking

"When Jesus saw his mother and the disciple whom he loved standing beside her, he said to his mother, "Woman, here is your son." Then he said to the disciple, "Here is your mother."

—John 19:26–27

Bartholomew was able to recover from his wounds, but Philip, credited as the one whose prayers had slain the temple serpent, was not.

Bartholomew might have escaped death in Phrygia, but legend gives him a far more gruesome end than that of his friend Philip.

Bartholomew the Flayed

The Bible doesn't say much about Bartholomew, but church legend has filled in the gaps. Bartholomew (who was probably also known as Nathanael) was, according to one tradition, born with the name Jesus (a fairly common name at the time). To avoid confusion, he changed it. After Jesus' crucifixion, writers of the early church say that Bartholomew traveled to Phrygia to destroy the snake cult there (surviving his crucifixion by way of a miraculous earthquake), founded Christian churches in India, and then moved on to Armenia. It is there that he met his doom.

> **note**
>
> Philip the Apostle should not be confused with Philip the Evangelist (Acts 6:1–7 and 8:4–40), the deacon responsible for spreading Christianity into Samaria and Ethiopia.

As shown in Table 24.1, most of the apostles suffered violent deaths. Bartholomew's, however, was probably the most gruesome of all. After converting Polymius, king of Armenia, to Christianity, he met the wrath of Polymius' pagan brother, Astyages. Astyages had the power to order Bartholomew's death, so he had the apostle skinned (flayed) alive and then crucified upside down.

Table 24.1 The Fates of the Apostles, According to Tradition

Apostle	Fate
Simon Peter	Crucified upside down in Rome in 64 or 67 A.D.
Andrew	Crucified on an X-shaped cross in Greece.
James the Great	The first of the loyal apostles to die, he was struck down by the sword of a Roman guard in 44 A.D.
John the Beloved	The last of the original 12 apostles to pass away. He died of natural causes in Ephesus, Turkey, possibly as late as 110 A.D.
Philip	Crucified in Phrygia, Turkey.
Bartholomew	Skinned alive and crucified upside down in Armenia.
Thomas	Impaled by four spears on a hill outside Madras, India, in 78 A.D.
Matthew	Martyred in Hierapolis, Turkey, by unknown means.
James the Just	Stoned to death in Jerusalem in 62 A.D.
Jude Thaddeus	Beaten to death and beheaded in Armenia in 65 A.D.
Simon the Zealot	Sawed in half in Armenia in 65 A.D.
Matthias	Stoned to death in Colchis, Georgia (in the former Soviet Union).

Thomas the Doubter

Perhaps none of the 12 apostles represents the challenge modern Christians face better than Thomas. In the Bible, Thomas does almost nothing but doubt—he receives virtually no mention in Matthew, Mark, and Luke, but the Gospel of John gives three accounts, all of which share a common thread:

- After Jesus leads His disciples away from the area surrounding the city of Bethany, where some had wanted to stone them to death for blasphemy, He becomes aware of the fact that Lazarus, sister to Martha and Mary of Bethany, has died. He tells His disciples this, and tells them that they are returning to Judea to visit the deceased Lazarus. In a moment of dark humor, Thomas turns to the other disciples and quips, "Let us also go, that we may die with him." (11:7–16)

- When Jesus tells the disciples that they "know the way to the place where I am going," Thomas responds, "Lord, we do not know where you are going. How can we know the way?" (14:4–5)

- In the story about Thomas that most people remember, Jesus returns from the dead. Disciples who have seen Him tell Thomas of His resurrection, and Thomas—perhaps suspecting that the other apostles had been hoodwinked by an impostor—responds that he'll believe Jesus is resurrected when he puts his fingers in the wounds himself. Jesus, of course, obliges. (20:24–29)

Perhaps the most remarkable fact about Thomas is that his skepticism does not make him a villain. There is no indication that he ever denies Jesus or that his questioning mind and sardonic wit in any way anger the Son of God. Jesus seems to take it all in stride, patiently welcoming every opportunity to answer Thomas's questions and relieve his doubts.

The skeptical apostle is called Thomas and Didymus, which mean "twin" in Greek and Aramaic, respectively—probably a nickname. Many scholars suspect that he was actually Jude (Judas), the brother of James and Jesus credited with writing the Epistle of Jude. If this was the case, then giving him a nickname like Thomas would have made good sense—there were already two other disciples named Judas, one of them infamous.

note

Although most historians believe that it was written long after the apostle's death, the Gospel of Thomas, the most well-known and widely read of the noncanonical gospels, tells the story of a Jesus who bears a strong resemblance to a Buddhist sage. For more information on this and other noncanonical gospels, refer to Chapter 18, "Nowhere in the Bible."

Whatever the case, it is clear from the amount of material written about Thomas that he played a significant role in the development of the early church. Legend has it that Thomas traveled to Syria after Jesus' death and then founded the church in India where he would spend most of the rest of his life. In Madras one can still visit St. Thomas' Cathedral Basilica, where his mortal remains are said to be stored. On a hill outside the city, known as St. Thomas' Mount, it is said that, as an old man, Thomas met his martyrdom at the hands of four spear-wielding soldiers.

Matthew the Tax Collector

Among religious Jews in Roman-occupied Palestine, few occupations were more reviled than that of the tax collector. The Roman empire that demanded worship of the emperor—the same Roman empire that crushed insurgencies by crucifying scores of rebels naked in the public square and leaving their bodies there to rot as a warning to others—demanded payment from the very people it spent that money oppressing. A tax collector was often a fellow Jew who had, by the standards of his peers, sold out to the Roman regime.

Tax collectors were complicit in oppression and were symbols of greed, cowardice, and disloyalty. They were despised, and despised for a reason.

And one of these tax collectors, a man referred to as Matthew in the gospels of Matthew and John and as Levi in the gospels of Mark and Luke, had gotten very rich off his tax collecting. So rich, in fact, that when Jesus came to town, Matthew held a banquet for Him, where other tax collectors, along with prostitutes and other undesirables, attended, laughing and drinking wine with the man whom some had called the Messiah.

> ### Biblically Speaking
>
> "As Jesus was walking along, he saw a man called Matthew sitting at the tax booth; and he said to him, 'Follow me.' And he got up and followed him. And as he sat at dinner in the house, many tax collectors and sinners came and were sitting with him and his disciples. When the Pharisees saw this, they said to his disciples, 'Why does your teacher eat with tax collectors and sinners?' But when he heard this, he said, 'Those who are well have no need of a physician, but those who are sick. Go and learn what this means, "I desire mercy, not sacrifice." For I have come to call not the righteous but sinners.'"
>
> —Matthew 9:9–13

It was a scandal. Local Pharisees were understandably outraged at Jesus' willingness to rub shoulders with the most despised of society, with those people who represented both oppression from above and corruption from below. But their presence, the Gospels say, was exactly what Jesus wanted. It was a difficult message to accept—and Matthew accepted it, giving up life as a tax collector to become a disciple.

Other than being credited with writing the Gospel of Matthew, the tax collector is not mentioned often in the New Testament. Even the legendary information about

Matthew is somewhat sketchy; we have reason to believe that he traveled east and possibly to north Africa, but little else has been recorded. Epiphanius, Bishop of Cyprus, recorded that he had been martyred in Hierapolis, a city in what is now known as Turkey, but the means of Matthew's death and the circumstances surrounding it remain a mystery.

James, Brother of Jesus

The exact relationship between James and Jesus is not clear. Although he is repeatedly and clearly identified as the brother of Jesus, and even arguably as a son of Mary and Joseph (as in Matthew 13:55), some believe that James was Jesus' brother by adoption rather than by blood. The epistle attributed to Jude—Jesus' other brother—claims authorship from "Jude, a servant of Jesus Christ and brother of James" (1:1), and the traditional Roman Catholic doctrine of Mary's perpetual virginity (which teaches that she never had sexual relations with Joseph, even after Jesus' birth) clashes with the idea that Jesus had blood siblings. For this reason, many believe that James and Jude were not born of Mary, but were instead either Jesus' cousins or Joseph's sons by way of a previous marriage.

While the other apostles scattered after Jesus' death, James stayed put in Jerusalem, the city where his brother had died. There he became bishop and is credited with writing—or at least having his ideas recorded in—the epistle of James. The epistle stands out from Paul's letters in that it clearly establishes good works as the standard of Christian life (2:17–19), a fact that led Protestant reformer Martin Luther (who did not believe in salvation by works) to refer to it as "an epistle of straw."

> **note**
>
> In 2002, archaeologists discovered an *ossuary*—a small coffin used to store human bones—bearing the inscription *James, son of Joseph, brother of Jesus.* Biblical archaeologists initially rejoiced, but later study revealed that the words *brother of Jesus* had almost certainly been carved fairly recently, much later than the other text. Most archaeologists now believe that the ossuary is a forgery and was almost certainly not used to house the remains of the apostle James.

But James, for his part, was devoted to strict moral ideals; he inspired the name "the Just" by voluntarily living by the Nazirite purity code described in Numbers 6:1–28, even though he was not required to do so according to the Christian theology of his time. He was stoned to death in Jerusalem, the same city where his brother had been executed by the Romans 29 years earlier.

Jude Thaddaeus, Patron Saint of Lost Causes

The identity of the apostle Jude, brother of James and Jesus, is shadowed in mystery; very little is written about him in the Bible, and there has been much speculation as to his identity. If the apostle Thomas was in fact Jude (see the previous section, "Thomas the Doubter"), then it seems reasonable to suppose that Jude Thaddaeus is the "Jude, son of James" mentioned in Luke 6:16. In any case, it is clearly Jesus' brother who is credited as author of the epistle of Jude, even though he identifies himself only as the brother of James (1:1)—perhaps because, given Jesus' parentage, he did not feel worthy to claim the name "brother of Jesus."

The only quote attributed to Jude in the gospels comes from John 14:22, where "Judas (not Iscariot) said to him, 'Lord, how is it that you will reveal yourself to us, and not to the whole world?'" But this might or might not be Jude Thaddaeus—it sounds like the sort of question Thomas would ask.

The best known story of Jude Thaddaeus is said to have taken place while Jesus was still alive, but it is not recorded in the gospels. According to tradition, King Abgarus V of Edessa (a region that is now part of modern Turkey) suffered leprosy and sent word to Jesus asking to be healed. Jesus reportedly pressed a cloth against His face, leaving His image on it. Jude Thaddaeus then took the cloth to Abgarus, who was healed. Some traditions suggest that the Image of Edessa might in fact be the cloth now called the Shroud of Turin, a relic that allegedly bears the image of Jesus.

Tradition has it that, at some point after Jesus' death, Jude Thaddaeus traveled to Armenia with Simon the Zealot where, in 65 A.D., they were both martyred.

Simon the Zealot

Also known as Simon the Canaanite, Simon the Zealot is the most obscure of the 12 apostles. Legends about his life tend to be far-reaching and diverse, the most reliable accounts having to do with his martyrdom alongside Jude Thaddaeus in Armenia in 65 A.D.

Matthias the Chosen

Matthias is the first apostle not directly chosen by Jesus, which makes him the first example of *apostolic succession*—the belief that some modern clergy, usually bishops, are empowered by the Holy Spirit to fill the shoes of the apostles.

Little is known about Matthias, which is not surprising given his late arrival in the story; tradition states that he spent time spreading Christianity in Palestine before traveling elsewhere. Although most legends place him in Colchis, Georgia, in what is now the former Soviet Union, and suggest that he was martyred there, other legends say he was martyred in Jerusalem or Ethiopia. Reports also differ on the means of execution, with some suggesting that he was stoned to death, others that he was crucified, and still others testifying that he was beheaded. Whatever the case, he's certainly dead now.

note

For more on Jesus' betrayal, refer to Chapter 23.

That's the Spirit

The Gospel of John and the epistles describe a Holy Spirit that came to earth after Jesus' death and worked through the disciples in more subtle and, in some respects, more powerful ways. When Jesus speaks of this spirit, He describes it with the Greek word *paraclete*—usually translated as "the helper" or "the advocate." This stands in sharp contrast with the Hebrew root of the word Satan, which means "the accuser" or "the adversary." When the two words are examined parallel, it is as though Satan is the prosecutor of humanity and the Holy Spirit its defense attorney.

In the Christian tradition, the holiday of *Pentecost* celebrates the Holy Spirit's descent into Jesus' followers on earth and, with it, the birth of the Christian church. In the Pentecost story (described in Acts 2), the Holy Spirit appears above the followers' heads as small flames and grants them the power of *glossolalia*—the ability to speak in languages they don't know. In Christian denominations, this phenomenon has generally been referred to as *speaking in tongues*. In some denominations—most notably those influenced by the Pentecostal movement—new converts are expected to speak in tongues as a way of demonstrating that the Holy Spirit is present in them.

In traditional Christian theology, the Holy Spirit is the third person of the Holy Trinity, existing alongside the Father and the Son. The Spirit is represented by a dove—symbolism inspired by the description of Jesus' baptism in Mark 1:10, where the Holy Spirit descended on him "like a dove"—and represents the work of God on earth today. The letter of Paul to the Galatians (in verses 5:22–23) lists nine fruits of the spirit, signs that the Holy Spirit is at work on a person. They are

- Love
- Joy

> ## Biblically Speaking
>
> "[And Jesus said] 'When the Advocate comes, whom I will send to you from the Father, the Spirit of truth who comes from the Father, he will testify on my behalf.... I tell you the truth: it is to your advantage that I go away, for if I do not go away, the Advocate will not come to you; but if I go, I will send him to you.'"
>
> —John 15:26, 16:7

> ## Biblically Speaking
>
> "When the day of Pentecost had come, they were all together in one place. And suddenly from heaven there came a sound like the rush of a violent wind, and it filled the entire house where they were sitting. Divided tongues, as of fire, appeared among them, and a tongue rested on each of them. All of them were filled with the Holy Spirit and began to speak in other languages, as the Spirit gave them ability."
>
> —Acts 2:1–4

- Peace
- Patience
- Kindness
- Generosity
- Faithfulness
- Gentleness
- Self-control

note

Theology dealing with the spiritual presence of God—whether it focuses on Jewish concepts of the *ruach* or Christian concepts of the Holy Spirit—is referred to as *pneumatology*.

The Jewish tradition teaches that God is one (*echad*) and has no doctrine of the Trinity. As such, its concept of the Holy Spirit is as a property of God—God's breath, which reflects His will or His soul. It is this breath (*ruach*) that blows across the face of the water in the creation account (Genesis 1:2). In the rabbinic tradition, the idea of God's spirit develops into something very much like another person of God: God's presence (*shekhinah*), or His physical expression on Earth. It is said, for example, that God's *shekhinah* was in the Temple, or that it led the Hebrews out of slavery in Egypt.

Although the *paraclete* and the *ruach* are very different ideas, both express a radical theological idea: That God pours the divine into human beings and works through them. Far from suggesting a fatalistic belief system centered on the idea that we play no role in the story of God, these ideas imply that human beings can be vessels for God's will and that human hands can do God's work in the world. It is this notion that forms the basis of the Christian church.

Biblically Speaking

"So Moses went out and told the people the words of the LORD; and he gathered seventy elders of the people[e]. Then the LORD came down in the cloud and spoke to him, and took some of the spirit [*ruach*] that was on him and put it on the seventy elders; and when the spirit rested upon them, they prophesied. But they did not do so again."

—Numbers 11:24–25

THE ABSOLUTE MINIMUM

- The 12 apostles were giants of early Christianity who created the church—aided, according to scripture, by the Holy Spirit—and dedicated the rest of their lives to evangelism.

continues

- In Christian theology, the Holy Spirit is the most subtle person of the Holy Trinity. While the Father and the Son influence the world through dramatic, miraculous events, the Spirit influences the world by moving human beings to do great things. In the Hebrew Bible, God's spirit (*ruach*) also influences human beings but represents the breath of God, not a separate person.

- The Pentecost event described in Acts 2 centers on *glossolalia*, or speaking in tongues. According to the Acts account, the Holy Spirit descended upon the apostles and gave them the power to speak in languages they could not previously understand.

RESOURCES

- **The Holy See**—www.vatican.va
- **The Search for the 12 Apostles**—www.biblepath.com/apostles.html
- **Pneumatology (Wikipedia)**—en.wikipedia.org/wiki/Pneumatology
- **Speaking in Tongues (Ontario Consultants)**—www.religioustolerance.org/tongues.htm

In This Chapter

- Christianity becomes an independent religion
- Early persecution of the Christian faith
- The life and influence of Paul of Tarsus

25

A New Religion

According to tradition, the Christian church began with the Pentecost event (described in Chapter 24, "The First Christians"). But the church that existed at the time was not one that we would recognize as Christian; it was essentially a sect of Judaism, where members obeyed Jewish law but also believed that Jesus Christ was the Messiah.

It would take the work of Paul of Tarsus, formerly one of Christianity's fiercest persecutors, to bring gentiles to the table and transform Christianity into a global faith.

The Spread of Christianity

According to the Gospels, Jesus never left Judea. His ministry was devoted primarily to the Jewish majority living in the region, although He was also kind to the gentile minority. After Jesus' death and the Pentecost event, the apostles continued to spread His teachings within Jewish communities. However, the implications of Jesus' own teachings as described in the Gospels were much broader than that, and disciples faced the problem of how to confront gentiles with Jesus' teachings. Would they need to convert to Judaism first, and then Christianity? Would they, like the 12 apostles, need to keep kosher law and practice circumcision? The character of Christianity was still very much that of a Christian Judaism of sorts—not so much an independent religion as a sect with some very unorthodox ideas.

It was a convert named Paul of Tarsus (discussed in greater detail in the following section, "The Apostle Paul") who changed everything by traveling throughout the Roman world, in modern-day Italy, Greece, and Turkey, spreading the teachings of Jesus among gentiles with the assurance that, under the terms of the Christian faith, no conversion to Judaism was

> ## Biblically Speaking
>
> "While Peter was still speaking, the Holy Spirit fell upon all who heard the word. The circumcised believers who had come with Peter were astounded that the gift of the Holy Spirit had been poured out even on the Gentiles, for they heard them speaking in tongues and extolling God. Then Peter said, 'Can anyone withhold the water for baptizing these people who have received the Holy Spirit just as we have?' So he ordered them to be baptized in the name of Jesus Christ."
>
> —Acts 10:44–48a

necessary. Suddenly the character of Christianity was changing: People who could not even understand Aramaic, the language of Jesus, were becoming Christians. According to Acts, Peter himself became convinced that Christianity was not strictly a Jewish tradition after having a vision indicating that he need no longer observe kosher law (Acts 10:9–16) and having some success of his own in converting gentiles to Christianity (Acts 10:44–48)—and, perhaps, after some fairly intense criticism by Paul (Galatians 2:1–21). Peter dealt with the issue directly when confronted by Jewish Christians in Jerusalem (Acts 11:1–18), and in a later meeting (Acts 15:1–29) he outlined four parts of Jewish law, outside of Jesus' teachings, that all converts must follow:

- They must not eat food sacrificed to idols (although Paul makes exceptions to this rule in 1 Corinthians 10:27–33). Those in early Christian communities were often poor, and food offered to Roman idols was easy to find.

- They must not engage in scandalous sexual practices.

- They must not eat meat from an animal that has been strangled.

- They must not drink blood. Blood has traditionally been regarded as sacred in the Jewish tradition. One of the commandments given to Noah in Genesis 9:1–7, applicable to all of humanity, forbade the consumption of blood. (For more on the Noachite commandments, refer to Chapter 6, "The Creation and the Flood.")

> **note**
>
> The term *Christian* ("little Christ") was originally a derogatory term and was not adopted right away. The first Christians described themselves as followers of the *hodos*—literally "the Way."

THE FIRST DEACONS

In Acts 6:1–6, the apostles are presented with a problem: They need to distribute food to the poor, but they can't fulfill this duty and still keep a full-time preaching schedule. They come up with a compromise by appointing seven disciples to oversee their ministry to the poor: Stephen, Philip, Prochorus, Nicanor, Timon, Parmenas, and Nicolaus.

Since that time, those who fulfill this role in the church have traditionally been described as *deacons* (from the Greek *diakonos*, or "servants"). Many of the epistles contain specific instructions for deacons, but the only other deacon identified by name in the New Testament is a woman named Phoebe (Romans 16:1).

From this point forward, the entire leadership of the church opened up to the idea of gentile Christianity and to the fact that Christianity was no longer a denomination of Judaism. It had become a new religion.

The Apostle Paul

He has been called the founder of Christianity—the man who turned it from a Jewish sect into a globe-spanning faith. If that's stretching it a bit, it's a forgivable mistake: With the possible exception of Peter, no apostle did more to build the early church than Paul.

Paul's introduction to Christianity was not particularly promising. After participating in the stoning of Stephen for blasphemy, Paul, then an angry young religious fanatic named Saul of Tarsus, was "still breathing threats and murder against the disciples of the Lord" (Acts 9:1) and about to head to Damascus in a very foul mood to root out more Christians. According to Acts, Saul was confronted by a vision of the risen Jesus who called out, "Saul, Saul, why do you persecute me" (Acts 9:4). Struck blind and then healed by a disciple, Saul of Tarsus, persecutor of Christians, became known as Paul of Tarsus, Christian evangelist.

It was Paul, tradition tells us, who brought Christianity to the gentiles and played perhaps the most central role in convincing the other apostles to accept gentiles into the Christian faith (Acts 15:12). It was certainly Paul who outlined what we now know as Christian theology in his epistles (described in Chapter 26, "Letters of the Early Church"). If Paul of Tarsus didn't build the Christian faith, he certainly installed its front door.

> **note**
>
> The deacon Stephen, one of the most beloved figures in the early church, was stoned to death for blasphemy (Acts 6:1–8:2). This event galvanized the early Christian community—and, according to tradition, introduced a slightly younger Saul of Tarsus to the Christian community in a less than ideal way, as he participated in the stoning (Acts 8:1).

PAUL SPEAKS OUT

Over the past two millennia, the words of Paul have been invoked in many contexts that he could have scarcely imagined. But what did Paul actually have to say about the controversial issues with which he is so often associated?

- **Women in the church**—It is difficult to ascertain exactly what Paul's beliefs were in this area. On the one hand, he praises women church leaders in Romans 16:1, including Phoebe—an ordained deacon and "a benefactor of many" ("help her in whatever she may require from you," he instructs his readers). And he praises Junia, a woman who is "prominent among the apostles." Yet in 1 Corinthians 14:34–36, he also writes that "women should be silent in the church," "should be subordinate," and rather than receiving instruction directly from religious leaders should "ask their husbands at home." What gives?

It could be that in these cases, Paul is addressing the concerns of the local church rather than more general issues. Corinth, in particular, had problems with local fertility cults that tended to be led by women with long hair—hence his concern, in 1 Corinthians, that women veil their hair (11:5 and 11:13). Also potentially relevant: 1 Corinthians was written in 54 A.D., four years *before* the Book of Romans. Could Paul's thinking on women have changed over time?

■ **Homosexuality**—The only explicit mention of sex between members of the same gender that Paul makes in the epistles is in Romans 1:26, as part of a catalog of complaints often leveled against the gentiles. This is most likely a reference to the orgiastic festivals that Roman pagans practiced at the time and not to homosexuality as such. The catalog of sins (which also includes covetousness, gossip, haughtiness, and rebellion against one's parents) is followed immediately by "therefore you have no excuse, whoever you are, when you judge others; for in passing judgment on another you condemn yourself" (Romans 2:1), continuing the discussion in Romans 1–3 on the sinful nature of all human beings. Sometimes 1 Corinthians 6:9 and 1 Timothy 1:9 are translated in such a manner that they appear to refer to homosexuality, but the Greek word sometimes translated as "homosexual," *arsenokotoi*, actually refers to male prostitutes.

Biblically Speaking

"You have heard, no doubt, of my earlier life in Judaism. I was violently persecuting the church of God and was trying to destroy it. I advanced in Judaism beyond many among my people the same age, for I was more zealous for the traditions of my ancestors. But when God, who had set me apart before I was born and called me through his grace, was pleased to reveal his Son to me, so that I might proclaim him among the Gentiles, I did not confer with any human being, nor did I go up to Jerusalem to those who were already apostles before me, but I went away at once into Arabia, and afterwards I returned to Damascus.

Then after three years I did go up to Jerusalem to visit Cephas [Peter] and stayed with him fifteen days; but I did not see any other apostle except James the Lord's brother. In what I am writing to you, before God, I do not lie! Then I went into the regions of Syria and Cicilia, and I was still unknown by sight to the churches of Judea that are in Christ; they only heard it said, 'The one who formerly was persecuting us is now proclaiming the faith he once tried to destroy.' And they glorified God because of me."

—Paul, writing in Galatians 1:13–24

THE ABSOLUTE MINIMUM

▦ In the beginning, Christianity was a sect of Judaism. It was only the innovations of Paul and Peter that transformed it into a faith in which gentiles, who did not observe Jewish law, could also participate.

▦ Persecution of the early Christian church was fierce, particularly in the years 64–68 A.D. when the Roman emperor Nero scapegoated Christians and treated them as a hostile revolutionary group.

▦ Paul of Tarsus is sometimes called the founder of Christianity because he was the first missionary to adapt the faith to the needs of gentiles on a large-scale basis and the first to outline a philosophically grounded and distinctively Christian theology in his epistles.

RESOURCES

▦ **Acts of the Apostles (Wikipedia)**—en.wikipedia.org/wiki/Acts_of_the_Apostles

▦ **Peter and Paul and the Christian Revolution (PBS)**—www.pbs.org/empires/peterandpaul

▦ **Paul and Women (*Theology Today*)**—theologytoday.ptsem.edu/apr1974/v31-1-editorial2.htm

▦ **Christian History (Ontario Consultants)**—www.religioustolerance.org/chr_ch.htm

▦ **Christian Martyrs (Wikipedia)**—en.wikipedia.org/wiki/Christian_martyrs

26

IN THIS CHAPTER

- An overview of the epistles (letters), which make up most of the New Testament

- Summaries of the 13 Pauline epistles

- Summaries of the 8 Catholic epistles

LETTERS OF THE EARLY CHURCH

Most of the New Testament is made up of open letters called *epistles*. Written by some of the giants of early Christianity and dealing with a host of issues facing the world's first Christian communities, these epistles have guided the tradition for over two millennia.

Message in a Bible

During the first years of the Christian tradition, the Gospel—the story of Jesus, particularly of his resurrection—was told by word of mouth. Early Christians traveled throughout Judea and the surrounding territories, spreading the word and bringing new people into the fold. The approach was effective, but it had its limits.

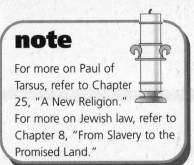

note

For more on Paul of Tarsus, refer to Chapter 25, "A New Religion." For more on Jewish law, refer to Chapter 8, "From Slavery to the Promised Land."

The first to stretch these limits completely was Paul of Tarsus, who transformed Christianity from a Jewish sect into an independent religion with multicultural appeal. Paul felt that his mission was to bring the Gospel to the gentiles, and to accomplish this goal he preached a radical new faith that did not require its members to observe Jewish law.

The trouble was that there was a great deal more land to cover once Christianity was expanded to include the non-Jewish world, and it soon became physically impossible for Paul and others to travel from city to city whenever they were needed.

Paul's solution was to write *epistles*, or open letters, that could be passed along to leaders of churches in various cities where Christianity had begun to take root. These epistles, which reflected on specific issues facing the individual church communities but also dealt with broader theological topics, were written over a period of decades (as shown in Figure 26.1). They were subsequently preserved and reread for centuries. By the time the New Testament canon took shape in the fourth century A.D., they had become so central to the faith that they were classified as holy texts.

How to Write an Epistle

Most New Testament epistles are made up of four parts:

- **A formal greeting**—In 1 Corinthians, this would be verses 1:1–3:

   "Paul, called to be an apostle of Christ Jesus by the will of God, and our brother Sosthenes, To the church of God that is in Corinth, to those who are sanctified in Christ Jesus, called to be saints, together with all those who in every place call on the name of our Lord Jesus Christ, both their Lord and ours: Grace to you and peace from God our father and the Lord Jesus Christ."

- **An opening blessing or thanksgiving**—In 1 Corinthians, this would be verses 1:4–9 (beginning "I give thanks to my God always for you because of the grace of God that has been given you in Christ Jesus…").

- **The body**—The bulk of the epistle can include a wide range of material, from specific advice on church issues to commendations of specific figures in the church to complex issues of theology.

FIGURE 26.1
Timeline of the
New Testament
epistles.

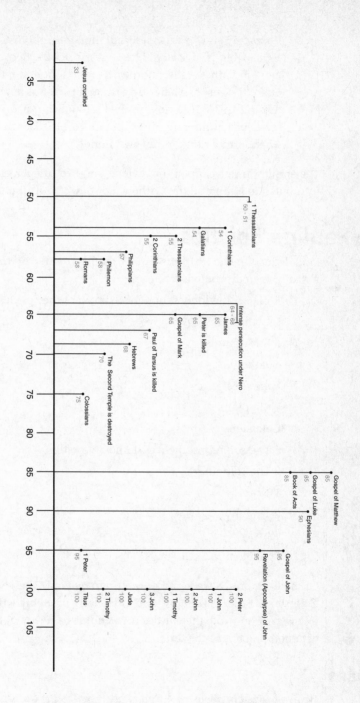

■ **Postscript**—This includes final thoughts and instructions and a blessing. In 1 Corinthians, this would be verses 16:13–24. Because most epistles were dictated to scribes rather than written out longhand, this is generally where the author "signs" the letter by writing a personal note. Here the postscript appears in 16:21, although the best-known passage along these lines is the self-deprecating humor in Galatians 6:11 ("See what large letters I make when I am writing in my own hand!").

The epistles in this chapter are divided into two categories: the Pauline Epistles (attributed to Paul) and the Catholic Epistles (not attributed to Paul).

The Pauline Epistles

Paul defined the genre of the New Testament epistle. Of the 21 epistles, 13 have historically been attributed to him:

■ Romans, the longest and best-known of the epistles

■ 1 Corinthians

■ 2 Corinthians

■ Galatians

■ Ephesians

■ Philippians

■ Colossians

■ 1 Thessalonians, the oldest known epistle

■ 2 Thessalonians

■ 1 Timothy

■ 2 Timothy

■ Titus

■ Philemon

Of these 13, only 8 were probably written by Paul. The other 5 (Ephesians, Colossians, 1 and 2 Timothy, and Titus) were probably written later by Paul's followers, who wrote the epistles in his name as a way of honoring his legacy (a common practice at the time).

Romans

Written by Paul in about 58 A.D. and addressed to the Christian community in the imperial capital of Rome.

Paul's epistle to the Romans was his masterpiece. The longest of the epistles, it was written for the church in Rome sometime near 58 A.D.; it may, in fact, be the last epistle Paul ever wrote. In it he addresses tensions between gentile Christians and traditional Jewish Christians and develops in great detail a theology of sin and resurrection that still defines orthodox Christianity to this day. The litany of sins in 1:16–32 is well remembered; less well remembered is verse 2:1, "Therefore you have no excuse, whoever you are, when you judge others; for in passing judgment on another you condemn yourself...."

1 Corinthians

Written by Paul in about 54 A.D. and addressed to the Christian community in Corinth (in Greece).

Paul's First Epistle to the Corinthians is technically not Paul's first epistle to the Corinthians (that document, mentioned in 5:9, has been lost). The surviving document is best known for chapter 13's "Hymn to Love" (see Appendix B, "Great Quotations from the Bible"), widely regarded as the most beautiful and memorable passage of all the epistles. Addressed to the struggling church in Corinth, it criticizes arrogant faith, affirms the supreme power of love, and includes a lengthy section (8:1–10:22) condemning the practice of taking and eating food that had been offered to idols.

2 Corinthians

Written by Paul around 55 A.D.

2 Corinthians is not a single letter, but is instead a collection of at least three, and possibly more, letters—all describing his relationship with the church of Corinth.

Galatians

Written by Paul around 54 A.D. and addressed to the Christian community in Galatia (in modern-day Turkey).

> ### Biblically Speaking
>
> "Owe no one anything, except to love one another; for the one who loves another has fulfilled the law. The commandments, 'You shall not commit adultery; You shall not murder; You shall not steal; You shall not covet'; and any other commandment, are summed up in this word, 'Love your neighbor as yourself.'"
>
> —Romans 13:8–9

> ### Biblically Speaking
>
> "Consider your own call, brothers and sisters: not many of you were wise by human standards, not many were powerful, not many were of noble birth. But God chose what is foolish in the world to shame the wise; God chose what is weak in the world to shame the strong; God chose what is low and despised in the world, things that are not, to reduce to nothing things that are, so that no one might boast in the presence of God."
>
> —1 Corinthians 1:26–29

In Galatians, Paul established his role as a counterpart to Peter—as the one "entrusted with the gospel for the uncircumcised, just as Peter had been entrusted with the gospel for the circumcised" (2:7). The chapter's primary theme is the assimilation of gentiles into the Christian faith, a central concern of Paul's ministry.

> **Biblically Speaking**
>
> "There is no longer Jew or Greek, there is no longer slave or free, there is no longer male and female; for all of you are one in Christ Jesus."
>
> —Galatians 3:28

Ephesians

Probably written by a follower of Paul around 90 A.D. and addressed to the Christian community in Ephesus (in modern-day Turkey).

Most scholars agree that Ephesians is the handiwork of one of Paul's followers writing near the end of the first century A.D. The first half of the epistle deals primarily with the role of gentiles in the new church, while the second half focuses on family relationships and household responsibilities. Much attention has been paid to verse 5:22, which calls on wives to be subject to their husbands—but verse 5:21, which also calls on husbands to be subject to their wives, has often gone overlooked.

Philippians

Written by Paul around 57 A.D., most likely while he was imprisoned in Caesarea Palaestina, and addressed to the Christian community in Philippi (in Greece).

Paul wrote his letter to the Philippians during a time when his death seemed like a very real possibility (2:13–26). Paul urged the church to remain united in his absence, and in the process helped to build an idea of church life that would survive him.

> **Biblically Speaking**
>
> "Therefore, my beloved, just as you have always obeyed me, not only in my presence, but much more now in my absence, work out your own salvation with fear and trembling; for it is God who is at work in you, enabling you both to will and to work for his good pleasure."
>
> —Philippians 2:12–13

Colossians

Probably written by an immediate follower of Paul—perhaps Timothy—near 75 A.D. However, it could have also been written by Paul himself while he was imprisoned in Rome near 62 A.D. Addressed to the Christian community in Colossae (in modern-day Turkey).

It is clear—based on the language and writing style—that Colossians was either written by Paul or compiled by an immediate follower shortly after his death. It primarily targets a new sect of religious ascetics (1:12–2:5), whose practices posed a distraction and possible threat to Christianity in that city.

1 Thessalonians

Written by Paul near 50 or 51 A.D. and addressed to the Christian community in Thessalonica (in Greece).

The first letter to the Thessalonians is Paul's earliest epistle, and among the friendliest and most cheerful in his repertoire. It is to a great extent a pep talk, urging members of the Christian community there to continue with their good work.

2 Thessalonians

Written by Paul around 55 A.D. and addressed to the Christian community in Thessalonica.

The second letter to the Thessalonians continues much of the cheerfulness of the first and includes discussion of the end of the world and the expected second coming of Jesus. For more on the apocalypse, see Chapter 27, "The End of the World."

> ## Biblically Speaking
>
> "As God's chosen ones, holy and beloved, clothe yourselves with compassion, kindness, humility, meekness, and patience. Bear with one another and, if anyone has a complaint against another, forgive each other; just as the Lord has forgiven you, so you must also forgive. Above all, clothe yourselves with love, which binds everything together in perfect harmony."
>
> —Colossians 3:12–14

1 Timothy

2 Timothy

Probably written by followers of Paul sometime near 100 A.D.

Although the epistles to Timothy are written from the perspective of a dying Paul seeking to preserve his tradition, a considerable majority of scholars consider the two epistles to be later works, written by Paul's successors to ensure that his teachings did not die over time. The epistles deal with Paul's moral teachings in a fairly general sense.

Titus

Probably written by followers of Paul sometime around 100 A.D.

Like the Book of Hebrews, the Book of Titus deals in a fairly general way with issues of Christian life.

Philemon

Probably written by Paul around 58 A.D., while he was imprisoned in Caesarea Palaestina.

In this, the shortest of the Pauline epistles, Paul writes to Philemon as an advocate for Philemon's slave Onesimus, whom Paul had befriended while in prison.

Describing Onesimus as "my own heart" (v. 12), Paul urges Philemon to forgive the slave's remaining debts and free him.

The Catholic Epistles

The eight remaining epistles are referred to as the Catholic ("universal") Epistles, or sometimes as the General Epistles. The distinction between the Pauline and Catholic epistles is fairly straightforward: The Pauline epistles are written under Paul's name (whether by Paul himself or by one of his disciples), while the Catholic epistles are not. The eight Catholic Epistles are

- Hebrews, which some attribute to Paul (though he is never mentioned in the letter)
- James, which was most likely written by James the Just, brother of Jesus, or by one of his immediate disciples
- 1 Peter
- 2 Peter
- 1 John
- 2 John
- 3 John
- Jude

> **note**
>
> For more information on the 12 apostles, refer to Chapter 24, "The First Christians."

Although the Catholic Epistles are not generally as well known as the Pauline Epistles, they play a crucial role in the New Testament and have been very important to the history of the Christian tradition.

Hebrews

Written by an unknown figure, probably around 68 A.D.

The purpose of the anonymous letter to the Hebrews is to define Jesus as a superior Jewish figure. It is remarkable in the way that it emphasizes the humanity of Jesus. The central portion of the epistle (chapters 4–10) describes Jesus as the eternal high priest, the intermediary between God and humanity.

> **Biblically Speaking**
>
> "Now faith is the assurance of things hoped for, the conviction of things not seen."
>
> —Hebrews 11:1

The authorship of the book is widely disputed by scholars, who don't really have any way of guessing who wrote it. One likely suspect is Priscilla, a well-known evangelist among Jewish Christians (Acts 18), but we can't say for sure. The 68 A.D. date is also approximate. It seems probable that the book was written prior to the destruction of the Second Temple in Jerusalem (which occurred in 70 A.D.), and after Paul's epistles had begun to be distributed, but alternative dates (ranging from 60 A.D. to 100 A.D. and beyond) have been proposed.

James

Written by James or a closely linked figure in the Jerusalem church near 65 A.D. to all Jewish Christians.

The epistle of James is one of the more controversial of the New Testament epistles because it proposes that faith is not enough to ensure salvation—good works are also needed. The great reformer Martin Luther referred to James as "an epistle of straw" for this reason and expressed a wish to remove it from the New Testament. But the emphasis on works was particularly relevant to early Jewish Christians, who had grown accustomed to operating in a faith tradition that valued morality over doctrine.

Biblically Speaking

"If any think they are religious, and do not bridle their tongues but deceive their hearts, their religion is worthless. Religion that is pure and undefiled before God, the Father, is this: to care for orphans and widows in their distress, and to keep oneself unstained by the world."

—James 1:26–27

1 Peter

Written by a follower of Peter around 95 A.D.

Although 1 Peter has traditionally been attributed to Peter, it bears the marks of a later text written by a different author. The style is complex Greek rather than Aramaic or Hebrew and assumes a Christianity that has taken on something of a non-Jewish character. The epistle focuses to a great extent on the relationship between Christians and the larger society.

2 Peter

Written by a follower of Peter around 100 A.D.

The second epistle of Peter is written in the form of a last will and testament, summarizing Peter's long-term wishes for the Christian community.

1 John

2 John

3 John

Written by early Christians near 100 A.D.

The three epistles of John were most likely composed by the same author, who may very well have been named John—but was probably not the apostle John, nor the John who wrote the Gospel of John or Revelation. The first epistle deals primarily with the importance of love and the nature of faith, while the latter two deal with questions of hospitality.

Jude

Written by early Christians around 100 A.D.

Attributed to the apostle Jude, this short epistle is remarkable because it quotes from the Book of Enoch, which is no longer regarded as canonical (refer to Chapter 18, "Nowhere in the Bible"). It focuses on retelling stories from the books of Genesis and Exodus to make broader points about Christian membership and the nature of God's vengeance.

THE ABSOLUTE MINIMUM

- The Epistles are letters—usually addressed to churches, but sometimes addressed to individuals—that were written by early Christian leaders to help guide these small churches as they grew. Over time, they have come to be regarded as holy texts in their own right—a sign of the Holy Spirit's influence over the early church.

- The 21 books of the epistles can be divided into two categories: The 13 Pauline Epistles and the 8 Catholic Epistles.

- The Pauline Epistles are those attributed to Paul, whether he was the actual author or not.

- The 8 Catholic Epistles are those attributed to other authors.

RESOURCES

- **Epistles (Wikipedia)**—en.wikipedia.org/wiki/Epistles
- **The General Epistles (Ontario Consultants)**—www.religioustolerance.org/chr_ntb4.htm
- **The Pauline Epistles (Ontario Consultants)**—www.religioustolerance.org/chr_ntb3.htm

27

THE END OF THE WORLD

The Revelation of John (referred to as the *Apocalypse of John* in the Roman Catholic and Eastern Orthodox traditions) is a visionary account of Armageddon, the final battle between good and evil. Rich with highly complex, sometimes disturbing, and nearly always surreal imagery, it is challenging to read and impossible to completely understand.

Signs and Visions

The Revelation was written by a disciple named John at some point near 100 A.D. It is by no means certain that this is the same John who wrote the Gospel of John or the Epistles of John. The dates and literary styles are very different, and John was not an uncommon name at the time. This John had clearly been subject to the wrath of Roman authorities and found himself exiled on the island of Patmos in modern-day Greece. It was there that he experienced what Christians have called the *apocalypse*—"the revealing of the hidden" (through visions), a word so identified with John's Revelation that it is now commonly used to refer to the end of the world. It is worth noting that in apocalyptic writing, images should *not* be taken literally—they are used as symbols to convey information.

If you feel that the Revelation of John seems a little bizarre, you're not alone. It is the last book in the New Testament not because it comes last in the story, but rather because it was the last to be recognized as a holy book. Early readers often found it as confusing as modern readers do. Over time, it has been subject to a great deal of criticism. The reformer Martin Luther, for example, once wrote that he could "in no way detect that the Holy Spirit produced it."

> ## note
>
> The idea of the Rapture—in which all faithful Christians are swept up and saved in advance of Armageddon—is not mentioned anywhere in Revelation. Instead it comes from 1 Thessalonians 4:17: "Those who are alive, who are left, will be caught up in the clouds together with them to meet the Lord in the air; and so we will be with the Lord forever."

But it is an exciting book for many reasons. It completes the story of the New Testament, telling us that God will win the final struggle between good and evil. Its jarringly vivid, chaotic images contrast sharply with the 21 epistles that precede it. It provides the most detailed accounts of heaven and hell in the entire Bible. Critics have had much to say about it, but few would call it dull. It is a bold stripe, emboldening early Christians and perhaps sometimes striking fear into the hearts of their oppressors.

Revelation essentially consists of one vision in 12 parts:

1. **The encounter with the Son of Man (Chapter 1)**—While in an altered state of consciousness (1:10), the exiled John hears a voice ordering him to witness a vision and write down what he sees and then send it to the churches of Ephesus, Smyrna, Pergamum, Thyatira, Sardis, Philadelphia, and Laodicea. The voice comes from a glowing, white-haired figure identified as the Son of Man, who refers to himself as "the first and the last, and the living one" (1:17–18). The Son of Man is neither Jesus nor God, but an angel representing God's dominion over the earth.

2. **God's messages for the seven churches (2–3)**—This section is made up of personal messages from God to be sent to the seven churches that will receive this revelation from John.

3. **The throne of God (4)**—John actually sees God Himself sitting on a throne, although the closest thing we get to an actual physical description (4:3) is that He looks like "jasper" (a multicolored, primarily light red stone) and "carnelian" (a deep, bold red stone). His throne is surrounded by 24 other thrones, each with a white-robed, crowned elder sitting on it. Thunder and lighting come from behind the throne, and placed in front of it are seven torches and a sea of glass.

4. **The seven seals and the four horsemen (5:1–8:1)**—God writes something down on a scroll, but no one is worthy to break its seals and read it—until a mutilated lamb, with seven horns and seven eyes (5:6, representing spirits that God had sent out into the world), approaches to choruses of praise. That lamb, representing Jesus, begins to open the scroll but must first remove its seven seals.

   ▪ **The first four seals (6:1–8)**—Each of the first four seals releases one of the four horsemen of the Apocalypse: a white horse with a crowned rider (sometimes called War); a bright red horse with a sword-wielding rider (sometimes called Pestilence); a black horse with a rider carrying a pair of scales (sometimes called Famine); and a pale green horse with a rider named Death, who is given authority to kill one-fourth of the world's population.

   ▪ **The fifth seal (6:9–11)**—The souls of martyrs cry out for vengeance.

   ▪ **The sixth seal (6:12–17)**—The world is rocked by a massive earthquake, the sun turns black, the moon turns red, the stars fall from the sky "as the fig tree drops its winter fruit when shaken by a gale" (6:13), the sky disappears, all mountains collapse, and all islands sink.

   ▪ **The seventh seal (8:1)**—The opening of the seventh seal prompts 30 minutes of total silence, possibly in parallel with the Sabbath on the seventh day of creation (refer to Chapter 6, "The Creation and the Flood").

5. **The seven trumpets (8:6–11:19)**—Angels appear, each of whom blows a trumpet, in sequence:

   ▪ **The first trumpet (8:7)**—Hail, fire, and blood rain from the sky, destroying one-third of the earth.

   ▪ **The second trumpet (8:8–9)**—A great mass of flaming rock is thrown into the sea, turning one-third of the sea into blood and destroying the ships and living creatures therein.

- **The third trumpet (8:10–11)**—A star called Wormwood falls from the sky, polluting one-third of the world's fresh water.

- **The fourth trumpet (8:12)**—The sun, moon, and stars are all struck, reducing their light output by one-third. It is not clear how this relates to the sixth seal, through which the sun already turns black, the moon already turns red, and the stars already fall from the sky; it is at times like these that it's important to remember that the language of Revelation is highly metaphorical.

- **The fifth trumpet (9:1–12)**—A star falls from the sky, opening a passage to the bottomless abyss where deadly locust-human hybrids fly into the world under instructions to spare Christians but torture everyone else for 5 months.

- **The sixth trumpet (9:13–21)**—Fire-breathing creatures with the heads of lions and the bodies of horses slaughter one-third of the world's population.

- **The seventh trumpet (11:15–19)**—The seventh trumpet announces God's reign on Earth, opens up the temple in heaven, and restores the Ark of the Covenant.

6. **The pregnant woman and the dragon (12)**—A woman wearing a crown made up of 12 stars (each probably representing one of the tribes of Israel) is pregnant and in labor pangs and is being chased by a giant red dragon—explicitly identified as Satan. She's rescued by God, so the infuriated dragon turns his wrath against surviving followers of God.

7. **The mark of the beast (13)**—The dragon (Satan) brings forth the great beast of the sea (identified with the antichrist, though the word is never actually used in Revelation), with 10 horns and seven heads (probably representing various nations under his control), who is called upon to rule all

note

In 13:18, John calls for "anyone with understanding [to] calculate the number of the beast, for it is the number of a person": 666 (or, according to some translations, 616). This is almost certainly a reference to Gematria, an ancient Hebrew practice popular at the time of the early Christian church that encoded words by adding up their numerical values in Hebrew. The insane Roman emperor Nero, the most vicious oppressor of Christianity, responsible for the deaths of both Peter and Paul (among many others), was known as Neron Caesar—or, as the name would be represented in Gematria, 666. (If the name is shortened to Nero Caesar, then it becomes 616 in Gematria.) Because Nero was already dead by the time Revelation was written, the verse probably refers either to Nero as resurrected through unholy means or to a new persecutor in the mold of Nero.

non-Jewish and non-Christian survivors for 42 months (13:5). A second beast rises from the earth (13:11) and demands that the beast of the sea be worshipped. Anyone who does not receive the mark of the beast (13:16–17) on the right hand or on the forehead will be prohibited, by the beast and his followers, from buying or selling goods. Anyone who refuses to worship the beast must either somehow escape or face violent death.

8. **The lamb and the angels (14)**—In one of the strangest and most difficult passages in the entire book, Jesus (as the slaughtered lamb) appears with 144,000 Jews who have been spared destruction (see 7:4). At this point, the Son of Man—not Jesus, but the figure described in chapter 1—appears with three angels, each armed with sickles. In a somewhat disturbing image, a great wine press crushes "the vine of the earth," flooding all the land within a 200-mile radius with blood the height of a horse's bridle (probably about 5 feet). As that would work out to a bare minimum of 17.5 trillion gallons of blood (equivalent to the blood of 15 trillion people), this is presumably a symbolic statement.

9. **The seven plagues (15–16)**—Angels pour out seven bowls, each creating a plague. There are many parallels between these plagues and the seven plagues inflicted on the Egyptians (for more on this, refer to Chapter 8, "From Slavery to the Promised Land"):

   - **The first plague (16:2)**—Painful sores appear on the bodies of all of the beast's followers.

   - **The second plague (16:3)**—The seas turn to blood, and every living creature in the seas dies.

   - **The third plague (16:4–5)**—The rivers and springs turn to blood.

   - **The fourth plague (16:8–9)**—The sun burns hotter, scorching everyone with its great heat.

   - **The fifth plague (16:10–11)**—The throne of the beast itself is cursed, and his kingdom begin to collapse.

   - **The sixth plague (16:12)**—The water in the Euphrates dries up. Here, again, is an obvious symbolic statement—given that the third plague had already turned all the rivers into blood.

note

The similarities between Rome and Babylon are notable: Each destroyed one of the two Jewish temples (Babylon destroyed the first in 586 B.C.; Rome destroyed the second in 70 A.D.), each was organized around a major city, and each was highly hostile to the religion of the Bible (the Babylonians toward Judaism, the Romans toward Christianity). Christians began referring to Rome as *Babylon* fairly early on in the movement, which functioned both as invective and code.

■ **The seventh plague (16:17–21)**—Every city on earth is split by an earthquake, every mountain on earth collapses, every island sinks, and the world is battered with 100-pound hailstones. Many of these effects would have already been achieved with the sixth seal (6:12–17), which had destroyed every mountain and island, and so on.

10. **The whore of Babylon (17–19)**—A woman of ill-repute, representing Babylon (Rome), rides a scarlet beast with seven heads and 10 horns (each representing a king). She is promiscuous and "drunk with the blood of the saints" (17:6). She will eventually be eaten by the beast (17:16), symbolizing the fall of Rome at the hands of smaller kingdoms.

11. **The reign of Christ and the last judgment (20)**—Jesus binds the beast and rules for 1,000 years (some see this as a reference to the Christian church); then He releases the beast to gather up any who are eager to rebel against Jesus into a massive army. When they began to lay siege to the cities of loyal Christians, they are consumed by fire. The lamb judges all humans according to their works, saving the blessed and tossing the beast and all the beast's followers into an eternal lake of fire.

12. **The new Jerusalem (21–22)**—An unimaginably beautiful city descends from heaven, where God and His people will remain for all eternity.

> ## Biblically Speaking
>
> "Then I saw a new heaven and a new earth; for the first heaven and the first earth had passed away, and the sea was no more. And I saw the holy city, the new Jerusalem, coming down out of heaven from God, prepared as a bride adorned for her husband. And I heard a loud voice from the throne saying,
>
> 'See, the home of God is among mortals.
>
> He will dwell with them,
>
> they will be his peoples,
>
> and God himself will be with them;
>
> he will wipe every tear from their eyes.
>
> Death will be no more;
>
> mourning and crying and pain will be no more,
>
> for the first things have passed away.'"
>
> —Revelation 21:3–4

Missed It By *That* Much

Predicting judgment day is not an exact science. For as long as the Revelation of John has existed, readers have seen their own circumstances in it—confident that it will be their generation, at last, that sees the end of the age. Here are a few particularly notable near misses:

> **note**
>
> One Christian tradition, called *preterism*, holds that the events described in Revelation already occurred during the first century A.D. and that the new Jerusalem or the lake of fire await everyone at the moment of death.

- **793**—In 786, a Spanish monk named Beatus of Liébana wrote his masterpiece, the *Commentary on the Apocalypse*. There he predicted that, based on his interpretation of the Revelation (the Apocalypse of John), the world would come to an end within 14 years. On the night before Easter 793, he caused a riot by announcing that the world would end by dawn.

- **1000**—Many predicted that the world would end 1,000 years after what was understood to be the birth of Christ.

- **1033**—When the world didn't end in 1000, some suggested that the effective date would be 1,000 years after Jesus' crucifixion in 33 A.D.

- **1284**—Pope Innocent III believed that Islam represented the beast and that the world would end 666 years after its founding in 618.

- **1656**—In his *Book of Prophecies*, Christopher Columbus predicted that the world would come to an end in 1656 A.D. (which he believed to be 1,656 years after the coming of Jesus), just as he suspected that the world was flooded 1,656 years after the creation in Genesis.

- **1666**—Believing that the end of the world would come after the millennium plus the number of the Beast (666), some predicted the end—especially in England, which was ravaged by the terrifying Great Fire of London.

- **1697**—In 1692, New England minister Cotton Mather was alarmed by the increasing number of alleged witches. He interpreted this as a sign that they were the Devil's Army and that the world would come to an end within 5 years. When 1697 came and went, he revised his predictions and said that the world would end in 1716, then later revised them once more to say that the world would end in 1736.

- **1799**—American author and socialite Hester Thrale Piozzi believed that Napoleon Bonaparte was the incarnation of Satan and would bring about the end of the world in 1799.

- **1914**—Charles Taze Russell, founder of the Jehovah's Witnesses, wrote in 1874 that he believed the world would come to an end in 1914. When the year came, the outbreak of World War I (1914–1918) made this seem like a very distinct possibility.

- **1988**—Some Christian leaders expected the end of the world to approach in 1988, sparking such book titles as *Watch 1988: The Year of Climax* and *88 Reasons Why the Rapture Will Be in 1988*.

- **1992**—The Rapture Movement, a coalition of Korean fundamentalist churches, purchased a full-page advertisement in an October 1991 issue of *USA Today* predicting that Armageddon would take place on October 28, 1992.

- **2000**—Throughout the world, many religious leaders predicted that 2000 would be the end. Some U.S. survivalists hid in underground bunkers with years of supplies—either because of predicted computer issues (where old computers were not equipped to recognize the year 2000) or in anticipation of the global thermonuclear war that would theoretically precede the Apocalypse.

THE ABSOLUTE MINIMUM

- The Revelation (Apocalypse) of John describes Armageddon—the final battle between good and evil. It culminates in the rise of a host of evil entities (probably symbolizing nations) who are defeated by a returning Jesus Christ. The language of Revelation is highly symbolic and very abstract.

- Ever since Revelation was written, readers have applied it to the crises of their own age in anticipation of the Apocalypse.

RESOURCES

- **Apocalypse! (PBS)**—www.pbs.org/wgbh/pages/frontline/shows/apocalypse
- **Scholarly Resources for Study of the Book of Revelation**—www.book-of-revelation.com
- **Eschatology (Wikipedia)**—en.wikipedia.org/wiki/Eschatology
- **Apocalyptic Literature**—www.piney.com/ApocalypticIndex.html

PART VIII

APPENDIXES

A

BIBLICAL PHRASES WE USE EVERY DAY

The 1611 King James Bible transformed the English language, introducing a number of words, phrases, and figures of speech that are still in common use today. The 12 examples of biblical English provided here only hint at the massive role the Bible has played in the development of secular western culture.

A Man After His Own Heart

In the Hebrew Bible, Saul—the first king of Israel—rises to power as a promising figure but soon proves himself to be petty, corrupt, and disobedient. The aging prophet Samuel, who ruled Israel before Saul was anointed, warns the king that he will not create a dynasty. Instead, the crown will pass to a new figure—someone whose heart comes closer to reflecting that of God.

---

1 SAMUEL 13:14

"But now thy kingdom shall not continue: **the LORD hath sought him a man after his own heart**, and the LORD hath commanded him to be captain over his people. . ."

A Still, Small Voice

Elijah is sometimes remembered as the greatest of Israel's prophets. Certainly he is described as having special favor with God, who spares him death and brings him directly up to heaven on a whirlwind. It is in the description of Elijah's prophecy that the voice of God is first depicted as a "still, small voice."

---

1 KINGS 19:11–12

"And, behold, the LORD passed by, and a great and strong wind rent the mountains, and brake in pieces the rocks before the LORD; but the LORD was not in the wind: and after the wind an earthquake; but the LORD was not in the earthquake: And after the earthquake a fire; but the LORD was not in the fire: and **after the fire a still small voice**."

By the Skin of My Teeth

Today when someone speaks of escaping by the skin of their teeth, it refers to a close call—a narrow escape. But in the Book of Job, which originated the phrase, the reference is to escaping *with* the skin of his teeth—a poetic way of saying that he has escaped with his own life, but nothing else.

JOB 19:20–21

"My bone cleaveth to my skin and to my flesh, and **I am escaped with the skin of my teeth**. Have pity upon me, have pity upon me, O ye my friends; for the hand of God hath touched me."

The Land of the Living

Chapter 28 of the Book of Job is a lengthy, anonymous discussion of the nature of wisdom. The world of this life might give up precious metals, the author argues, but it will never give up understanding.

JOB 28:12–13

"But where shall wisdom be found? and where is the place of understanding? Man knoweth not the price thereof; neither is it found **in the land of the living**."

Out of the Mouths of Babes

Although scholars aren't quite sure which specific event this Psalm refers to, the phrase "out of the mouths of babes" now brings to mind an uncannily wise or otherwise surprising statement uttered by a child.

PSALM 8:12

"**Out of the mouths of babes** and sucklings hast thou ordained strength because of thine enemies,

that thou mightest still the enemy and the avenger."

The Apple of Your Eye

A parent might refer to a child as the apple of his or her eye. The term is sweet enough, but a little strange when taken at face value. What's the connection between eyes and apples?

It turns out that in Hebrew idiom, the apple of the eye is the pupil. The Psalmist asks God to guard him as he might guard the pupil of his own eye—and, through happy coincidence, in very much the same way that a doting parent would guard a child.

PSALM 17:8–9

"Keep me as **the apple of the eye**, hide me under the shadow of thy wings,

From the wicked that oppress me, from my deadly enemies, who compass me about."

At Wit's End

In the Psalm, storms and high waves drive ancient Jewish sailors to the verge of insanity. When the phrase is used today, it's usually applied to far less desperate—but, perhaps, comparably frustrating—situations.

PSALM 107:23–27

"They that go down to the sea in ships, that do business in great waters;

These see the works of the LORD, and his wonders in the deep.

For he commandeth, and raiseth the stormy wind,

which lifteth up the waves thereof.

They mount up to the heaven, they go down again to the depths:

their soul is melted because of trouble.

They reel to and fro, and stagger like a drunken man,

and are **at their wits' end**."

The Powers That Be

When Paul wrote in Romans 13:1 that earthly institutions deserve obedience by virtue of divine authority, he clearly was not referring to all earthly institutions—Paul himself would later be executed for defying the Roman authorities, and the letter to the Romans itself was part and parcel of what amounted to an illegal underground movement. Scholars believe that the reference here is meant to be specific to the issues of the letter.

ROMANS 13:1

"Let every soul be subject unto the higher powers. For there is no power but of God: **the powers that be** are ordained of God."

In the Twinkling of an Eye

One of the things that makes people nervous about the whole idea of physical resurrection is the time spent in the grave. The mental image of lying dead until Armageddon doesn't sit well. Paul knew this and assured members of the early church that, from their vantage point, no time would elapse between their death and their resurrection. It would all be over in the twinkling of an eye.

1 CORINTHIANS 15:51–52, 55

"We shall not all sleep, but we shall all be changed. In a moment, **in the twinkling of an eye**, at that last trump: for the trumpet shall sound, and the dead shall be raised incorruptible, and we shall be changed.… O death, where is thy sting? O grave, where is thy victory?"

A Labor of Love

In the Gospel of Mark (chapter 12), Jesus Christ himself identified love of God and neighbor as the fundamental commandments and the proper basis of all moral law. Paul understood the work of church-building to be a labor of love, a reflection of those two fundamental values.

1 THESSALONIANS 1:2–4

"We give thanks to God always for you all, making mention of you in our prayers; Remembering without ceasing your work of faith, and **labour of love**, and patience of hope in our Lord Jesus Christ, in the sight of God and our Father; Knowing, brethren beloved, your election of God."

Fight the Good Fight

Paul was an older, established figure in the church nearing his inevitable martyrdom at the hands of the Roman empire. In the epistles titled 1 Timothy and 2 Timothy, Paul offers advice to Timothy—whom he addresses as "my son"—on how to conduct the dangerous business of building the Christian church.

1 TIMOTHY 6:12

"**Fight the good fight** of faith, lay hold on eternal life, whereunto thou art also called, and hast professed a good profession before many witnesses."

Stranger in a Strange Land

In his 1961 novel *Stranger in a Strange Land*, science-fiction writer Robert Heinlein tells the story of Valentine Smith, a human raised by aliens on Mars and then returned to Earth as an adult. The book introduced the word *grok*—a verb meaning "to absorb," "to become one with," or "to comprehend intuitively"—to the English language. It also draws heavily on religious symbolism.

The title of the book comes from Exodus chapter 2, where Moses, far from his home of Egypt, settles into the household of a priest named Reuel. Reuel's daughter, Zipporah, bears Moses a son, and he names the boy Gershom ("foreigner") because Moses has been "a stranger in a strange land." To this day, Gershom remains a somewhat common Jewish name.

The phrase *stranger in a strange land* is poetic and sums up alienation in a way that few other phrases can. Because Moses is a foreigner, he is a stranger to the local residents; at the same time, the local culture is equally foreign to him.

EXODUS 2:16–22

"Now the priest of Midian had seven daughters: and they came and drew water, and filled the troughs to water their father's flock. And the shepherds came and drove them away: but Moses stood up and helped them, and watered their flock. And when they came to Reuel their father, he said, How is it that ye are come so soon to day? And they said, An Egyptian delivered us out of the hands of the shepherds, and also drew water enough for us, and watered the flock. And he said unto his daughters, And where is he? Why is it that ye have left the man? Call him, that he may eat bread. And Moses was content to dwell with the man: and he gave Moses Zipporah his daughter. And she bare him a son, and he called his name Gershom: for he said, **I have been a stranger in a strange land**."

B

GREAT QUOTATIONS FROM THE BIBLE

On God

When I look at the heavens, the work of your fingers,

the moon and the stars that you have established;

What are human beings that you are mindful of them,

mortals that you care for them?

Yet you have made them a little lower than God,

and crowned them with glory and honor.

—Psalm 8, verses 3–5

A voice cries out:

"In the wilderness prepare the way of the Lord,

make straight in the desert a highway for our God.

Every valley shall be lifted up,

and every mountain and hill be made low;

the uneven ground shall become level,

and the rough places a plain.

Then the glory of the Lord shall be revealed,

and all people shall see it together,

for the mouth of the Lord has spoken."

He will feed his flock like a shepherd;

he will gather the lambs in his arms,

and carry them in his bosom,

and gently lead the mother sheep.

Have you not known? Have you not heard?

Has it not been told you from the beginning?

Have you not understood from the foundations of the earth?

It is he who sits above the circle of the earth,

and its inhabitants are like grasshoppers;

who stretches out the heavens like a curtain,

and spreads them like a tent to live in;

who brings princes to naught,

and makes the rulers of the earth as nothing.

—Isaiah 40:3–5, 11, 21–23

On Love

If I speak in the tongues of mortals and of angels, but do not have love, I am a noisy gong or a clanging cymbal.

And if I have prophetic powers, and understand all mysteries and all knowledge, and if I have all faith, so as to remove mountains, but do not have love, I am nothing.

If I give away all my possessions, and if I hand over my body to be burned, so that I may boast, but do not have love, I gain nothing.

Love is patient; love is kind; love is not envious or boastful or arrogant or rude. It does not insist on its own way; it is not irritable or resentful; it does not rejoice in wrongdoing, but rejoices in the truth. It bears all things, believes all things, hopes all things, endures all things.

Love never ends. But as for prophecies, they will come to an end;

as for tongues, they will cease; as for knowledge, it will come to an end.

For we know only in part, and we prophesy only in part; but when the complete comes, the partial will come to an end. When I was a child, I spoke like a child, I thought like a child, I reasoned like a child; when I became an adult, I put an end to childish ways.

For now we see in a mirror, in a riddle, but then we will see face to face. Now I know only in part; then I will know fully, even as I have been fully known. And now faith, hope, and love abide, these three; and the greatest of these is love.

—1 Corinthians 13:1–13

Beloved, let us love one another, because love is from God; everyone who loves is born of God and knows God. Whoever does not love does not know God, for God is love. No one has ever seen God; if we love one another, God lives in us, and his love is perfected in us.

God is love, and those who abide in love abide in God, and God abides in them. There is no fear in love, but perfect love casts out fear; for fear has to do with punishment, and whoever fears has not reached perfection in love. We love because he first loved us. Those who say "I love God," and hate their brothers or sisters, are liars; for those who do not love a brother or sister whom they have seen, cannot love God whom they have not seen. The commandment we have from him is this: those who love God must love their brothers and sisters also.

—1 John 4:7–8, 12, 16, 18–21

On the Meaning of Life

Vanity of vanities, says the Teacher, vanity of vanities! All is vanity.

What do people gain from all the toil at which they toil under the sun?

A generation goes, and a generation comes,

but the earth remains forever. . . .

All streams run to the sea,

but the sea is not full;

to the place where the streams flow,

there they continue to flow.

All things are wearisome;

more than one can express.

The eye is not satisfied with seeing,

or the ear filled with hearing.

What has been is what will be,

and what has been done is what will be done;

there is nothing new under the sun. . .

The people of long ago are not remembered,

nor will there be any remembrance of people yet to come

by those who come after them.

—Ecclesiastes 1:2–4, 8–9, 11

"With what shall I come before the Lord,

and bow myself before God on high?

Shall I come before him with burnt offerings,

with calves a year old?

Will the Lord be pleased with thousands of rams,

with ten thousand rivers of oil?

Shall I give my firstborn for my transgression,

the fruit of my body for the sin of my soul?"

He has told you, O mortal, what is good;

and what does the Lord require of you

but to do justice, and to love kindness,

and to walk humbly with your God?

—Micah 6:6–8

When Jesus saw the crowds, he went up to the mountain; and after he sat down, his disciples came to him. Then he began to speak, and taught them, saying:

"Blessed are the poor in spirit, for theirs is the kingdom of heaven.

Blessed are those who mourn, for they will be comforted.

Blessed are the meek, for they will inherit the earth.

Blessed are those who hunger and thirst for righteousness,

for they will be filled.

Blessed are the merciful, for they will receive mercy.

Blessed are the pure in heart, for they will see God.

Blessed are the peacemakers, for they will be called children of God.

Blessed are those who are persecuted for righteousness' sake,

for theirs is the kingdom of heaven.

"You are the light of the world. A city built on a hill cannot be hid. No one after lighting a lamp puts it under the bushel basket, but on the lampstand, and it gives light to all in the house. In the same way, let your light shine before others, so that they may see your good works and give glory to your Father in heaven."

—Matthew 5:1–11, 14–16

C

25 GREAT BIBLE WEBSITES

Online Bibles and General Reference Sites

For centuries, looking up a specific Bible verse meant using a *concordance*, a massive book-length index of words found in the Bible. These huge books are still published, and there are advantages to using them—flipping around a 12-pound *Strong's Concordance* for hours on end is a great way to build up your pecs—but if you'd rather type than bench press, clicking "Search" on an online Bible site usually works just as well.

There are other benefits to using online Bibles. For starters, there are the many translations you have to choose from; most people won't ever need St. Jerome's Latin Vulgate, but if you always wanted to flip through one, StudyLight.org (listed in this section) has a searchable edition—as well as the Emphasized Bible, the New Living Translation, the New Life Bible, and enough other versions to take up a whole bookshelf. And that's just *one* online Bible site; there are plenty of others.

The Bible @ Beliefnet

bible.beliefnet.com

The interfaith site Beliefnet runs a nifty general Bible page, which features a lot of articles. I'd tell you what the articles are about, but the site is updated so often that by the time you read this, I'd be wrong.

The Bible Gateway

www.biblegateway.com

If you're looking at this list of online Bible sites and don't know where to begin, you could do a lot worse than the Bible Gateway. You can search up to 19 English translations (including the King James, the New International Version, and the New American Standard Bible), but what really makes this site stand out is the huge number of non-English translations available. If you've ever wanted to read Leviticus in Haitian Creole, now's your chance.

BibleMaster

www.biblemaster.com

No, it isn't a new exercise machine endorsed by Suzanne Somers; it's a searchable online Bible with five English translations, plus thousands upon thousands of searchable pages covering personal advice and issues in biblical scholarship from a conservative Christian perspective.

Biblenotes

www.biblenotes.com

Want to know your Bible without actually reading it first? This site has short, easy-to-read summaries of every book of the Bible, with study questions and other helpful features.

Bible Resource Center

www.bibleresourcecenter.org

This huge site features a Bible dictionary, charts, graphs, daily readings, and many research articles and devotionals addressing issues in the Bible from an ecumenical Christian perspective.

Biblical Studies on the Web

www.bsw.org

If you're interested in studying the Bible from a scholarly perspective and want to dig deeper, this site is for you. It features a scholarly search engine, its own e-journal, searchable indices of academic journals and Bible commentaries, study tools, and a large links section.

The Blue Letter Bible

www.blueletterbible.org

Sure, this site has a searchable Bible, but what *really* makes it special is what you can do to a Bible verse after you find it. Whether you want interlinear Hebrew or Greek or would just like to know what John Calvin had to say about what you're reading, this site will probably fit the bill.

The New Testament Gateway

www.ntgateway.com

Maintained by Mark Goodacre, a theology professor at England's University of Birmingham, this is the single best general New Testament directory of any kind on the Web. It includes everything from online New Testaments (in any language), to email discussion listservs, to relevant academic organizations. If you can't find it here, it probably isn't online.

StudyLight

www.studylight.org

If what you're looking for is a regular, searchable online Bible, you're not likely to find anything better than StudyLight. Featuring 36 English translations, from the 1365 Wycliffe Bible to The Message, this site is the perfect place to go if you're hunting down a verse and aren't quite sure where to look.

The Unbound Bible

unbound.biola.edu

Sponsored by Biola University, this site lets you search among 10 English translations or choose among hundreds of other options, including the original Hebrew and Greek versions and enough non-English translations to rival Bible Gateway. The most compelling feature of this site, though, is its parallel search option; by selecting up to 4 Bible translations at a time, you can display multiple translations side-by-side and see how they read differently.

Jewish Bible Study Resources

The vast majority of Bible-related websites are maintained by Christians. Christian online Bibles work great for citation searches, but for Jewish readers there's nothing like looking up study material on the Book of Deuteronomy and finding a 15-page meditation about Jesus.

Fortunately, the tradition of Torah study is alive and well on the Internet. Whether you're looking for a weekly *parsha* or a detailed discussion of Rashi's commentaries, odds are you'll be able to find what you need here.

Project Genesis

www.torah.org

This site features commentaries on weekly Torah *parshas* (readings from the first five books of the Bible), a lot of articles, an "Ask the Rabbi" feature, and some online discussion forums. There's no substitute for a Thursday night roundtable at a local synagogue, but sometimes this comes pretty close.

Tanach Study Center

www.tanach.org

"Had it not been for Chet Ha'Egel," begins this week's Torah study, "would Bnei Yisrael have needed a Mishkan?" If you want a crash course in high-level Torah study, visit this site with a dictionary handy and get ready for some of the most intensive biblical reflection you will find anywhere on the Internet.

Virtual Beit Midrash

www.vbm-torah.org

Located about 12 miles south of Jerusalem, Yeshivat Har Etzion (YHE) is a highly rigorous and nontraditional yeshiva (rabbinical school) combining religious and military training in a single five-year program. To accommodate those (military or civilian, Jew or non-Jew, Israeli or non-Israeli) who would like to study Torah online, YHE sponsors the Virtual Beit Midrash, a rigorous online self-study program. The site also features thoughtful and intensive weekly Torah commentaries.

Quizzes and Entertainment

There's plenty of opportunity for serious online Bible study, but we all know what the Internet is *really* for. Besides, all work and no play makes Hezekiah a dull boy.

Bible Games

www.biblestudygames.com/biblegames

This site features three delightful online Bible games: a trivia game, a word search, and a crossword puzzle.

Bible Quizzes

www.biblequizzes.com

As of press time, this site is up to 53 Bible quizzes and counting. They're all multiple-choice, with topics ranging from "Birds and Creeping Things" to "Biblical Feet." If you really feel like an expert on the Bible, this site—the best Bible quiz site on the Internet, bar none—will reacquaint you with the virtue of humility.

The Brick Testament

www.thebricktestament.com

Brendan Powell Smith had a vision What if he retold the greatest stories of the Bible using Lego kits? The end result—featuring dozens of Bible stories, retold using more than 2,000 captioned photographs—is even more fascinating than it sounds.

Organizations

If you're interested in carrying your study of the Bible a step further, these organizations can help.

The American Bible Society

www.americanbible.org

Founded in 1816, the nondenominational Christian charity The American Bible Society (ABS) works to distribute Bibles to everyone who might need them, in every imaginable language or format.

Catholic Biblical Federation

www.c-b-f.org

The Roman Catholic Church has produced many of the twentieth century's top-notch biblical scholars, and the Catholic Biblical Federation (CBF) combines this legacy of scholarship with an equally strong emphasis on devotional Bible reading.

The Society for Biblical Literature

www.sbl-site.org

If you're looking for a more scholarly organization, the Society for Biblical Literature (SBL) is for you. As the leading biblical scholarship organization in North America, the SBL publishes the *Journal for Biblical Literature*, sponsors regular conferences and seminars, maintains an online forum, and makes plenty of articles available on its website. If the SBL ever schedules its annual meeting in a city near you, don't miss it. A morning or afternoon wandering the aisles of its booksellers' exhibition is a treat.

Miscellaneous

If you still haven't found what you're looking for, it's probably here.

Bible Query

www.biblequery.org

This scholarly, conservative Christian website addresses criticisms scholars and non-scholars have made regarding the Bible's reliability as a historical document. For a real thrill, read it in tandem with the Skeptic's Annotated Bible (covered later in this section).

The Christian Classics Ethereal Library

www.ccel.org

In addition to being the Internet's largest archive of Christian theological classics, this website also features the World Wide Study Bible, audio excerpts, and the online World Wide Encyclopedia of Christianity.

Daily Bible Reading

www.dailybible.com

This site features a daily short and long Bible reading. If you go with the long readings and visit every day, you'll have read the entire Bible in a year.

Early Christian Writings

www.earlychristianwritings.com

This huge site includes the New Testament, noncanonical sources, and the writings of the Church Fathers.

Early Jewish Writings

www.earlyjewishwritings.com

Here you can find the entire Hebrew Bible, the Talmud, the Dead Sea Scrolls, writings of some classical Jewish philosophers (including Philo of Alexandria), and noncanonical sources (Jewish and non-Jewish) dealing with themes in the Hebrew Bible.

The New Media Bible

www.newmediabible.org

The American Bible Society is presently working on a multimedia, interactive Bible that can be accessed for free online. At the present time, only a few stories have been finished, but the completed multimedia Parable of the Good Samaritan is extremely promising.

The Skeptic's Annotated Bible

www.skepticsannotatedbible.com

Every anachronism, contradiction, or otherwise difficult statement in the Bible can be found on this site, organized by chapter and by type. If you want an experience comparable to reading the Bible with 3D glasses, try looking at this site side-by-side with the Bible Query page (listed previously).

12 GOOD BOOKS BASED ON THE GOOD BOOK

The Bible is full of haunting, thought-provoking stories. They were told and retold by the faith traditions that spawned the Bible, and they have been told and retold by every generation since. Contemporary authors, struck by a particularly compelling biblical narrative, are often obliged to tell a Bible story in an entirely new way.

Jesus Reimagined

Little is known about the life of Jesus, but the information the Gospels do provide has been more than enough to form the basis of the world's largest religion—and to inspire the imagination of many great authors, including the following two.

Shusaku Endo, *A Life of Jesus*

Endo, arguably the best known Japanese Christian novelist who has ever lived, produced an astonishingly warm, gentle, and humble work in his *A Life of Jesus*. Placing more emphasis on Jesus' friendship with John the Baptist than most other accounts, Endo's novel humanizes Jesus in a unique way. If the story of Jesus has always seemed a little strange and abstract to you, this book will bring it down to Earth.

Nikos Kazantzakis, *The Last Temptation of Christ*

This book by the renowned Greek novelist Kazantzakis, best known in America as author of *Zorba the Greek*, retells the story of Jesus Christ from Christ's own perspective and portrays Jesus as a flawed, reluctant messiah suffering from existential doubts.

Nobel Endeavors

Awarded every year, the Nobel Prize in Literature instantly establishes its recipient as a global literary giant. Two Americans of the past century relied on the Bible when writing some of their best-known work.

William Faulkner, *Absalom, Absalom!*

The Mississippi novelist Faulkner, winner of the 1949 prize, based his story of Thomas Sutpen on the tragic biblical account of David's oldest and most rebellious son, Absalom.

John Steinbeck, *East of Eden*

Steinbeck, winner of the 1962 prize, wrote his sprawling saga of two families around the biblical story of Cain and Abel.

Women of the Hebrew Bible

These include the story of a victim, of a consort, of a matriarch, and of a revolutionary. These novels of the Hebrew Bible bring fresh perspectives and contemporary relevance to some of the Bible's most memorable characters, retelling their stories for a new generation of readers.

Anita Diamant, *The Red Tent*

Under the Torah's purity codes, women gathered in a red tent to give birth, during menstruation, or while ill. In this bestselling novel, Jacob's daughter Dinah tells of what she learned as a girl in the red tent—the stories she was told, the confidences she kept, and the conflicts she observed.

India Edghill, *Queenmaker: A Novel of King David's Queen*

Michal, David's first wife, was treated shamefully in the biblical account. After falling in love with young David and marrying him, she is sent away by King Saul to marry a farmer. After 10 years, she has learned to love the farmer and her new life—but David, who has finally succeeded Saul and ascended to the throne, demands that she return to his side.

Marek Halter, *Sarah*

The first volume of a planned trilogy by the French novelist Halter, this novel recounts the life of the biblical matriarch Sarah and fleshes out the story of her life before Abram.

Rebecca Kohn, *The Gilded Chamber*

Queen Esther was one of the boldest figures of the Hebrew Bible, and her story is retold in great detail in this novel.

Men of the Hebrew Bible

In some ways, the Hebrew Bible is a book about patriarchs—young, heroic men who become old, powerful men with God's help.

Thomas Mann, *Joseph and His Brothers*

In this massive saga, made up of four books (*The Tales of Jacob*, *The Young Joseph*, *Joseph in Egypt*, and *Joseph the Provider*) that are usually published as one volume, Mann (who, like Faulkner and Steinbeck, earned a Nobel Prize for his work) tells the story of Joseph and his father, Jacob.

Orson Scott Card, *Stone Tables*

In this retelling of the story of Moses and Aaron, science-fiction writer Card—who is also author of a series of novels on the lives of biblical women—invokes Christian symbolism, as well as material drawn from his own Mormon faith, to tell the Hebrew Bible story in a new light.

Zora Neale Hurston, *Moses, Man of the Mountain*

Hurston's retelling of the story of Moses draws on both the biblical narrative and African-American folklore. In Hurston's novel, Moses is a powerful figure—the Great Emancipator, the visible sign of the Hebrews' confrontation with their Egyptian oppressors.

Joel Cohen, *Moses: A Memoir*

Cohen's first-person retelling of Moses' life is remarkable for its psychological complexity. Cohen's objective is to put the reader in the mind of Moses—to show what it might have been like to become the leader of an entire people and develop a close, mutual friendship with the Almighty.

E

12 GREAT MOVIES BASED ON THE BIBLE

During medieval times, plays based on the Bible were extremely popular. In many ways, film has replaced the stage as our primary storytelling medium; movies get higher budgets than other media and usually end up raking in more money, and popular movies inevitably leave their mark on popular culture. Great movies are those movies whose mark does not easily fade.

La Vie et la Passion de Jésus Christ (1905)

This silent French film on the life of Christ, filmed over a three-year period between 1902 and 1905, was the first feature-length film ever released (although at 44 minutes, it would be an extremely short feature by today's standards). The makers of *La Vie et la Passion* made no attempt to be realistic, and the movie's almost comically elaborate style clashes with today's movies. Still, there's something to be said for being the first on the scene—and silent films have a charm of their own.

Quo Vadis (1951)

The story of a Roman general who faces a moral dilemma under the reign of the anti-Christian emperor Nero, *Quo Vadis* (a Latin phrase meaning "Where are you going," as Jesus once asked Peter) deals with the persecution early Christians faced.

The Ten Commandments (1956)

This version of *The Ten Commandments*, starring Charlton Heston as Moses and Yul Brynner as Pharaoh, is widely regarded as the grandest and most impressive biblical epic of all time. But the 1923 silent version is also considered a classic. Cecil B. DeMille directed both versions, remaking his own film 33 years later.

Ben-Hur (1959)

The winner of 11 Academy Awards, this movie features the character of Judah Ben-Hur (Charlton Heston), a wealthy Jewish merchant who is captured and enslaved by the Romans. The events of his life run parallel to those of Jesus, whom he encounters several times. As in the case of *The Ten Commandments*, this is a remake of a silent classic that has also been acclaimed by many.

King of Kings (1961)

This is a film version of the life of Christ, beginning with events prior to his birth. *King of Kings* places a great deal of emphasis on political struggle—the Roman occupation and the Jewish revolutionaries who fight against them—and hope that Jesus will aid them in their cause.

Il Vangelo secondo Matteo (1964)

Perhaps the greatest testimony to the power of *Il Vangelo secondo Matteo* is that this classic film, the brainchild of an openly gay Italian communist art-film director named Pier Paolo Pasolini, is beloved by conservative American evangelicals. Considered by many critics to be the best movie ever filmed on the life of Christ, *Il Vangelo secondo Matteo* retells the story of the Gospel of Matthew without pomp or elaboration.

The Greatest Story Ever Told (1965)

And speaking of pomp and elaboration, *The Greatest Story Ever Told* (featuring Max von Sydow as Jesus) co-stars such notables as Charlton Heston, Telly Savalas (in his first bald role), Angela Lansbury, Robert Blake, Sidney Poitier, John Wayne, Shelley Winters, and Pat Boone (yes, Pat Boone). At just over three hours long in its original, uncut edition, *The Greatest Story* has joined *The Ten Commandments* and *King of Kings* as an Easter television rebroadcast tradition.

The Bible (1966)

Retelling the first half of the Book of Genesis, *The Bible* (originally subtitled *In the Beginning...*) was intended to be the first in a long series of Bible retellings. Watch for George C. Scott as Abraham.

Jesus of Nazareth (1977)

Although Franco Zeffirelli's *Jesus of Nazareth* was not the first movie to depict a blue-eyed Jesus, it is probably the only movie specifically remembered for doing so (thanks no doubt to Robert Powell's piercing gaze). Featuring a star-studded cast that includes Anne Bancroft, Ernest Borgnine, James Earl Jones, Sir Laurence Olivier, Christopher Plummer, Anthony Quinn, and Peter Ustinov, this six-hour miniseries is a favorite of many.

The Last Temptation of Christ (1988)

Based on Nikos Kazantzakis's novel by the same name (profiled in Appendix D, "12 Good Books on the Good Book") and directed by Martin Scorsese, this is probably the most controversial film on the life of Christ ever released to a wide market. Against the backdrop of a haunting soundtrack provided by Peter Gabriel, Jesus Christ (Willem Dafoe) suffers acute headaches and acute doubt as he tries to decide whether to take up the cross. The movie features David Bowie as an eerily compelling Pontius Pilate.

The Prince of Egypt (1998)

This big-budget animated version of the life of Moses, which resembles a Disney film in many respects, takes a unique turn by portraying Moses (Val Kilmer) and the Pharaoh Ramses (Ralph Fiennes) as brothers. The story, animation, and soundtrack are all outstanding and appeals to both adults and children.

The Passion of the Christ (2004)

The top-grossing Bible movie of all time, this retelling of the last 12 hours of Jesus Christ's life was seen as a major risk for its producer, director, and bankroller, Mel Gibson. Filmed in Latin and Aramaic with subtitles, the movie is extremely gory (film critic Roger Ebert once described it as the most violent movie he had ever seen)—and its apparent marketability was reduced even further when the movie was denounced by many as antisemitic. The success of *The Passion* surprised many and firmly reestablished the biblical epic as a viable movie genre.

F

CHOOSING A STUDY BIBLE

Aside from paying me or another writer to study the Bible with you, you
have two options —either read it out loud at a bar on karaoke night or
buy a study Bible. I recommend the second option. So do the people at
the bar on karaoke night.

The New Oxford Annotated Bible—New Revised Standard Version with the Apocrypha, Third Edition. **Oxford University Press, 2001. 2,180 pages. $33 paperback, $45 hardbound.**

- **Pros**—It includes detailed introductions to each book, page-by-page (frequently verse-by-verse) running commentaries, maps, diagrams, scholarly essays, and a concordance. This is probably the most complete one-volume scholarly study Bible you'll ever find.

- **Cons**—It doesn't give much attention to religious commentary. The same qualities that make it a perfect scholarly edition make it a much less useful devotional edition.

The Catholic Study Bible—New American Bible. **Oxford University Press, 1990. 2,336 pages. $35 paperback, $52 hardbound.**

- **Pros**—In addition to the features you'll find in the New Oxford Annotated Bible, the Catholic Study Bible also has vastly superior, more user-friendly book introductions that break each book down into sections for easy reference (for example, "Genesis 1–3—The story of God's creation and the first human sin"). The Catholic Study Bible also includes a glossary, which the New Oxford doesn't have. If you're relatively new to the Bible, you'll probably find this study Bible more useful, in general, than the New Oxford because it's much more approachable, for both Catholics and non-Catholics. Catholics will find the lectionary index in the back of the book particularly useful, but the overall perspective of the book is more scholarly than devotional.

- **Cons**—The book-by-book commentaries in the Catholic Study Bible only use up a few inches at the bottom of the page; contrast this with the New Oxford, where often a full quarter of the page is made up entirely of commentary. If you're looking for a KGB dossier on each verse of the Bible, this probably isn't your cup of tea.

The Zondervan NIV Study Bible. **Revised edition. Zondervan Publishing Company, 2002. 2,240 pages. $40 hardbound.**

- **Pros**—Of the study Bibles discussed so far, this is by far the most user-friendly. The writing style is warmer, the tone less scholarly, and the discussion more like a conversation and less like an encyclopedia. It is also a devotional commentary in many respects—it favors a more traditional interpretation of the origins of Scripture than either of the study Bibles discussed previously, and it connects biblical principles together with an eye for fostering a consistent worldview based on the Bible.

- **Cons**—This is not, strictly speaking, a scholarly Bible commentary. Although it assesses scholarship in a serious and even-handed way, it unapologetically makes a case for a moderately conservative Christian understanding of the Bible. It is, however, fairly gentle with its opinions, and most readers—regardless of their beliefs—would probably find some value in its straightforward and engaging approach.

***Etz Hayim—Torah and Commentary*. Jewish Publication Society of America, 2001. 1,559 pages. $72.50 leatherbound.** *(This is not a full Bible commentary; rather it's a commentary on the Torah [Pentateuch], the first five books of the Bible.)*

■ **Pros**—The actual text of the Torah (with interlinear Hebrew) makes up perhaps 20% or 30% of the text at the top of the page; the rest is magnificent commentary, with paragraph upon paragraph of warm, lucid, and readable exposition on every verse. This commentary, prepared by a massive team of Conservative Jewish scholars (including Harold Kushner and Chaim Potok), is always easy to comprehend—even when it addresses the obscure details of Hebrew etymology.

■ **Cons**—Although issues of scholarship are sometimes addressed in the accompanying essays, this is a literary-devotional commentary; it makes no pretense of being focused on secular scholarship. It also has a very clear Conservative Jewish theological bias, although most readers—from other traditions of Judaism or from another faith entirely—are likely to find the general discussion warm, thoughtful, and provocative.

***The Stone Edition Chumash*. Mesorah Publications, 1993. 1,339 pages. $50 hardbound.** *(This is a Torah commentary, not a full Bible commentary.)*

■ **Pros**—For centuries, rabbinical students have studied the classical commentaries on the Bible written by Rashi, Rambam (Moses Maimonides), Ramban (Moses ben Nachman), Ibn Ezra, and so forth. With the Stone Edition Chumash, Mesorah Publications took these classic commentaries and assembled them into a single study Bible—with each English and interlinear Hebrew Bible verse surrounded by English summaries of commentaries from Judaism's greatest theologians. Although the volume is not a comprehensive presentation of Jewish thought on the Bible (no single volume of this kind could ever be), it is the single finest one-volume rabbinic Bible that anyone will ever find. Laced with folklore, provocative questions, and disparate views on the interpretation of specific verses, this surprisingly readable volume is a wonderful introduction to the rabbinic approach to Bible study.

■ **Cons**—This isn't just an Orthodox Jewish study Bible; it's an Orthodox Jewish study Bible that draws its views from ancient sources. There is very little historical-critical scholarship of any kind in this book. Rabbinic commentary is its own genre—containing parallel literary, devotional, and theological streams of thought—and while some love it, others find it bizarre and impractical. If you're not familiar with rabbinic commentary, however, this book is certainly worth a look; you might be surprised at how much you enjoy reading it. Once you have a taste for it, rabbinic commentary is highly addictive.

Index

NUMBERS

Matthew (the Gospel of)
  age of, 20
  as the chronologically first Gospel, 197
  date of creation, 197
  intended audience written for, 197
  possible origins of, 197
  movie translations, 302-303
  novelizations, 298
  Q Gospel, the, 198
  Thomas (the Gospel of), 186
goy kadosh, 94
Greatest Commandment, the (Gospel teaching), 216-217
Greatest Story Ever Told, The (movie), 302
group reading. *See* **Bible groups**
Gutenberg, Johann, 24

H

Habakkuk, 135
Hadassah. *See* **Esther (Book of)**
haftorah, 36
Hagar as mother of Ishmael, 66
haggadah, 38-39
Haggai, 135
Hail Mary, origin of, 203
halakha, 38-39
Halter, Marek, *Sarah*, 299
Ham, origin of races controversy, 64
Haman the Agagite, 141-142
hamantaschen, 142
Hanukkah, 39, 180
hebel, mistranslation of, 170
Hebrew, etymology of, 76
Hebrew Bible
  canonical variations, 21
  canonization of, 21
  Dead Sea Scrolls, 19
  Jewish canonical divides, 36
  Masoretic Text, 19
  origins of, 17-18. *See also* Tanakh
  Septuagint, 19, 23
  Targumim, 19
  Targums, 22

Hebrews (Epistle to), 264
Hermas (the Shepherd of), 186
Herod Antipas, 205
hidden teachings. *See* **Deuterocanonical Books (of the Bible)**
higgaion, 154
historical accuracy, controversy over, 28
historical psalms, 156, 161
historical reading of the Bible, 28
Holiness Code, the, 86
Holy Grail, 206-207
holy scripture, reading the Bible as, 26-28
Holy Spirit, the, 248-249
homosexuality
  Biblical controversy, 66-67
  Paul's stance, 255
Horeb, 77
horns of Moses, 85
Hosea, 133
Hoshea, 116
Huldah, 129
Hurston, Zora Neale, *Moses, Man of the Mountain*, 299
hymns
  ancient Israeli, 154
  spirituals, origins of, 79-80
hymns of praise, 155-156

I

Ibzan, 102
Iddo, 129
***Il Vangelo secondo Matteo* (movie), 302**
"in the twinkling of an eye," origin of phrase, 280
individual Bible study, 27
Internet Bibles. *See* **online Bibles**
Isa (Prophet), 207
Isaac, Abraham's near sacrifice of, 68
Isaiah
  story of, 130
  wife of, 129
Isaiah (Book of), 130

Ishmael, birth of, 66
Islam
  as the beast, 273
  Ishmael as father of, 66
Islamic texts, the Gospel of Barnabas, 186
Israel
  fall of, 122
  history of, prophets, 126
  Jacob as, 71
  North versus South, 112-113
  tribes of, 71-72
  versus Judah, kings of Israel, 113-116
Israelites, 40 years in wilderness, 87-89
Issachar (tribe of), 71

J

Jabesh-gilead, atrocities at, 105
Jacob
  rape of Dinah, 73
  story of, 69-71
Jacob's daughter, novels based on, 298
Jair, 102
James (brother of Jesus)
  as mentioned in Antiquities of the Jews, 198
  life of, 246
James (Epistle of), 265
James (the Great), life of, 240
Jeduthun, 154
Jehoahaz, 115, 120
Jehoash, 115, 118
Jehoiakim, 121
Jehoram, 118
Jehoshaphat, 117
Jehovah, origin of name, 78
Jehovah's Witnesses, predictions of, 273
Jehu
  as a prophet, 128
  story of, 115
Jephthah, 102-103
Jeremiah
  as author of Lamentations (Book of), 132
  story of, 131